Antithetical Arts

Frontispiece: The Alhambra Palace, Granada, Spain
Photograph by Joan Pearlman

Antithetical Arts

On the Ancient Quarrel between
Literature and Music

Peter Kivy

CLARENDON PRESS · OXFORD

OXFORD

UNIVERSITY PRESS

Great Clarendon Street, Oxford OX2 6DP

Oxford University Press is a department of the University of Oxford.
It furthers the University's objective of excellence in research, scholarship,
and education by publishing worldwide in

Oxford New York

Auckland Cape Town Dar es Salaam Hong Kong Karachi
Kuala Lumpur Madrid Melbourne Mexico City Nairobi
New Delhi Shanghai Taipei Toronto

With offices in

Argentina Austria Brazil Chile Czech Republic France Greece
Guatemala Hungary Italy Japan Poland Portugal Singapore
South Korea Switzerland Thailand Turkey Ukraine Vietnam

Oxford is a registered trademark of Oxford University Press
in the UK and in certain other countries

Published in the United States
by Oxford University Press Inc., New York

© Peter Kivy 2009

The moral rights of the author have been asserted
Database right Oxford University Press (maker)

First published 2009

British Library Cataloguing in Publication Data

Data available

Library of Congress Cataloging in Publication Data

Kivy, Peter.
Antithetical arts: on the ancient quarrel between literature and music / Peter Kivy.
p. cm.
Includes bibliographical references and index.
ISBN 978–0–19–956280–0
1. Music and literature. 2. Absolute music. I. Title.
ML3849.K57 2009
780′.08–dc22
2008048452

Typeset by Laserwords Private Limited, Chennai, India
Printed in the UK
on acid-free paper by
MPG Books Group

ISBN 978–0–19–956280–0

10 9 8 7 6 5 4 3 2 1

*To Anthony Pryer
and the music students
at Goldsmiths' College,
University of London,
but for whom I would
have been a stranger
in a strange land.*

Preface

The "ancient quarrel" with which I deal in this book is neither ancient in the sense of dating back to antiquity, nor ancient in the sense of being very very old. It is *old*, to be sure, by ordinary standards, having its beginnings in the rise of pure instrumental music in the second half of the eighteenth century. Thus it is close on two hundred and fifty years old, which is old enough: a good deal older, one supposes, than the Ancient Mariner, who, Coleridge thought, deserved the epithet.

Philosophers will, of course, recognize the allusion, in my title, to Plato's description, in *Republic* X, of "an ancient quarrel between philosophy and poetry; of which there are many proofs...."[1] That is Jowett's translation, by the way; and both Cornford, and Davies and Vaughan, to adduce two examples, render it rather as simply, a "long-standing" quarrel.[2] So there is, really, no reason to make heavy weather of the distinction between ancient and old. But "ancient quarrel" is the phrase that has endured and is how Plato's assertion is customarily quoted. So "ancient quarrel" is how *my* quarrel will be characterized, although "long-standing" is closer to the literal truth.

My ancient quarrel is not between philosophy and any one of the arts, although *that* quarrel has certain affinities with mine, as we shall see. It is, rather, an "internal" quarrel, as it were: an internecine conflict within the arts, between the emerging art of absolute music, as the Romantics called it, "music alone," as I sometimes refer to it, and the truly ancient, long-established art of literary fiction. And it arises, as we shall see, in the attempt to understand, interpret, appreciate the newly emerging absolute music canon, on the part of those who were "present at the creation." It is, in other words, a quarrel between those who insist on understanding, interpreting, appreciating music

---

[1] Plato, *The Republic*, *The Dialogues of Plato*, trans. B. Jowett (New York: Random House, 1937), vol. I, 865 (607).

[2] *The Republic of Plato*, trans. Francis MacDonald Cornford (New York and Oxford: Oxford University Press, 1960), 339. *The Republic of Plato*, trans. John Llewelyn Davies and David James Vaughan (London: Macmillan, 1950), 352.

alone in, broadly speaking, literary terms, and those, customarily called "formalists," who insist on understanding, interpreting, appreciating absolute music in, broadly speaking, its own terms, whatever those terms may ultimately turn out to be.

I am no neutral observer of this ancient quarrel. I am on the side of the formalists. But this book will be more a critique of the opposition than a defense of absolute music's autonomy. For it seems to me that although the progress to formalism in the early years was a struggle *against* the literary crowd, after it was a going concern it became and, I believe still is, the one to beat, not the one in need of defense. The burden of proof, I strongly believe, is on those who wish to place—it is very tempting for me to say *impose*—literary and other semantic interpretations on the absolute music canon.

In Part I, I have tried to lay bear what, from a philosopher's point of view, at least *this* philosopher's point of view, seem to be the conceptual origins of musical formalism, and the origin of its "quarrel" with the literary arts. It is decidedly *not* meant to be a history of musical formalism, which so far as I know, has never been written, nor am I qualified to write it, or interested in writing it, even if I could.

Part II is composed of chapters that engage the literary interpreters of the absolute music canon. It is critical throughout.

Finally, in Part III, although I continue to engage the literary interpreters in debate, I also try to say something *positive* about the future of musical formalism—how it must proceed if it is to address the very real philosophical problems that it faces. For formalism, it is not all beer and skittles, as I know full well. And this book ends, alas, not with the solution, but with the problem.

Although some of the chapters started life as separate essays, this is not an essay collection but a book with an argument, begun in the first chapter and concluded in the last. Nevertheless, there are bound to be some readers who will not be keen on working their way through the intricacies of scholarship and interpretation in Part I, where the historical foundations of formalism are laid out. For those readers, no great harm will be done by skipping the historical material altogether and going straight on to Part II, where the contemporary argument begins. Naturally, though, I hope those so inclined will overcome their aversion, and begin at the beginning—that is because I think knowing the historical origins of the debate makes the current debate itself far more understandable. Had I not thought so, I would have cut to the chase. But here, as elsewhere, what precedes the chase makes sense of the chase.

Chapter 4, "Mood and Music," appeared previously in the *Journal of Aesthetics and Art Criticism*, 64 (2006), parts of Chapter 5, "Persona Non Grata," in the *British Journal of Aesthetics*, 46 (2006), and Chapter 10, "Musical Morality," in the *Review Internationale de Philosophie*, 62 (2008).

Contents

Preface   vii

Part I: The Founding of Formalism   1

1. First the Music, and Then the Words   3

2. Designs À La Grecque   29

3. Body and Soul   53

Part II: The Fortunes of Formalism   77

4. Mood and Music   79

5. Persona Non Grata   101

6. Action and Agency   119

7. Shostakovich's Secret?   157

Part III: The Fate of Formalism   177

8. The Failure of Formalism and the Failure
of its Foes   179

9. Attention, Ritual, and the Additive Strategy   201

10. Musical Morality   215

11. Empty Pleasure to the Ear   235

Bibliography   263
Index   269

The slow progress of music's history amply demonstrates how hard it has been for music to cut herself free from her sisters—mime and word—and to establish herself as an independent art.

Johann Gottfried Herder

PART I:

The Founding of Formalism

1

First the Music, and Then the Words

Introduction

"First the Music, and Then the Words," is the title, translated into English, of a one-act opera by Antonio Salieri, called, in Italian, *Prima la musica, e poi le parole.* It was first performed in Vienna, 7 February 1786, in the Orangery of the Schönbrunn Palace on a double bill with Mozart's *Der Schauspieldirektor.* The two were commissioned by Joseph II, obviously as a matched pair of satires on Italian and German opera, respectively. The whole thing, as Volkmar Braunbehrens suggests, "might have been interpreted as a little contest between the two composers—and may even have been deliberately planned as such."[1]

Mozart's contribution to this unusual musical event is familiar territory and requires no further comment. But Salieri's deserves, I have come to think, serious consideration from, believe it or not, a *philosophical* perspective. Not, needless to say, on account of anything distinctive about Salieri's music. Music, in any case, cannot be a source of philosophical insight and illumination—the music of Salieri least of all (if there can be less than nothing). So it may be more correct to say that it is the contribution of Salieri's librettist, Giambattista Casti, that I am concerned with. For it is he, we must assume, who was responsible for the central idea of Salieri's opera; and it is this central idea that, it seems to me, deserves philosophical scrutiny. Indeed, I think Casti

---

[1] Volkmar Braunbehrens, *Maligned Master: The Real Story of Antonio Salieri*, trans. Eveline L. Kanes (New York: Fromm International Publishing Corporation, 1992), 118.

managed to lay bare, in this idea, the crucial philosophical issue at the heart of arguably the most epoch-making artistic innovation of the eighteenth century: the rise to prominence of pure instrumental music. That issue gave rise to the subject of this book: the ancient quarrel between music and literature.

Pure instrumental music's ascendancy, at the end of the eighteenth century, as a major art form, and a primary concern of composers, raised a philosophical question both new and enduring: namely, the question of whether, or how such music could be described, and understood, in ordinary linguistic terms. The problem was, to put it another way, how to put words to music.

The Western world, since time out of mind, had been, of course, thoroughly familiar with what might be thought of as the reverse problem: putting music to words, which is to say, making a musical setting of a text. As an artistic practice, the putting of music to words seemed unproblematic, as the putting of words to the new instrumental music, that is to say, *describing* it, did not.

Theories of whether or how words might be put to what the nineteenth century came to call absolute music or, in other words, how it might be *described*, have ranged from the claim that absolute music is "ineffable," and cannot be described at all, to the formalists' insistence on structural and syntactic language only, to the more "permissive" descriptions of absolute music in emotive and narrative terms. And what is particularly interesting is that the "economy," if I may so put it, of musical descriptions, seems to wax and wane in periodic fashion. We seem now, however, to be in a pluralistic stage, characteristic of our times in many areas and disciplines, with more promiscuous, "luxurious" theories and schools of musical description existing alongside of traditional formalism, "enhanced formalism," as I like to call my view (to be defended here), and even theories to the effect that absolute music is "ineffable."

With these preliminary remarks in mind, I want now to turn briefly to Salieri's opera, or, rather, Casti's libretto, for a closer look. It holds the key to the origins of musical formalism in the late eighteenth century, and to the origins of the "quarrel" with which we are concerned.

An Impossible Project?

The joke around which Casti's libretto is organized, and which is the whole point of the exercise, is, needless to say, already made in the title: *First the Music, and Then the Words*, which suggests a complete reversal of the order, since time immemorial, the making of music with texts has followed in the West. There are, of course, well-known exceptions to this order of business, and I shall have occasion to mention some of them later on. But that the customary, the *rational* way of doing things is first the words and then the music, is the assumption without which Casti's libretto would lack its point and its humor.

The outline of the plot, in a nutshell, is this. Count Opizio commissions "a new opera that must be written, rehearsed, and performed in four days... The librettist considers the task impossible, but the music is already completed and needs only a text."[2] That is the general idea; but here it is in a little more detail.

After a brief, brisk, and unpretentious overture, in more-or-less sonata form, the real business of the opera begins with a duet between the composer, Maestro, and the librettist, Poeta, bass baritone and baritone respectively, in the nature of a comic argument. The composer informs the poet that "the Count [Opizio] wants music and words [of an opera] ready in four days," and assures him (later on) that "The matter is absolutely possible and has to be done this way."[3]

Poeta, whom Lorenzo Da Ponte, by the way, took to be a caricature of himself, replies that Maestro is mistaken, for the Count "is a man of wisdom and cannot have such a foolish and absurd idea in mind." The composer then threatens to get another collaborator: "If you worry me a bit more I'll look for a better poet." And the poet replies indignantly: "Dear Signor Master, you cannot order one's inspiration. Heavens! What a blunder! A Drama in four days?"

---

[2] Ibid., 119.

[3] I have relied for my quotations from Casti's libretto on the translation provided in the booklet accompanying the recording by Domenico Sanfilippo and the Orchestra della Filarmonica della Bohemia del Nord, 18–20. The translation is frequently unidiomatic. (No translator is credited.)

The duet is followed by a recitative which begins with the composer putting it to the poet: "Well now: decide: yes or no?" To which the poet responds: "Then you think we can write words and music in four days?"

Now follows the principal joke and, if I may say so, the philosophical point of the opera. "Don't worry as to the music: it is ready" the composer reassures the poet: "you have only to adapt the words to it," the poet responding irately: "It is as if one makes a suit and then makes the man who can wear it." And here the composer pulls rank, putting it to the librettist that in opera it is the composer who is the principal artist. "You poets are mad. My friend, persuade yourself: whoever do you think will pay attention to your words?"

Poeta then plays his final card in this game of opera aesthetics. "But... music must express one's feelings, either good or bad," he avers, obviously intending the thought that the emotive expression of the music must be made to match the emotive expression of a previously existing text. And Maestro trumps it with the opera's second joke. "My music is excellent in that, it can be adapted to anything very well," the implication being that the emotive expression of the music can match the emotive expression of *any* text. At this point the poet acquiesces in the scheme, and gets on to more practical matters. "Who's going to sing?"

Here we have what I am emboldened to call the philosophical understructure of Casti's text, It is embellished, necessarily, with the usual incidents of such satires on operatic practice. But none of these familiar antics needs detain us here.

Casti, then, is operating under the assumption that it is not only absurd, but so absurd as to be laughable, to propose an operatic project in which the composer writes the music, for which the librettist *then* writes the words, rather than the other way around. But *why* is it absurd? *Why* is it funny?

The librettist in the opera suggests that the absurdity of "first the music, and then the words" lies in its contradiction of the universally accepted aesthetic principle that the emotive character of the music should be made by the composer to coincide with the emotive character of the words. To this the composer gives what

Casti obviously takes to be the laughably absurd reply that his music is suitable to *any* expressive character at all.

Thus, there are two jokes to Casti's libretto. There is the main, thematic joke that an opera is to be composed music first, words afterwards. And there is what might be called the subsidiary joke, which the thematic joke implies, that the composer's music, once composed, is suitable to any emotion a text might express. One size fits all!

But just as we can ask why it is written in stone that the composer can write music to the poet's words, but not vice versa, we can ask whether, indeed, it is absurd, laughably absurd at that, to claim that a given piece of music might be suitable to any emotion a text might express. I think it is absurd. But Eduard Hanslick, for one, as we shall see, came very close to asserting its truth in chapter II of his famous and influential book, *Of Musical Beauty*. The conclusion is, indeed, implied by what Hanslick says in that chapter, and he as good as says it outright on more than one occasion. Casti's absurdity became formalist orthodoxy in not much more than fifty years.

I hope these brief and somewhat diffuse remarks on Casti's libretto will have, nevertheless, convinced you, as I have come to be convinced, that a tender philosophical nerve has been exposed by Salieri's collaborator, perhaps unwittingly, although I am inclined to give him the benefit of the doubt. So let us pursue this matter further.

Words to Music

Let us, to begin with, imagine what the composer must have presented to the librettist, given the laughable premise of Casti's and Salieri's opera. I will suppose, to keep things simple, that the composer has given his librettist an overture, and a string of wordless recitatives and arias. And again, to keep things simple, I will only consider the arias.

The arias will, of course, all be self-contained musical movements, in recognizable musical forms. Some might even be in the larger instrumental forms such as sonata form or rondo. The librettist's job is to write texts for these songs without words: these textless instrumental movements. Not only that, the texts must be expressively appropriate, and appropriate in every other way, to the music for which they are provided. And this stipulation, of course, is what provokes the librettist's skepticism when the project is first proposed to him.

Putting words to pre-existent music is not, as a matter of fact, unknown or so unusual. There are familiar circumstances in the history of music where the usual order of "first the words, and then the music," is reversed. Furthermore, there are actually two compositional processes that might fairly be described as reversing the conventional order; although only one of them is the extreme case that Casti's libretto puts.

The more usual case is where a composer reuses a piece of pre-existent music for a pre-existent text. The most familiar example that comes immediately to mind is Handel's reworking of previously composed material for the text of *Messiah*. He had Charles Jennens' words, selected from scripture, before him and adapted music previously written by him for radically different words. It is a compositional procedure common in the Baroque era, and still existent, although perhaps not so prevalent, at the time of Salieri's opera. Hanslick makes very heavy weather of it in *On Musical Beauty*; and what he says is relevant here.

"Many whole vocal pieces," Hanslick remarks, "have used different texts with the same music."[4] And he cites, among other well-known examples, Handel's use of his secular Italian love duets for Jennens' sacred text. As Hanslick puts his point:

> If the music in itself, however, were capable of representing devotion in its content, such a quid pro quo would be impossible. Our greatest masters of sacred music, Handel in particular, offer abundant examples in support of what we are saying here. He proceeded in this with great nonchalance. Winterfeld has shown that many of the most famous pieces in *Messiah*, including some of the ones most admired for their godly sentiments, are for the most part transcribed from the secular and mainly erotic duets which Handel composed in 1711–12 for Princess Caroline of Hanover to madrigal texts of Marrio Ortensio.[5]

A famous case in point is Handel's use of music originally set to an Italian text which translates as "No, I will not trust you,/blind love,

---

[4] Eduard Hanslick, *On the Musically Beautiful: A Contribution towards the Revision of the Aesthetics of Music*, trans. Geoffrey Payzant (Indianapolis: Hackett, 1986), 18.
[5] Ibid., 18–19.

cruel beauty,/you are too deceitful,/flattering deity!'' to the text from Isaiah, chapter ix, verse 6: "For unto us a child is born, unto us a son is given."[6] It is known to all choral singers that Handel has put the accent on the wrong syllable by making "For" the downbeat, as the melody demands, and which is right in the original Italian setting, where the first word is "Nò." (It is not clear whether Handel did this because he just did not care, or because English not being his native language, he was unaware of the mistake. But that is beside the point.)

Hanslick's point is that from the, shall we say, emotive, expressive point of view, the music fits both texts perfectly; but the texts are so radically different in meaning and emotive tone that there couldn't be anything emotively or expressively specific in the music, or it couldn't possibly be, which it manifestly is, expressively suited to *both* texts. And, after all, how could two texts be more radically different than an erotic Italian love poem and a verse from scripture announcing the birth of the Christ?

What Hanslick meant to elicit from such examples, which he had no trouble finding in abundance, was the conclusion that, emotively, music is but a protean clay, to which a text can give whatever expressive character it, the text, may possess. As he puts this conclusion, in its most radical form, "expressive passages of vocal music will, when separated from their texts, at least only allow us to guess which feelings they express. They are like silhouettes whose originals we cannot recognize without someone giving us a hint as to their identity."[7]

So here is irony. What for Casti and Salieri was a capital joke, music appropriate to the expressive character of *any* text, was, for Hanslick, a basic premise of his formalist aesthetic credo.

Of course nothing of the kind follows from the examples Hanslick adduces. And the idea that *any* music is suitable to *any* expressive text is as ludicrous as Casti and Salieri thought it was. In all of Handel's so called "borrowings" from his own music, and from the music of other composers, in setting texts, it is quite obvious that he is careful to choose music that is expressively appropriate to the new words, and on the rare occasion when he is not, the disparity is immediately apparent. The music he reused for "For unto us a child is born . . ."

---

⁶ Ibid., 18 and 18n.   ⁷ Ibid., 18.

would *clearly* be inappropriate for the passion texts that follow in Part Two of *Messiah*.

The reason that reusing pre-existent music for pre-existent texts is not a laughing matter should be fairly clear. No composer starts with a *tabula rasa*. Composing is, in part, a matter of *selecting* musical materials, whether they are in the form of already composed music, or in the form of musical fragments already in the composer's tool box: pre-existent themes or thematic fragments; harmonic vocabulary; contrapuntal figures and snippets; and so forth. I am not by any means suggesting that musical composition consists solely in the selection of pre-existent materials, merely that there may be more of that in the process than the lay person thinks. That being the case, the gap between selecting pre-existent music that is appropriate to a given text, and composing music that is appropriate to a given text, is not as wide as one might think.

In any case, it is a *fact* of musical history in the West that composers, particularly in periods when music was written to order, and in a hurry, reused music in the setting of texts, other people's music as well as their own, and when the music was well chosen, the tracks were well covered. It has taken historical musicology to detect the borrowings. To the musical ear it sounds as if the music were made for the place it occupies.

Thus, the joke of *Prima la musica* is not the reuse of pre-existent music for pre-existent texts. There is nothing funny in that; it was a common practice in Salieri's time, and I have no doubt that he indulged in it. (Mozart did.)

The joke is about the *second* kind of case in which the music precedes the words: the case in which the composer presents the music to the poet and says in effect, as Handel once said to one of his librettists: "Hear the passage again. There! Go you, make words to that music." But, clearly, the very fact that Handel demanded his librettist to put words to already composed music suggests that even *this* order of business is not unheard of, or always the object of raillery. Consider the following case.

The opening chorus of Bach's Cantata 110, for the first Sunday of Christmas, is more or less note-for-note identical to the overture of the previously composed Fourth Suite for Orchestra.[8] The author of the text is unknown, and might well have been the composer himself. The point is that the pre-existent music was not, apparently, chosen to fit a pre-existent text, but the words were expressly written to fit the already composed music. The thing is all the more remarkable because the pre-existent music is not vocal music at all but a pure instrumental piece: in fact a French overture, with the usual slow introduction in dotted-eighth-and-sixteenth-note rhythm, a fast fugal section, elaborately worked out, and a return to the slow introductory material as a conclusion.

Another truly remarkable thing about the opening chorus of Cantata 110 is how perfectly the text conforms to the music, in expression, in rhythmic character, and, quite extraordinarily, in the way the music, so to speak, "represents" the text. Of course there is no particular difficulty in writing a joyful text to go with joyful music. And the overture to the Fourth Orchestral Suite was chosen for a Christmas cantata, obviously, because the instrumental work has an exuberantly joyous character, well suited to the Festival of the Nativity.

Somewhat more difficult is the fitting of a text to pre-existing music, so that the musical accents and rhythms match those of the words. (Recall Handel's misplaced accent in "For unto us a child is born . . . .") This would have been particularly difficult in the given instance because the pre-existing music is instrumental music; and instrumental lines, particularly those of Bach, are notoriously long, and intricate, with little place to breath—very difficult for the human voice to negotiate: in a word, "unvocal." On the other hand, Bach is well known for his instrumentally conceived vocal lines, and the way that, in his vocal music, instruments and voices are called upon to utilize the same, interchangeable musical material. In any event,

---

[8] See Wolfgang Schmieder, *Thematisch-systematisches Verzeichnis der Musikalischen Werke von Johann Sebastian Bach* (Leipzig: Breitkoph und Härtel, 1950). The cantata is dated by Schmieder "not before 1734" (p. 147). The suite he dates as "Leipzig between 1727 and 1736 (or earlier in Köthen?)" (p. 498). Obviously it is difficult to date many of Bach's works with any exactitude. But it seems obvious too from these estimates of Schmieder's that the probability of the cantata's composition antedating that of the suite is pretty slim, given that the suite might even have been composed before Bach came to Leipzig, and the earliest possible date for the cantata is only two years before the very latest possible date for the suite.

1. (Chor) Sopr., Alto, Ten., Basso; Tromba I, II, III, Timp.; Flauto trav. I, II coll' Ob. I, Ob.I, II, III, Fag.;Viol. I, II,

not only do the words fit the music accentually and rhythmically, but the word *Lachens*, "laughter," is set to dotted-eighth-and-sixteenth-note figures, and triplets, that when sung appear as an unmistakable representation of laughter in musical sound. Indeed, one cannot sing the melismas without making the syllables ha..ha..ha..

J.S. Bach, Cantata 110, *Unser Mund sei voll Lachens*, First Chorus:

If I am right, that the words of this chorus were written especially for the pre-existing music, and it was not a case of matching pre-existent music to pre-existent text, then two important points emerge from the example.

The first point is that we can think of the poet's (Bach's?) words as, in effect, a "literary interpretation" of a pure instrumental work: a work of absolute music. It is as if a program annotator were to say, in the inflated lingo of his profession, "In the massive overture of Bach's Fourth Suite for Orchestra we hear the cosmic laughter of the cherubim and seraphim celebrating the savior's birth." I shall return to this point later on.

The second point can be put, initially, in the form of a question. If it is an accepted practice in Western art music of writing words to precomposed instrumental music, witness the first chorus of Cantata 110, what's so funny—what's funny at all—about Salieri's *Prima la musica*, the whole point of which is to mine the supposed humor from a request by a composer that a poet write a libretto for music already composed? Indeed, when the composer in Salieri's opera throws up to the poet the taunt that the music, not the text, is the primary component of an opera, he is stating an unquestioned truth about the genre, albeit in a highly exaggerated way. After all, opera scores are shelved in the *music* section of the library, not the drama section. As Maestro puts it to Poeta: "You poets are mad. My friend, persuade yourself: whoever do you think will pay attention to your words?"

Isn't that close to being the whole truth of the matter? And if it is, then it would not seem funny, but entirely reasonable, for the order of business to be *first the music, and then the words*. If the music is most important, then the music *should* come temporally first, and the librettist should write his words to go with it. The music should call the tune.

But, clearly, the aesthetics of text-setting in Western art music, in Salieri's time, as in Bach's, embodied two apparently incompatible precepts: that music *is* the principle player, *and* that the text should (temporally speaking) come *first*. In order to understand this apparent contradiction, indeed, perhaps more real than apparent, we must go back to the second half of the sixteenth century: back to the musical events that were forming the modern aesthetics of text setting, and the contradiction of which I am now speaking. I have more than once found in this crucial period of music history food for philosophical thought, and I am not surprised, then, that, in considering the philosophical problems raised by Casti's libretto, I am returning to it yet again for enlightenment.[9]

Master or Slave?

Two events in the second half of the sixteenth century had a profound effect on what I have been calling the aesthetics of text setting. First, hardly just an event in music history, was the so-called counter-reformation, and the Council of Trent, during which many of its precepts and principles were formulated.

It is part of musical folk lore that the ruling clergy, at the Council of Trent, seriously considered the abolishing of polyphony in the liturgy, because the complexity of the musical texture obscured the spiritual meaning of the words. As one of the proclamations of the Council put it: "The whole plan of singing in musical modes should be constructed not to give empty pleasure to the ear, but in such a way that the

---

[9] For two of my previous discussions of this historical period, see *Osmin's Rage: Philosophical Reflections on Opera, Drama, and Text* (2nd edn.; Ithaca and London: Cornell University Press, 1999), Part I; and "Making the Codes and Breaking the Codes: Two Revolutions in Twentieth-Century Music," *New Essays on Musical Understanding* (Oxford: Clarendon Press, 2001), 44–67.

words may be clearly understood by all . . . ."[10] The rest of the folk legend, the subject of Hans Pfitzner's opera, *Palestrina*, has it that the composer saved the day with the *Missa Pape Marcelli*, proving to the clergy that it was indeed possible to write a kind of polyphonic music in which the words could be clearly understood.

It is now well known that *Palestrina's* active role in the Council of Trent, and the special place of the *Missa Pape Marcelli* in the "reform" of Catholic church music, is largely a myth. And there is, as well, a growing suspicion among musicologists, that the Council's interest in the whole matter of religious music has been somewhat exaggerated. Nevertheless, I don't think there can be any doubt that changes in the aesthetics of text setting had indeed occurred, and that the music of *Palestrina* satisfied, as previous polyphony had not, the Council's demand that "the words may be clearly understood by all . . . ." In effect, the aesthetics of text setting had become, not just temporally, but *artistically*, "first the words, and then the music."

A far more obvious and direct influence on what might well be called a "revolution" in the aesthetics of text setting is to be found in the development of opera, at the close of the sixteenth century, as well as in the theoretical literature that both accompanied and immediately preceded it. This new aesthetics is best summed up in the precept of Claudio Monteverdi's, as attributed to him by his brother, that "in this kind of music, it has been his intention to make the words mistress of the harmony and not the servant."[11] But what do the words command; and how does their slave, the harmony, serve?

As is pretty well known, the group of Florentine intellectuals known as the Camerata, proposed, at the close of the sixteenth century, a project they perceived as a revival of the dramatic practice of the ancient Greeks, and which, in fact, resulted in the musical form

---

[10] Quoted in Gustave Reese, *Music in the Renaissance* (New York: Norton, 1954), 449.

[11] *Source Readings in Music History*, ed. Oliver Strunk (New York: Norton, 1950), p. 406n. But see Tim Carter, "Two Monteverdi Problems, and Why They Matter," *The Journal of Musicology*, 19 (2002). Carter asks, apropos of this, whether Monteverdi "really meant it" (p. 419), the implication being that his practice was not in accordance with his precept. Of course he meant it, just as a smoker really means that he wants to give up his habit all the while he continues to smoke. He is addicted to tobacco, just as Monteverdi was addicted to musical composition. As Carter wisely puts the point later on, "he was a musician through and through" (p. 420).

we know as opera. Their stated purpose was to musically represent dramatic speech, following as close as possible in the music, the pace, rhythm, accent, and emotive expression of the spoken text. As Giulio Caccini, one of the first composers of such music, put it, "... I have endeavored ... to bring in a kind of music by which men might, as it were, talk in harmony...."[12] This kind of music became known as the *stile rappresentativo*, the style of the actor.

Now it is clear that such an aesthetics of text setting requires the text to come first, both temporally and aesthetically. It is the composer's task to make his music fit the pace, rhythmic accent, and emotive expression of the words. In order for him to do that there must be words antecedent to his task, and they must dictate, to a very significant degree, his aesthetic choices. This is the sense in which the new aesthetics of text setting mandated that the composer be the poet's slave.

Furthermore, it is surely this aesthetics of text setting that underlies the joke of Casti's and Salieri's opera. Obviously the music cannot serve the text if the music comes first; and, in particular, as Poeta puts it to Maestro, "The connoisseur seeks in the music of an opera the expression of the feelings that are in the words and the action," a sentiment with which the Camerata would have whole-heartedly concurred. "First the music, then the words," therefore, contradicts the most basic premise of text setting, in place since the closing years of the sixteenth century, that "the words [are] mistress of the harmony and not the servant."

But if the history of the text setting aesthetics, from the beginning of the Baroque era, can tell us why the premise of Casti's libretto, "first the music, then the words," is funny, can it also tell us why the composer's taunt to the poet is not funny but rings true? "Who in the world is going to notice your rhymes and verses? It's nothing compared to the music. The music alone is what people really want."

Perhaps we can get a handle on this contradiction by quoting from the composer who shared the double bill with Salieri on the night *Prima la musica* was premiered. Mozart writes to his father (26 September 1781) of his own aesthetics of operatic text

---

[12] Strunk, *Source Readings*, 374.

setting: "music, even in the most terrible situations, must never offend the ear, but must please the hearer, or, in other words must never cease to be *music*...."[13] To stay close to our previous metaphor, it is Mozart's precept that in serving the words and dramatic situation the music must, as well, serve itself. The servant must be master as well: master in his own house. Or, as Mozart put it, again to his father (13 October 1781): "I should say that in an opera the poetry must be altogether the obedient daughter of the music... [T]here the music reigns supreme and when one listens to it all else is forgotten."[14]

It is not too much to say that in the setting of texts, operatic texts especially, the precept that the music must be slave to the words has been in continual conflict with the precept that the result of musical text setting is a *musical* work, not a literary one. Which of these precepts is dominant? It is certainly the former that is most frequently enunciated. Which, indeed, should lead us to believe that the latter is the more basic axiom, indeed the defining one. For it is always the unspoken assumptions that lie closest to the center. They are unspoken, of course, because there is no need to speak them: their authority is unquestioned. But sometimes even the most obvious must be said. And when Gluck famously enunciated, for another age, in the dedication of *Alceste*, that music must be restrained to "its true office of serving poetry by means of expression...,"[15] a critic at the time felt compelled, in reply, to state the all too obvious: "When I go to the Opéra, it is to hear music."[16]

Interpreting the Wordless

Let us return to the beginning, to Salieri's opera, in fact, and take stock. The opera is a joke. The joke is that an opera is to be written backwards: first the music, and then the words. The reason it is a joke

---

[13] *Letters of Mozart and His Family*, trans. Emily Anderson (London: Macmillan, 1938), vol. III, 1145.

[14] Ibid., vol. III, 1150–1.

[15] Quoted in Alfred Einstein, *Gluck* (London: Dent, 1954), 98.

[16] *The Collected Correspondence and Papers of Christoph Willibald Gluck*, trans. Stewart Thomson, ed. Hedwig and E. H. Mueller von Asow (New York: St. Martin's Press, 1962), 106.

is that the underlying principle of text setting since the close of the sixteenth century is: music must be the servant to the text. Yet that precept exists alongside another, which the composer throws up to the librettist: the most important part of an opera, by far, is the *music*; operas are *musical* works.

And yet, finally, the joke of Salieri's opera is not *always* a laughing matter. For there is a musical practice, if not common, yet common enough to be familiar, of words being written for already composed music, even music originally composed for instruments. Furthermore, it was not, in Salieri's time, an outmoded practice. Indeed, Mozart himself used music from the unfinished Great Mass in C-minor (K. 429) for his cantata, *Davide penitente* (K. 469). And, even more relevant to the present point, he reveals in one of his letters to his father (26 September 1781), concerning the composition of an aria for *Die Entführung aus dem Serai* (K. 384): "I have explained to Stephanie [the librettist] the words I require for this aria—indeed I had finished composing most of the music for it before Stephanie knew anything whatever about it."[17] In fact then, Mozart did just that thing that Casti and Salieri held up to ridicule in one of his greatest works for the stage. And, ironically, Salieri himself seems to have done so, on at least one occasion, as well. For Lorenzo Da Ponte tells us that when he finally delivered his libretto of *Il ricco d'un giorno* to his collaborator, after a long delay—it was his first attempt at libretto writing—Salieri "had already written part of the music."[18] Nor is that an end to the irony, as *Prima la musica* may also have been created music first.[19]

Imagine, now, against this backdrop of assumptions and practices of the text setting aesthetics, the meteoric rise of pure instrumental music in the latter part of the eighteenth century, and the early part of the nineteenth. There is no doubt whatever that this music posed a theoretical and, if I may say so, a philosophical problem for the people who thought about such things. From the point of view of hard-core philosophy, the struggle of Kant and Hegel to understand the significance of this music or, in fact, to accept it is fine art at all,

---

[17] *Letters of Mozart and His Family*, vol. III, 1144.
[18] Sheila Hodges, *Lorenzo Da Ponte: The Life and Times of Mozart's Librettist* (Madison, · Wisconsin: University of Wisconsin Press, 2002), 52.
[19] Ibid., 71–2.

is ample evidence of the theoretical difficulties it posed. But what concerns me principally in the present chapter is theory at a somewhat lower level: the theory of how absolute music is to be talked about: how, in other words, it is to be interpreted to would-be listeners, or to the interpreter himself.

It is obvious from even a cursory perusal of the literature that critics and theoreticians of these times felt a deep need to talk about the newly emerging instrumental idiom. What one cannot discuss one cannot understand, or explain to another. To put it more grandiosely, words give us power over things. But where to find the words? Is it too bizarre to suggest that the first model for absolute music talk was the practice, already in place, of putting words to already existing music? Casti's and Salieri's joke, in other words, became the critics' and theoreticians' stock-in-trade. As Bach, or his collaborator, wrote words for the overture to the Fourth Orchestral Suite, as Stephanie wrote words for Mozart's already composed aria, so the theoreticians and critics wrote words for symphonies and string quartets. They were the instrumental composers' librettists *ex post facto*.

Not only is this not a bizarre suggestion, it does, in fact, help us to understand why so much of the early Romantic interpretation took narrative form. It is not merely that Romantics "like to do that sort of thing." That, no doubt, is true. But surely it is also that such an interpretive strategy already existed in the accepted musical practice of putting words to previously composed music. What is ready to hand one tends to pick up if one needs a tool.

Furthermore, the assumption on which specific narrative interpret-ations of the growing absolute music canon were based, namely, that absolute music really *is*, generally, wordless drama, to which words must be put by the would-be interpreter, did not go unspoken. Witness, for instance, August Apel, writing in the early nineteenth century that "instrumental music should have such a character as can be rendered in poetry...," and providing, as an example, one of Mozart's large-scale symphonies.[20] Further instances are easily provided.

---

[20] *Music and Aesthetics in the Eighteenth and Early-Nineteenth Centuries*, ed. Peter le Huray and James Day (Cambridge: Cambridge University Press, 1981), 392. I have not actually

More frequently, it is well to point out, absolute music is described, in the late eighteenth and early nineteenth centuries as a "language" of "emotive expression." Thus Johann Georg Sulzer, one of the most influential aestheticians of the late eighteenth century, wrote that "the sole function of a perfect musical composition is the accurate expression of emotions and passions in all their varying and individual nuances."[21] But that this "expression theory" of music is not inconsistent with narrative interpretation of pure instrumental music—indeed is *part* of it—becomes clear as we continue on to Sulzer's advice to the composer as to *how* emotive expression is to be achieved.

Every piece of music must have a definite character and evoke emotions of a specific kind. This is so both of instrumental and vocal music. Any composer would be misguided if he started work before deciding on the character of his piece . . . Having determined the character of his piece, he must put himself into the emotional state that he wishes others to experience. His best course of action is to imagine some drama, happening or situation that will naturally induce the kind of state that he has in mind; and if his imagination is sufficiently fired by this, he should at once set to work . . . .[22]

The reason I say that the expression theory of absolute music is really part and parcel of the narrative theory, and not a rival, is the close association, in music with text, and, especially, operatic music, of musical text setting with following in the music the expressive character of the words. Opera is, after all quintessentially, emotive drama, with the music's role—not entirely, of course, but in very large measure—the highlighting of the emotive states of characters, and the emotive import of the situations in which they find themselves. What we can glean from Sulzer's discussion, then, is that the composer imagines an emotive drama in composing absolute music, and the music itself, if the compositional process has been successful, embodies that drama. Narrative interpretation is re-imagining, as it were, the emotive drama that the composer has imagined, and putting words to that drama. *Prima la musica, e poi le parole.*

been able to consult the writings of August Apel. The view is attributed to him by Peter Lichtenthal (1780–1853).

[21] Ibid., 124.   [22] Ibid., 126–7.

This method of analysis or description of absolute music was carried to its extreme, its absurd extreme, one is tempted to say, and made quite explicit by Jerome-Joseph de Momigny, in his *Cours complet d'harmonie et de composition*, of 1803, where he actually contrived an operatic text, in French, of a lamenting Dido, and put it to the first movement of Mozart D minor Quartet (K. 421), as a commentary on the movement. Peter le Huray writes, "Momigny thus thought of an instrumental composition (and particularly the highly dramatic first movement of Mozart's D minor Quarter) as a wordless operatic aria . . . ."[23] And as Momigny described what he did:

The style of this *Allegro moderato* is noble and full of pathos. I believe that the best way to make my readers aware of its true quality is to set words to it . . . The feelings expressed by the composer are to be imagined as those of the beloved who is on the point of being deserted by her hero. Dido . . . immediately sprang to mind. The nobility of her rank, the warmth of her love, the greatness of her misfortune, all these persuaded me to make her the heroine of this piece.[24]

Here is what the opening measures of the Mozart look like, in Momigny's "operatic" version (see pp. 21–2).[25]

In sum, then, the first wave of musical interpreters of the new absolute music, faced with the phenomenon of a rapidly growing instrumental repertoire, turned to the familiar, if somewhat less than commonplace practice of writing words to precomposed music, for their interpretive method. What they heard in absolute music was wordless drama. And, as interpreters, they became the composers' (sometimes unwelcome) librettists.

Interpretations without Stories

But it would be a mistake to represent this first period of absolute music's interpretation as single-minded in its approach. For while narrative, dramatic interpretations may have been the more abundant, critics and theoreticians were also struggling with another concept of

---

[23] Peter le Huray, *Authenticity in Performance: Eighteenth-Century Case Studies* (Cambridge: Cambridge University Press, 1990), 115–16.

[24] Ibid., 121.   [25] Ibid., 117.

absolute music that would lead to Hanslick's formalism, and other formalisms to come. It was the concept of absolute music as a pure sonic structure with no secret or underlying meaning at all.

Perhaps one of the most startlingly advanced expressions of this proto-formalism is to be found in the late eighteenth-century writer, Wilhelm Heinrich Wackenroder, a name unfamiliar to philosophers, no doubt, but well known to the music historians. Here is how Wackenroder describes the experience of absolute music in one place:

Whenever I go to a concert, I always enjoy the music two ways. Only one of them is the true one. This involves attentively following the progression of sounds, yielding completely to this stream of overwhelming sensations, and banishing and withdrawing from every disturbing thought and every alien sense-impression. A certain effort is involved when one drinks in the sounds so avidly, and it cannot be sustained for any length of time.[26]

I am struck by the similarity of this description to that of an author far from unfamiliar, Clive Bell, whose formalist credentials are beyond reproach:

when I am feeling bright and clear and intent, at the beginning of a concert, for instance, . . . I get from music that pure aesthetic emotion I get from visual

---

[26] Peter le Huray, *Authenticity in Performance*, 249.

art . . . [A]t moments I do appreciate music as pure aesthetic form, . . . as pure art . . . with no relation at all to the significance of life . . . Tired or perplexed, I let slip my sense of form . . . and I begin weaving meaning into the harmonies . . . the ideas of life . . . .[27]

Even though, with the benefit of hindsight, Wackenroder's characterization of the purely musical experience seems to us very like the formalism of such figures as Bell, Fry, and their musical counterparts, it is obvious that it was no easy path from the narrative model of musical interpretation and appreciation to the formalism of Hanslick, which we tend to think of as the first substantial version of the doctrine in music. Herder described what he saw as the struggle of music to become an autonomous art form, free of "foreign entanglements." "The slow progress of music's history amply demonstrates how hard it has been for music to cut herself free from her sisters—mime and word—and to establish herself as an independent art."[28] It was a struggle too, to find a way of understanding, describing, appreciating the "new" absolute music in absolutist terms, free of narrative content—a struggle it seems to me in lock step with the struggle of Kant and Hegel to conceive of music, free of text, as an art form at all.

Hanslick saw the alternatives being not between absolute music as dramatic narrative, and absolute music as pure formal structure, but being between absolute music as emotively expressive, and as pure formal structure, a false dichotomy, as will become apparent. Narrative interpretation was, for Hanslick, anyway, no longer a live option.

We are the heirs to two conflicting ways of appreciating and describing the absolute music canon. There is the way of narrative interpretation, the way that the first critics and theorists of the new instrumental music naturally fell into, through the practice of putting words to pre-existing music, and there is the later way of formalism.

Wackenroder already saw these as two ways of listening to and describing absolute music; and he averred that "Only one of these is the true one," the "true one" being, of course, what *we* call formalism, and I prefer to call, since it is my own view, enhanced formalism (to be elucidated later on). Was he right that there is only one "true"

[27] Clive Bell, *Art* (New York: Capricorn Books, 1958), 30.
[28] *Music and Aesthetics*, 257.

way, and that it is formalism? That, as we used to say, before inflation, is the sixty-four dollar question.

Historicism or Progress?

There was a period in my own professional lifetime when formalism reigned supreme. It was not that narrative descriptions of absolute music were unheard of or uncommon. But they were considered by the "experts" pabulum for the uneducated masses: appropriate for program notes at symphony concerts and what was called when I was in grade school "music appreciation" (which mostly consisted, as I remember, in turning every piece of music into *Till Eulenspiegel*). Formalism was an escape from the excesses of early Romantic criticism. It was the discovery, by an enlightened age, of absolute music's true essence.

But that is all behind us now; and "the bottom rail is on top" (as a former slave told Abraham Lincoln). For there is no doubt that, at least in musicological circles, narrative interpretation of the now "so-called" absolute music canon is accepted practice. As for formalism, even of the "enhanced" kind, it is represented as a narrow-minded, "positivistic" doctrine that tends to make of absolute music, which is absolute in name only, a thing apart without what any art worth the name must have: without, in a word, *meaning*.

Furthermore, whereas formalism represented itself as providing a true understanding of the new absolute music that its first hearers could not possess, the neo-narrative critics, true to the historicist spirit of modern musicology, have tended to represent themselves as returning to a true understanding of the absolute music canon that has been lost, and that only its first hearers could possess. It is this stand-off between what I will call the "doctrine of historicism" and the "doctrine of progress" that is another way in which the ancient quarrel between the literary and the musical now expresses itself. And the question as to whether formalist description or narrative description of the absolute music canon is the right kind of description may not be resolvable solely on grounds internal to the conflicting practices themselves but rather on external grounds in addition: on whether you adhere to the doctrine of historicism or the doctrine of progress.

The doctrine of historicism in artistic appreciation, as I am under-standing it here, has it as a general principle of interpretation and appreciation that the first audiences to a work of art are the ones most likely to comprehend it in the right way, because they share with the artist a common experience, and common knowledge, which the passage of time gradually erases. So if it is the case, as I do think it is, that the first audiences and critics to experience the burgeoning new instrumental idiom tended for the most part to hear these works as, and describe them in terms of, dramatic narrative or, so to speak, opera without words, for which *they* were to supply the words, then that is the correct way of reacting to and describing them, according the doctrine of historicism.

The doctrine of progress, which I take to be deeply implicated in what I would describe as the good old fashioned, romantic concept of *genius*, has it that audiences are ill-prepared to understand and appreciate the art works of their own times, when these are the works of genius, because geniuses are "ahead of their time." Beethoven is, of course, the legendary case in point, in the absolute music tradition, the reception of the Rasoumowski Quartets being a cornerstone of the legend. As one contemporary writer reports: "I said to him [Beethoven], that he surely did not consider these works to be music?—to which he replied, 'Oh, they are not for you, but for a later age.' "[29]

I am an inveterate, entirely unrepentant believer in the good old romantic concept of genius, and in the doctrine of progress that it supports, when that doctrine is taken to apply to our understanding of the works of artistic genius. That is *my* artistic and aesthetic world view.[30] What follows from it is the conviction that those who comprised the first audiences to the new instrumental repertory were struggling with a strange and unfamiliar idiom which they were not in a position to fully understand and appreciate. In their struggle they, quite naturally, fell back on the most readily available and familiar way of describing, understanding, and appreciating this new and frequently

---

[29] Alexander Wheelock Thayer, *The Life of Ludwig van Beethoven* (Carbondale, Illinois: Southern Illinois University Press, 1960), vol. II, 75.

[30] On this see, Peter Kivy, *The Possessor and the Possessed: Handel, Mozart, Beethoven, and the Idea of Musical Genius* (New Haven: Yale University Press, 2001), especially chapter XIII.

difficult music. They put words to the music, the words of musical drama.

It was necessary then, for people to discover that what they were confronted with was not wordless drama to be augmented by an audience of self-appointed librettists, but a sonic structure to be grasped in a very different way, as I will argue in the closing chapters of this book. And if Eduard Hanslick was not the first to fully realize this, he was certainly the first to put it in a way accessible to the general musical public, amply attested to by the ten editions his "little book" went through between 1884, the date of the first edition of *On Musical Beauty*, and 1904, the date of his death.

If I am right that lying at the heart of the conflict between those who want to put narrative words to absolute music and those who want only to put structural, syntactic, and expressive words to it is what I have described as conflicting artistic and aesthetic "world views," then resolution is certainly going to be difficult, although if I thought it impossible I would not be writing this book.

Seeming intractability usually invites councils of despair. And disputes about how absolute music can correctly be described have tempted some to conclude that it cannot be described at all. "Music is ineffable" said one theorist at the beginning of the nineteenth century,[31] and the view perennially recurs. Such skepticism to the contrary notwithstanding, it does seem reasonable to believe that if we can find language to describe the inner structure of the atom and the outer structure of the cosmos, we can do so for the familiar, everyday (to us) phenomenon of absolute music as well. The late eighteenth century and early nineteenth struggled with this problem in an era when absolute music was a more or less new rather than familiar experience, at least as a major player in the art world. And although putting words to absolute music—the problem that, I have suggested, Salieri's comic opera lays bear—was initially, and naturally, seen as putting a libretto to an already written opera, in other words, a narrative strategy, the formalist strategy had also been "discovered" early on.

[31] *Music and Aesthetics*, 273.

Not only had the formalist strategy been discovered by such critics and theoreticians of music as Wackenroder, however, but, most would agree, by a singularly unlikely candidate in the philosophical world, the markedly unmusical Immanuel Kant, whose genius prevailed over his lack of musical sensibility. And it is really to Kant's third *Critique*, not to such writers as Wackenroder, that we must turn for the first philosophically significant venture into formalism in absolute music. For it was Kant who first gave the literary interpreters of the absolute music canon something philosophically deep to quarrel with. But ironically, as we shall see, Kant's so-called "musical formalism" itself was not entirely free of "extra-musical" content. The "quarrel," indeed, lay just beneath the surface.

2

Designs À La Grecque

Introduction

Kant's philosophical reflections on music, we are forced to believe, were not motivated by any particular interest in the subject on his part but, it seems apparent, merely by a desire to fill out the scheme, to which he wasn't even sure music belonged, that Paul Oskar Kristeller designated as "the modern system of the arts."[1] For what we quite naturally think of as "the fine arts," were only just beginning to be thought of as such in the eighteenth century. And as late as Hegel's *Lectures on the Fine Arts*, which is to say, the early nineteenth century, it was still an issue in some philosophers' minds, Hegel's and Kant's included, whether music, at least absolute music, really *did* belong to "the system."

In the eighteenth century, when music was talked about at all by philosophers and other "theorists" of the arts, it was almost always vocal music that was being talked about, even when that was not explicitly stated. And there wasn't any real problem with vocal music's membership in the family of the fine arts. For one thing, it had a poetic text, and there was never any doubt that *poetry* was a fine art: indeed it was the paradigm case. For another, what the fine arts were supposed to have in common, as their defining principle, was *representation*. And vocal music, since the end of the sixteenth century, had been understood as a representational art: it represented the passionate tones of the human speaking voice, as we have seen.

---

[1] See Paul Oskar Kristeller, "The Modern System of the Arts (I)," and "The Modern System of the Arts (II)," reprinted in Peter Kivy (ed.), *Essays in the History of Aesthetics* (Rochester: Rochester University Press, 1992).

The bone of contention was pure instrumental music: music without a text, what came to be called "absolute music" in the nineteenth century. And it did not become a major philosophical issue until, at the end of the eighteenth century, pure instrumental music emerged as a major player in the game, at the hands of Haydn, Mozart, and Beethoven. The problem was that it was difficult to see how, if representation was to be the defining property of the fine arts, that principle could apply to absolute music. For it seemed to have no plausible object of representation: the human voice seemed an unlikely candidate, although it was proposed from time to time; and there was no other in evidence to serve the purpose, if the human voice could not. (Storms and battles were pretty weak candidates.)

It is in the context of the debate over whether or not absolute music is one of the fine arts that we must view Kant's philosophy of music as a whole, and his musical formalism in particular. And so I turn now to Kant's contribution to it.

Form

It is one of the most obvious aspects of Kant's entry into the debate over absolute music's credentials as a fine art that he radically transforms it from a debate over how or whether absolute music can be narrative, or representational to a debate, with himself, over how or whether it can possess perceivable *form*. For form, in the Kantian system, is the bearer of *beauty*, and the fine arts, for Kant, are the beautiful arts: *schöne Kunst*. In other words, no perceivable form, no beauty; no beauty, no fine art, no *schöne Kunst*. This is, of course, the move to formalism that so characterizes Kant's philosophy of art, and has been identified by many as the source of modern formalism, in music particularly and in the fine arts in general.

That Kant was the major source of formalism in philosophy of art I have no doubt. That Kant himself was a formalist, in the sense of someone who thinks form is the *only* art-relevant property, is totally false, as shall become apparent later on in this chapter. First, though, to the debate over musical form.

What is puzzling to all readers of Kant, when they come to the question of musical form, is the peculiar candidate Kant seems at least to propose for it in the first place. For the musical reader, in any period of the modern era, musical form is taken to be the overall plan, the patterned sequence of events instantiated by a musical composition: sonata form, or da capo form, or theme-and-variation form, and so forth. It is the general outline of a musical composition, be it a whole composition or a movement in it. But for Kant, musical form seems to be the form of musical sound's "vibrating movements," as Kant calls them;[2] *Zitterungen*, in German:[3] in other words, what we call, loosely speaking in colloquial English, "sound waves."

The question, then, of whether absolute music is a fine art, apparently turns out, for Kant, to be the question of whether we can consciously perceive the forms of these vibrating waves, or whether we merely perceive their effects on the auditory sense. Furthermore, it is a question formed in terms of a choice between music as a *fine* art, which is to say, in Kant's terms, a *beautiful* art, or what Kant calls an *agreeable* art. Interestingly enough, Kant does not seem to think that the choice is of very great importance. Here is what he says:

> The difference which the one opinion or the other occasions in the estimate of the basis of music would, however, only give rise to this much change in its definition, that either it is to be interpreted, as we have done, as the *beautiful* play of sensations (through hearing), or else as one of *agreeable* sensations. According to the former interpretation alone, would music be represented out and out as a *fine* art, whereas according to the latter it would be represented as (in part at least) an *agreeable* art.[4]

Kant had no real conception of the significance absolute music had even then, and has now, for serious, reflective audiences. He would, I imagine, be quite astonished were he to see the commanding statue of Beethoven in Bonn, or the shrine to Mozart that the whole city of Salzburg has become. Clearly, he did not realize the importance of the philosophical issue he had raised.

[2] Immanuel Kant, *Critique of Aesthetic Judgement*, trans. James Creed Meredith (Oxford: Clarendon Press, 1911), 189 (§51). All quotations from the *Critique of Judgment* are from this edition unless otherwise indicated.

[3] Immanuel Kant, *Kritik der Urteilskraft* (Hamburg: Felix Meiner Verlag, 1959), 181 (§51).

[4] Kant, *Critique of Aesthetic Judgement*, 190 (§51).

For us to understand both the terms in which Kant framed the question of whether music is a beautiful or an agreeable play of sensations, which is to say a fine or an agreeable art, we must for a bit get into some more or less picky Kantian minutiae. But it does have a philosophical payoff.

Kant's theory of beauty and the fine arts, in other words what we would call his aesthetics and philosophy of art, is put forward in his Critique of Aesthetic Judgment, which is Part I of his *Critique of Judgment*, first published in 1790, and frequently referred to, as I shall do at times, as the third *Critique*. It went through three editions in the author's lifetime, the significance of which will become apparent in a moment.

Fairly early in the Critique of Aesthetic Judgment, before he gets to his account of the fine arts, Kant writes, according to the first and second editions: "If we assume with Euler that colours are isochronous vibrations (pulsus) of the ether, as sounds are of the air in a state of disturbance, and—what is the most important—that the mind not only perceives by sense the effect of these in exciting the organ, but also perceives by reflection the regular play of impressions (and thus the form of the combination of different representations)—which I very much doubt—then colours and tone cannot be reckoned as mere sensations, but...as beauties."[5]

The reference to Euler, is to Leonhard Euler, the Swiss mathematician and physicist, whose work on color Kant is invoking here. And he is, apparently, denying the possibility that the form of Euler's vibrations, either in the case of color, or of sound, is such that one, as he puts it, "perceives by reflection the regular play of impressions...." That one could do that, with regard either to color vibrations or sound vibrations, he says, "...I very much doubt...." Thus, it seems, musical sound cannot be perceived as form, so music cannot be a fine, but must be an agreeable art.

There is a catch, however, namely, that in the *third* edition of the *Critique of Judgment*, "I very much doubt" is altered to read: "which I

[5] Immanuel Kant, *Critique of Judgment*, trans. J. H. Bernard (New York: Hafner, 1951), 60 (§14).

still in no way doubt . . . ."[6] The reading of the third edition completely
reverses the meaning of the sentence from apparently denying that we
actually perceive sound vibrations cognitively, rather than just sensing
their effect, to apparently affirming that that is exactly what we do.
Which is the authentic reading? The version of the first and second
editions certainly seems to make it a more plausible claim, at least if
we are interpreting Kant correctly here. And in the absence of other
textual evidence, that might decide us in its favor. But there are other
considerations that support the reading of the third edition, and the
Kant experts with whose work I am acquainted, who think about
this textual problem, are generally in favor of it.[7] In the past I have
acquiesced in their judgment. But I will, later on, come back to
consider whether we have really understood correctly just *what* Kant
was saying here.

With this textual problem out of the way, at least for the moment,
let us return again to the section of the third *Critique* where Kant
tackles the question of whether music is a fine or an agreeable art.
It seems to turn, remember, on whether we perceive the forms of
vibrations of musical tone, Euler's vibrations, cognitively, or whether
we merely feel their effect.

One of the puzzling things about Kant's mode of expression here
which, by the way, is §51 of the third *Critique*, is that it evinces
diffidence and uncertainty. If we accept the third edition reading
of §14, then Kant can be understood as expressing more or less
confidently that we do indeed perceive, cognitively, the forms of the
individual musical sound vibrations. He says: ". . . I still in no way
doubt [it] . . . ."

But in §51 he is far less confident than that. He says: "we cannot
confidently assert whether a colour or a tone (sound) is merely an

---

[6] Kant, *Critique of Aesthetic Judgement*, p. 66 (§14). Cf. Immanuel Kant, *Critique of Judgment*,
trans. Werner S. Pluhar (Indianapolis: Hackett, 1987), 70 (§14): "which, after all, I do not
doubt at all . . . ," and Immanuel Kant, *Critique of the Power of Judgment*, trans. Paul Guyer and
Eric Matthews (Cambridge: Cambridge University Press, 2001), 109 (§14), "about which I
have very little doubt . . . ."

[7] See, especially, Theodore E. Uehling, Jr., *The Notion of Form in Kant's "Critique of
Aesthetic Judgment"* (The Hague: Mouton, 1971).

agreeable sensation, or whether they are in themselves a beautiful play of sensations and in being estimated aesthetically, convey, as such, a delight in their form."[8] The indecision is expressed in the form of a kind of informal dilemma. On the one hand, Kant observes, it seems quite repugnant to common sense to think that we can perceive light waves or sound waves in the same way we perceive the waves of the ocean or ripples on a pond. For the velocity of these vibrations "in all probability far outstrips any capacity on our part for forming an immediate estimate in perception of the time interval between them . . . ." And that being the case, "we should be led to believe that it is only the *effect* of these vibrating movements upon the elastic parts of our body, that can be evident to sense . . . and that, consequently, all that enters into combination with colours and tones is agreeableness, and not beauty, of their composition."[9]

The word "composition," *Komposition*, as it is used by Kant in the musical context is going to be an important issue in a little while. But as it is necessary to read the passage just quoted, the "composition" referred to is the composition, that is the structure, of the individual tones themselves, not the musical composition which might be made of them. This structure, of which the tones are composed, Kant is saying, seems not possible to perceive by sense in the manner in which we can see, for example, the waves that "compose" the ocean.

But on the other hand, Kant says—and here is the other horn of the dilemma—"we may feel compelled to look upon the sensations afforded by both [colours and sounds], not as mere sense impressions, but as the effect of an estimate of forms in the play of a number of sensations."[10]

Now a dilemma, or "antinomy," as Kant famously called some well known dilemmas, is supposed to be made up of two intuitively plausible theses, both of which cannot be true, or so it seems: for example, that there is free will, and that the universe is deterministic. The present one, however, presents, at least as it has been understood in the past, only *one* plausible thesis, namely, that we do *not* consciously perceive the form of the vibrations of musical sound. And it is the

---

[8] Kant, *Critique of Aesthetic Judgement*, 189 (§51).   [9] Ibid.
[10] Ibid., 190 (§51).

other, completely *implausible* thesis that, if the third edition of the third *Critique* is to be credited, Kant apparently was maintaining. But the experts seem agreed that the reading of the third edition is the correct one. For the moment (but only for the moment) I will let it stand, and get on with the argument.

Kant seemingly says in §14 that he is certain we do in fact perceive, cognitively, the form of the sound vibrations in musical tones. In §51 he says he is not sure whether we do or we don't, but recent commentators apparently think that the statement in §14 is Kant's true position. That being the case, we can conclude that Kant thought music was a fine art; because to be a fine art an art must be an art of the beautiful and to be an art of the beautiful it must have perceivable form. Music does have perceivable form, namely, Kant seems to say, in the sound vibrations of musical tone. Therefore, music has the necessary characteristic for being a fine art, an art of the beautiful. (It must also, of course, be an *art*, which is to say a man-made product, not a natural object, to qualify as a fine art.)

Alas, the case is not quite so simple. Here are two reasons why. First of all, in a series of lectures which Kant gave throughout his mature life, and published, in 1798, under the title *Anthropology from a Pragmatic Point of View*, he states quite explicitly: "it is only because music serves as an instrument for poetry that it is *fine* (not merely pleasant) art."[11] And second, at the end of §51 of the third *Critique*, Kant says, apparently, that if the sound vibrations are *not* consciously perceived, then music will be an agreeable art "in part at least," suggesting that it will, if the vibrations *are* consciously perceived, be a fine art "in part at least." In short, Kant thought it possible that art could be fine art in one respect but not in another; and, I suggest, he thought music was one such art.

Given these two important qualifications, I think we can now state more accurately and plausibly what Kant was saying. Absolute music, music without a text, has one of two necessary (not jointly sufficient) features of the fine arts: it has perceivable form. But it lacks a second feature, namely, ideational content. Vocal music, on the other hand,

[11] Immanuel Kant, *Anthropology from a Pragmatic Point of View*, trans. Mary J. Gregory (The Hague: Martinus Nijhoff, 1974), 114.

which is what Kant was talking about in the *Anthropology*, has both form and ideational content, the content being given by the text which music sets. So whereas vocal music is a fine art, having both form and ideational content, absolute music is "in part" a fine art since it has form, but in part not a fine art since it lacks ideational content.

This is, however, just a rough account of what Kant is claiming. More exactly, what he turns out to be saying is that absolute music does not lack ideational content: rather, it does have such content but, so to speak, not in the right way. Kant then was not a formalist with regard to the fine arts. He thought that a certain kind of ideational content, functioning in a certain way, was a necessary condition for the fine arts. And to understand how absolute music fails in this department, we must go briefly into the matter of *what* Kant thought the ideational content of the fine arts is, and how he thought it functions.

Content

The content of the fine arts that is peculiarly theirs Kant calls "aesthetic ideas." He explains, "by an aesthetic idea I mean that representation of the imagination which induces much thought, yet without the possibility of any definite thought whatever, i.e. *concept*, being adequate to it, and which language, consequently, can never quite get on level terms with or render completely intelligible."[12]

Kant's notion, as I read him, is motivated by these considerations. If the content of an artwork were merely what I would call its "manifest" content, susceptible of paraphrase, then there would be nothing special about it. You could get it from any number of other forms of expression, and that would leave artworks with no special role or function of their own. But our intuitions run in a different direction. We feel that artworks have ideational content in a very different way. We feel that their ideational content, unlike that of non-artistic means of expression, is somehow ineffable: you cannot express what an artwork "says" in any other form than that in which the artwork "says" it.

---

[12] *Critique of Aesthetic Judgement*, 175–6 (§49).

Artworks do indeed have manifest content, susceptible of paraphrase, and this content does indeed perform a vital function: it sets
going a train of aesthetic ideas. What I have been calling the fine arts'
manifest content, as Kant puts it, "stirs up a crowd of sensations and
secondary representations for which no expression can be found."[13] It
is this "crowd of sensations and secondary representations for which
no expression can be found," which is to say, the aesthetic ideas, that
constitutes the art-relevant content of the fine arts: the arts of the
beautiful.

But absolute music, too, on Kant's view, possesses both manifest
content and aesthetic ideas that that content sets in train. The manifest content turns out, not very surprisingly, to be what we might
call music's expressive or emotive content. For Kant bought into
the eighteenth-century doctrine, particularly prominent in Germany
under the title of the *Affektenlehre*, that is to say, doctrine of the
affections, which made music out to be a kind of language of the
emotions, which reflected the emotive tone of passionate human
speech.

It was a notion fairly ubiquitous in the Enlightenment that human
speech has an underlying emotive sub-text universal to the species.
As Kant puts it, "Every expression in language has an associated
tone suited to its sense. This tone indicates, more or less, a mode
in which the speaker is affected, and in turn evokes it in the hearer
also, in whom conversely it then excites the idea which in language is
expressed with such a tone."[14] The point is, then, that if the speaker
expresses, say, anger in her speech, the angry tone of her expression
will evoke, which I think is to say will arouse, anger in the hearer,
empathetically, and this will then provoke the hearer to have the
concept which that expressive tone is associated with, namely the
concept of anger.

Music, Kant thinks, follows the very same routine; and, furthermore,
it goes beyond it. For the end product in the case of music is not the
concept of an emotion, or emotions, but a chain of aesthetic ideas
stimulated by the concept. Thus, in Kant's words, "just as modulation
[of speech] is, as it were, a universal [emotive] language of sensations

---

[13] Ibid., 178 (§49).   [14] Ibid., 194 (§53).

intelligible to every man, so the art of [musical] tone wields the full force of this [emotive] language wholly on its own account, namely, as a language of the affections, and in this way, according to the law of association, universally communicates the aesthetic ideas that are naturally combined therewith."[15]

But, one is bound to ask, if absolute music possesses both form and an ideational content of aesthetic ideas, which are jointly sufficient for making an artifact a work of the fine arts, why does music not qualify? The answer, as I suggested earlier, is that it is not just that something initiate a train of aesthetic ideas, but how these aesthetic ideas *function*, that decides whether the train of aesthetic ideas is or is not a fine-art-making feature. And according to Kant the aesthetic ideas initiated by music do *not* have the proper function to make them fine-art-relevant. To understand this point, though, we must come to understand some of the basic machinery underlying the perception of beauty and what Kant calls the pure judgment of taste.

Taste

In the first part of his Critique of Aesthetic Judgment, which he calls the Analytic of the Beautiful, Kant poses the following question. How can judgments of the beautiful, which are based merely upon our feeling of pleasure, and therefore like the kinds of judgment we call purely subjective, also be judgments that seem to demand universal assent, as if they were objective judgments, based on commonly held concepts? For, as Kant says, when someone "puts a thing on a pedestal and calls it beautiful, he demands the same delight from others."[16] But how can this demand be justified if the judgment is based merely on the judger's personal feeling of pleasure? That is Kant's problem, as it had been David Hume's and others of his British predecessors'.

The answer to it that Kant gives is complicated, and fraught with interpretational difficulties. Fortunately, all that is necessary, for present purposes, is that we have the most basic grasp of the answer

---

[15] *Critique of Aesthetic Judgement*, 194 (§53).   [16] Ibid., 52 (§7).

Kant gives. And that I will try now to provide avoiding, I hope, an over-simplification that might amount to misrepresentation of Kant's views.

Let us begin with an item of what might be called epistemological ontology. According to Kant, what we might call factual and conceptual judgments are the result of an interaction between two mental faculties common to all: our *understanding* and our *imagination*. There is no particular need, for present purposes, to know how this all works. What we do need to know is that Kant thought there is an activity that these two cognitive faculties, the understanding and the imagination, can mutually engage in, which he called their "free play," and which produces a felt pleasure in the person whose cognitive faculties are so engaged.

Furthermore, because this pleasure issues from the free play of *cognitive* faculties, which, on that account, must be faculties common to all human beings, since cognition is common, the pleasure itself is universally felt, when the pleasure truly has its source in the free play of these faculties, and not in some other bodily source, from which so many of our pleasures arise. The free play of the understanding and imagination can be considered, then, as a kind of sense, common to us all, a *sensus communis*, as Kant calls it.[17] With regard to judgments of the beautiful, he says, "We are suitors for agreement from every one, because we are fortified with a ground common to all."[18]

How, then, are we to understand the perceptual process whereby we experience the pleasure of the beautiful? When I see things, for example, their perception may give me various kinds of pleasures; but it is quite possible that none of these pleasures is the pleasure of beauty: the pleasure of the cognitive faculties in free play that is the basis for a judgment that something is beautiful—what Kant calls a pure judgment of taste. The question then comes down to what kind of perception it *is* that thus engages the faculties of imagination and understanding. How does perception put them in free play?

The answer is—and here lies the heart of Kant's often misunderstood formalism—that when we achieve perception of the pure form

---

[17] Ibid., 82 (§20).   [18] Ibid. (§19).

of a perceptual presentation, untainted by an extraneous conceptual or practical interest in it, we then achieve a state in which our perception is completely purged of any personal idiosyncrasies, due to experience or physical differences. That being the case, we have a right to assume that *anyone* who has achieved this state will feel the same pleasure we do, because they too would have been purged of anything that makes their perceptual experience different from ours. But what has *form* do with this? Simply that when perception is pared down to this bare, skeletal state, all that remains to be perceived is the pure form of the perceptual presentation. Furthermore, that pure form of the perceptual presentation will be perceived by *anyone* who achieves this state; for he or she too will, as we have seen, have been purged of all personal interest in the object.

Kant had a characteristic way of expressing this thought that is famous and was of great influence both in the nineteenth and twentieth centuries. He said: "*Taste* is the faculty of estimating an object or mode of representation by means of a delight or aversion *apart from any interest*. The object of such delight is called *beautiful*."[19] What Kant is describing has, since his time, been called, by aestheticians and philosophers of art, "disinterested perception," and Kant himself refers to the pleasure that results from this kind of perception as "pure disinterested delight...."[20]

What is particularly distinctive about Kant's description of disinterestedness is the extreme to which he carries the concept. It is not merely that, in what Kant calls the "pure judgment of taste," we are supposed to be indifferent to the nature of the object of perception; we are to be indifferent as well to its very existence—that is, whether or not it even exists. As Kant puts the point in one place, "Now, where the question is whether something is beautiful, we do not want to know, whether we, or any one else, are, or even could be, concerned in the real existence of the thing, but rather what estimate we form of it on mere contemplation...."[21]

What Kant is getting at here is this. If the sight of an object (say) is giving me pleasure because of the good use to which I can put it,

<hr />

[19] *Critique of Aesthetic Judgement*, 50 (§5).
[20] Ibid., 43–4 (§2).   [21] Ibid., 42–3 (§2).

then that pleasure is not the pleasure of the beautiful, and is, of course, bound up with the real existence of the object; it will not survive its dissolution. But if the sight of the object pleases disinterestedly, purely in virtue of the form of the perceptual presentation, then it matters not at all if I discover that the perception is a hallucination, or a dream, and the object of the perception non-existent. For the pleasure is in the form, and the perceptual presentation will have that form regardless of whether it is a veridical presentation or some species of illusion. It is this disinterested perception that activates the free play of the cognitive faculties that in turn produces the disinterested pleasure of the beautiful: a pleasure shared by all who achieve the requisite state, and which is the basis of the pure judgment of taste.

Is Music an Art?

With this basic and, I hope, not over-simplified account of Kant's position on the perception of beauty in hand, we can return now to the aesthetic ideas, and to the question of why they are not, in absolute music, functioning in a way appropriate to the fine arts. And to answer *that* question we must, of course, ask the prior question of how the aesthetic ideas function when they *are* functioning in a fine-art-relevant way.

It is clear that Kant wants a unified theory of fine art in which form and content are not two separate, unrelated features of artworks. He achieves this unity by claiming that the ultimate payoff of content, that is, of the aesthetic ideas, is the *same* payoff as that of formal beauty, namely, the free play of the cognitive faculties. And it is just this payoff that the aesthetic ideas in music lack. For whereas the aesthetic ideas in literature and the visual arts have their payoff in their interaction with the cognitive faculties, the aesthetic ideas in absolute music, for reasons I do not thoroughly understand, but at least have some glimmerings about, only have a bodily payoff: a sense of bodily well-being. Here is how Kant puts his point. Music is a "play with aesthetic ideas, or even with representations of the understanding, by which, all said and done, nothing is thought." Hence: "In music the course of this play is from bodily sensation to aesthetic ideas (which are the Objects for the affections), and then from these back again, but with gathered strength, to the body."[22]

At this point the general outline of Kant's philosophy of musical formalism can be organized somewhat along the following lines

First, Kant thinks, there are at least two requirements for being a fine art, besides the obvious one of being an artifact: that the artifact in question has perceivable form, and that it excite aesthetic ideas that eventuate in the free play of the cognitive faculties. Second, he seems to think, implausibly, that the form of the vibrations of air, of musical tones, is consciously perceivable, as is affirmed in the third edition of the third *Critique*, but denied in the first and second editions. Third, therefore, he thinks that music has one necessary condition for being a fine art: perceivable form. Fourth, music, for Kant, like the literary and visual arts, excites aesthetic ideas in the perceiver; but they do not engage the free play of the cognitive faculties. So music fails to fully qualify as a fine art. Fifth, music is, therefore, fine-art-like in one respect: it possesses perceivable beauty of form, but it is *not* fine-art-like in another respect—its aesthetic ideas do not stimulate the free play of the cognitive faculties. Sixth, in placing musical form in the form of sound vibrations Kant was taking an absurd position, which reveals that he had absolutely no notion of where true musical form resides, namely, in the formal structure of musical compositions.

But is Kant really maintaining the sixth, obviously absurd point? I used to think so. Now, however, I am not so sure.

Form and Composition

Consider the following passage:

The *charm* of colours, or of the agreeable tones of instruments, may be added: but the *design* in the former and the *composition* in the latter constitute the proper object of the pure judgement of taste ... [T]hey make this form more clearly, definitely, and completely intuitable, and besides stimulate the representation by their charm, as they excite and sustain the attention directed to the object itself.[23]

---

[22] *Critique of Aesthetic Judgement*, 198–9 (§54).   [23] Ibid., 68 (§14).

Two things about this passage are extremely important. First, most important, and most obvious, Kant is using the word "composition" here in just the way we would. He is clearly not referring to the composition of musical tones themselves, as he was in the passage quoted previously, but to the composition which musical tones are used to make. This is clear from his juxtaposition of *composition*, in music, to *design* in painting. Design is the large outline, the form, if you will, of a visual artwork. And if composition in music is being analogized to design in painting, then what Kant is referring to are the larger outlines of musical form, sonata, theme-and-variations, rondo, and so forth, even though he probably had no specific knowledge of the particulars of musical forms, and what they are called.

Second, but perhaps less obvious, Kant seems to be denying that the forms of the vibrations of either color or sound can be consciously, cognitively perceived; for he says that only the design of painting and the composition of music are "the proper object of the pure judgement of taste." But the proper object of the pure judgment of taste is form; so if color and timbre are not its proper objects, as Kant seems to be saying, then it follows that their forms, their internal structure cannot be consciously perceived, a point I will return to in a moment.

Are there any other passages in the Critique of Aesthetic Judgment that directly suggest Kant's grasp of larger musical form? The answer is affirmative, although the pickings are pretty slim. I will adduce one other for you, the only one I have so far turned up. But as we shall see, two passages that I have already quoted, and that others quote frequently, take on an entirely different complexion when read with the two passages in mind that I am now discussing.

The second passage I want now to adduce will, I hope, not only support my claim that Kant did indeed have at least some notion of musical form as we understand it, but also perhaps will present a side of the great philosopher few of us suspected was there. I am going to quote, in fact, a passage in which the Sage of Königsberg, no less, bestows upon us his instructions for entertaining at table. Kant begins: "Agreeable arts are those which have mere enjoyment for their object. Such are all the charms that can gratify a dinner party . . ."; and among these "charms" Kant includes "the art of arranging the table for enjoyment, or, at large banquets, the music of the orchestra—a quaint idea intended to act on the mind merely as an agreeable noise fostering a genial spirit, which, without anyone paying the smallest attention to the composition, promotes the free flow of conversation between guest and guest."[24]

What catches our attention here is not simply Kant's use of the term "composition" and the music's being, as Kant puts it, "merely an agreeable noise." When the musical composition is not attended to, he is saying, it functions as "merely an agreeable noise": one of the agreeable arts, like "the art of arranging the table . . . ." But when, however, we *are* attending to the musical composition, it must be functioning as something else, presumably as, at least in one respect, a fine art. And the difference must be that when we are paying attention to the composition, we are paying attention to the larger aspects of musical form; for it is form, as we have seen, that is one of the two aspects of art that together lift it above the agreeable and into the realm of the fine arts.

If the two passages just cited are to be read as I have done, then it appears that I must withdraw my earlier claim, in my previous writings, that Kant had no notion at all of musical form as we understand it, but thought of musical form only as the form of the sound vibrations of musical tones. It was a doubly doomed view: doomed because it paid no attention to real musical form, and doomed because it made the monstrously implausible claim that we can perceive consciously the forms of sound vibrations in the same sense that we can perceive the ocean's waves or the ripples on a pond.

But even if it turns out that, as I have been arguing, Kant did recognize the larger aspects of musical form, there still remains the implausibility of his apparent view that we can perceive the form of the musical sound vibrations. Was he maintaining *both*? To that difficult question I now turn.

Vibrations Reconsidered

At this point I want to return to two passages I have quoted and discussed before. The first is the passage in §14 where Kant describes

---

[24] *Critique of Aesthetic Judgement*, 165–6 (§44).

what is happening when we do indeed consciously perceive vibrations of musical tone, according to the third edition, and the other is the passage in §51 where Kant, at least tentatively, entertains the hypothesis that we consciously perceive the vibrations, and again describes what is going on if we do. What I want to argue is that everyone I know of who has interpreted these passages, including myself, in my previous writings, has gotten them wrong; furthermore, when you get them right, they make perfect sense.

In §14, you may remember, Kant says, according to the third edition, "...I, still, in no way doubt..." that musical tones "are isochronous vibrations... of the air set in vibration by sound, and, what is most important, that the mind not alone perceives by sense their effect in stimulating the organs, but also, by reflection, the regular play of the impressions, (and consequently the form in which different representations are united)...."[25]

The general consensus among Kant scholars, in which, in the past, I have acquiesced, has this passage affirming that sound, like color, is the result of Euler's vibrations, and, in addition, as affirming that we perceive by reflection the forms of the waves themselves, as we do the waves of the ocean or the ripples on a pond, following the third edition. I now think this may be wrong.

I begin with the premise that "perceiving" the vibrations of sound—Euler's vibrations—in the way we "perceive" the waves of the ocean or the ripples on a pond is patently false, bordering on the absurd. And if, in §14, we accept the reading of the first and second editions of the third *Critique*, we can save Kant from that seemingly outlandish position. We read him as very much doubting it.

Furthermore, philosophical considerations aside, it appears more likely that the third edition has the misprint. For if the clause was misprinted in the first edition, why was it not corrected in the second? That the misprint crept into the third edition, unnoticed, seems altogether more plausible. Kant was no longer around to notice and correct it.

But if we take Kant as saying that he very much doubted we can consciously perceive sound vibrations, then the paragraph following

[25] Ibid., 66 (§14).

this expression of doubt raises another problem. For Kant *seems* to be saying there that "pure" colors are beautiful (and the argument applies, *pari passu*, to sounds as well). As he puts it, "all simple colours are regarded as beautiful, so far as pure."[26] If pure colors and sounds are beautiful, though, it must be for their consciously perceivable form, on Kant's view. And so it would appear that Kant is *not* denying that we can consciously perceive, in colors and sounds, Euler's vibrations. The third edition must be *echt*.

Notice, however, how Kant expresses himself here, which is to say, in the passive voice. He does not say that pure colors and sounds *are* beautiful or that *he* thinks they are beautiful. He says that they are "held to be beautiful,"[27] are "regarded as Beautiful,"[28] are "considered beautiful."[29] In the German it is *für schön gehalten*. What I suggest we understand Kant to be doing, here, is saying that pure colors and sounds are, *mistakenly*, "held to be beautiful," "regarded as beautiful," "considered beautiful," and offering an *explanation* for why this is so.

What does it mean for a color or sound to be pure? Kant writes: "But the purity of a simple mode of sensation means that its uniformity is not disturbed or broken by any foreign sensation. It belongs merely to the form . . . ."[30] And I take Kant to mean by "It [which is to say, the "uniformity"] belongs merely to the form . . . ," not that it belongs to the form as consciously perceived but to the form as *cause* of the sensation. In other words, we have pure sensations of color when the forms of the vibrations have their effect on us unperturbed by *extraneous* sensations; and we have impure sensations of color when the unperceived cause of the sensations, i.e. the vibrations, are affected by *extraneous* sensations. And the same is true of pure and impure sensations of sound.

So pure sensations of color and sound are like perceptions of the beautiful in that they are free of extraneous influences. And for that reason we mistakenly take pure sensations of color and sound to be

---

[26]   *Critique of Aesthetic Judgement*, 67 (§14).
[27]   *Critique of the Power of Judgment*, trans. Guyer and Matthews, 109.
[28]   *Critique of Judgment*, Bernard, 60, Meredith, 67.
[29]   *Critique of Judgment*, Pluhar, 71.
[30]   *Critique of Aesthetic Judgement*, 66 (§14).

beautiful. But they are not, because they do not possess consciously perceived form.

This, however, still leaves a problem in §51. For there Kant reintroduces the question of whether we do or do not consciously perceive Euler's vibrations in musical sounds. But on my reading of §51 the problem is more apparent than real.

First of all, as I read §51, although Kant does express the view that "we cannot confidently assert whether a colour or tone (sound) is merely an agreeable sensation, or whether they are in themselves a beautiful play of sensations . . . ," the gist of the passage strongly suggests to me that Kant inclines to the former alternative, particularly, as he says, "If we consider the velocity of the vibrations of light, or, in the second case, of the air, which in all probability far outstrips any capacity on our part for forming an immediate estimate in perception of the time interval between them . . . ."[31] Furthermore, that he at least entertains doubts here, as to whether we consciously perceive the Euler vibrations of sound, is quite inconsistent with the statement in §14, if the first and second editions of the third *Critique* are followed, that he "in no way" doubts it, but entirely consistent with the third edition reading of "I very much doubt" it.

This leaves Kant's final judgment on the question of whether absolute music is a fine art to be worked into the puzzle. The last sentence of §51 reads: "According to the former interpretation, alone, would music be represented out and out as a *fine* art, whereas according to the latter it would be represented as (in part at least) an *agreeable* art."[32] Which is to say, if we consciously perceive the forms of the Euler vibrations of the individual tones making up a musical composition, then we can call music, *without qualification*, out and out, a beautiful art: in other words a fine, not an agreeable art. But if we only perceive them in their effects on sensation, and do not consciously perceive their form, then we must conclude that absolute music is not completely an art of the beautiful, a fine art: it is, to be sure, in part an art of the beautiful, a fine art, in virtue of its large compositional forms; but it is as well, in part, an art of the agreeable because the individual tones that make up its larger forms

[31] Ibid., 189 (§51).   [32] Ibid., 190 (§51).

are themselves, as we perceive them formless, and therefore agreeable rather than beautiful in themselves. And, it should be added, the same would be true of paintings in color.

If I am right that in both §14 and §51 Kant is plumping for the conclusion that we do *not* consciously perceive the form of Euler's vibrations in musical tones, then Kant is also plumping for the conclusion that, in this respect, music is partly an art of the beautiful, partly an art of the agreeable, hence only in part a fine art (in this respect). Is this an implausible conclusion? Not at all. For all Kant is saying, in effect, is that the beauty of absolute music lies in its perceivable formal structure, not in its individual constituent tones. There is nothing absurd in the conclusion. It is wrong, I think, in denying that the individual tones of music can be beautiful; but being wrong is one thing, and being off the wall is another.

Thus it seems to me that in interpreting Kant in this way we are saving him from three absurdities in his account of music. We are saving him from the absurd notion that we consciously perceive the form of Euler's vibrations in musical tones. We are saving him from the absurd notion that music can only be a fine art if we acquiesce in the notion that the form of Euler's sound vibrations are consciously perceived in it. And, finally, we are saving him from contradiction by bringing §14 and §51 in line with one another.

Perhaps one further question is outstanding, at this point, with regard to the question of music as a fine art. Kant, after all, seems not to have had a very high opinion of absolute music. For even though it possess aesthetic ideas, their payoff is not a "cognitive" one but simply an enhancement of bodily well-being. The question can well be raised then, whether, even though Kant recognized works of absolute music as "compositions," not merely individual tones, whether he thought these compositions themselves can be perceived as formal structures worthy of the name of fine art, or whether they are merely, as the tones that compose them, agreeable not beautiful. Indeed, Kant's own example of musical background to a dinner party, where the *composition* is not attended to, but where the music merely provides an agreeable accompaniment to the meal and to conversation is an example of an agreeable rather than a beautiful play of sensations, by virtue of the fact that the sequence of sound sensations, even though it does have consciously perceivable form, is not being experienced in such a way as to consciously perceive the form. Is this the canonical way of perceiving absolute music, on Kant's view? If so, then in spite of the fact that Kant recognizes the larger compositional forms of music, they play, on his view, no part in the listening experience, *as perceived forms*, and hence do not redeem music from the realm of the agreeable.

However, there is no reason to believe that Kant thought "background" music to dinner parties, where music is indeed an agreeable rather than a fine art, is canonical for music listening. Indeed the tenor of the passage is quite the opposite. Background music for dinner parties is "a quaint idea." And when he describes the listeners to music in this setting as not "paying the smallest attention to the composition...," he is surely paying such listening no compliment, and implying that there is a more serious mode of listening, namely, the mode in which we *do* pay close attention to the composition.

It therefore appears not only mistaken to deny Kant had acquaintance with larger aspects of musical form; it is mistaken as well that he thought musical form resides in the vibrations of individual musical tones. We all should have known better. But there it is.

All well and good. We have, by laborious, not to say pedantic argumentation and interpretation, reached the conclusion that Kant thought music without text fulfilled one of two necessary conditions for being a fine art: it possesses a consciously perceivable formal structure. And we have concluded as well that he meant by formal structure one of the things that we ordinarily mean by it: which is to say, the formal pattern of sounds that constitutes such structures as sonata form, rondo, and the like, as well as the internal patterns within these structures, and the larger forms—symphony, sonata, concerto—that the smaller forms make up, even though Kant never mentions any of them by name, and gives no evidence of knowing anything specific about musical structure or theory. But was Kant a *formalist* in music? And if so, can we determine in any detail in what his musical formalism consisted? The answer to the first question I think is a clear affirmative, and to the second, alas, an equally clear negative.

Kant's Musical Formalism

In a passage early on, in the "Analytic of the Beautiful," long before, indeed, Kant gives his account of the fine arts in the "Analytic of the Sublime," he describes music as a free beauty of form that "presupposes no concept of what the object should be . . . ."[33] (Kant is thinking here of the distinction between something's being beautiful in being beautifully designed or adapted to a purpose and something's being beautiful in appearance without regard to what the thing might be.) The relevant passage is as follows:

> So designs *à la grecque*, foliage for framework or on wallpapers, &c., have no intrinsic meaning; they represent nothing—no Object under a definite concept—and are free beauties. We may also rank in the same class what in music are called free fantasias (without a theme), and, indeed, all music that is not set to words).[34]

It is not clear what Kant means by free fantasias, but I presume he is thinking of the kinds of flourishes, scales, and arpeggios that characterize toccatas and fantasias of both the Baroque and Classical periods, and, as he says, are without discernable musical themes. But, in any case, what he means is really irrelevant to present concerns. For he shortly extends his point—that such free fantasias are without intrinsic meaning—to "all music which is not set to words": that is to say, all pure instrumental music. And that, of course, is the relevant and vital claim.

Kant invokes numerous images to illustrate what he means by free beauty, those that are artifactual being examples of what we would call "decorative art": "*designs à la grecque* [i.e. *Arabesque*-like ornaments], foliage for framework or on wall papers." But beyond that, unfortunately, he tells us nothing further about what the special character of *sonic* "decoration" might be. That Kant apparently identified absolute music with the decorative arts will no doubt shock most music lovers whose objects of veneration are the instrumental works of Bach, Haydn, Mozart, Beethoven, and their ilk. Perhaps their shock might be ameliorated somewhat if they were reminded

---

[33] *Critique of Aesthetic Judgement*, 72 (§16).   [34] Ibid.

that the decorative arts include not only wallpaper and woodwork but those magnificent Persian rugs that are sublime works of art with price tags on them appropriate to their status, as well as the decorations of the Alhambra and Alcazar, a point I shall return to in the end.

In any event, Kant's characterization of music without words, whatever its lack of detail, was, undoubtedly, a *formalist* one—but with an important proviso. For Kant, as we have seen, thought that music *also*, at least in a somewhat attenuated sense, had a content: an ideational content in the form of the capacity to arouse the human emotions, bring the ideas of them before the mind, with the result of setting in motion a train of what he called "aesthetic ideas," whose main identifying characteristic was their ineffability. As Kant put his point:

> by an aesthetic idea I mean that representation of the imagination which induces much thought, yet without the possibility of any definite thought whatever, i.e. *concept*, being adequate to it, and which language, consequently, can never quite get on equal terms with or render completely intelligible.[35]

Now if we put Kant's musical formalism together with his doctrine of the aesthetic ideas then we get the mixed position that the pure formal structure of absolute music, which, as Kant says, has "no intrinsic meaning," arouses what I like to call the "garden-variety emotions," those in turn initiate a train of ineffable "aesthetic ideas," which have their ultimate payoff in the production of a physical sense of well-being: as he puts it, "gathered strength to the body." Well, is this formalism cum arousal cum aesthetic ideas *really* formalism or not?

That Kant was the father of modern formalism, in music, and, indeed in all of the arts, is beyond question. That he was not a "pure" formalist, even in music, is clear enough. However, it was the formalist aspect of his position that has always stood out as its most characteristic and well-worked-out one; and it is *that* aspect that has been the influential one in nineteenth- and twentieth-century aesthetics and philosophy of art. The murky doctrine of music's "content," in the *Affektenlehre* and "aesthetic ideas," although puzzled

---

[35] Ibid., 175–6 (§49).

over by scholars, has had little if any influence on modern aesthetic theory, so far as I know, except perhaps in a very indirect way.

Furthermore, it can well be asked just what Kant's *non*-formalism in music amounted to, in real substance. For the aesthetic ideas are an *ineffable* content. And it is a nice question whether an ineffable "content" is any content at all.

Be that as it may, that Kant never quite bit the pure formalist bullet, when it came to absolute music, shows how deep and pervasive the ancient quarrel was and is. The bullet was, of course, bitten, famously, by Eduard Hanslick. And to that much discussed author I shall devote the next chapter with, I hope, something new to say. It is at any rate new to me.

3

Body and Soul

Introduction

Eduard Hanslick's "little book" (as he called it), *Vom Musikalisch-Schönen*, has become, in recent years, a text *celebre* among those philosophers who began, not too long ago, to interest themselves in the special problems that music might present to their subject. That these philosophers, among whom I include myself, did not *invent* the importance of the work is amply attested to by the *ten* editions that appeared, from its first publication in 1854, to the author's death in 1904.

But for the philosophers of whom I speak, *Of Musical Beauty*, as I shall call it, has taken a special *philosophical* place in the history of their discipline. It is generally denominated the inaugural text in the founding of musical formalism as a position in the philosophy of art. And in that role, therefore, it is treated as a *philosophical* text, despite its author's lack of bona fide philosophical credentials. (Well, as the saying goes, it doesn't take a jockey to know a horse.)

But what *kind* of work is *Of Musical Beauty*? It was the well-known philosopher of art, Morris Weitz, who had the happy idea in the 1957 re-issue of the first English translation, by Gustav Cohen, of analogizing it to David Hume's first *Inquiry*. "It is to music," Weitz wrote in his introduction, "what Hume's *Inquiry Concerning Human Understanding* is to speculative philosophy, a devastating critique of unsupportable views and an attempt to state clearly and precisely the territories and boundaries of the areas they discuss."[1]

---

[1] Eduard Hanslick, *The Beautiful in Music*, trans. Gustav Cohen, ed. Morris Weitz (New York: The Liberal Arts Press, 1957), vii.

Hume, of course, famously had Kant to answer—or at least attempt to answer—his skepticism. Did Hanslick have a "Kant" to attempt to answer *his*? Apparently he did, although the fact, and the "Kant," are little known to philosophers of art

Hanslick's "Kant," Wilhelm August Ambros, is by no means a minor figure in the history of music or in the history of its history. He is well known to all musicologists as a pioneer in the study of the musical Renaissance: "an epoch in the history of music he helped to define and survey amply for the first time . . . ," as Lawrence F. Bernstein describes his accomplishment.[2] But what few, if indeed any philosophers of art know, even those who take a special interest in music, is that in 1855, one year after the appearance of Hanslick's little book, Ambros wrote an answer to it in another "little book," entitled *Der Grenzen der Musik und Poesie: Eine Studie zur Aesthetik der Tonkunst*.[3] It was translated into English in 1893, under the title: *The Boundaries of Music: A Study in Musical Aesthetics*. And it is no mere surmise that Ambros intended his book as an "answer" to Hanslick's "skepticism." For he makes his intention, in this regard, very plain in his Preface, where he writes of Hanslick's "clever treatise . . ." that from it ". . . I have obtained abundant inspiration," and adds: "I desire all the more to express my indebtedness in this place, as I am obliged to assert myself in the body of the book, and especially often to dispute Dr. Hanslick's view from my standpoint."[4]

Standing alone, as the inaugural work in the history of musical formalism as a philosophical position, Hanslick's little book has received close scrutiny in recent years by a number of aestheticians, including the present one. But viewed now in the light of Ambros's "answer" to it, we can get a better idea of its philosophical significance. And, in

---

[2] Lawrence F. Bernstein, " 'Singende Seele' or 'unsingbar'? Forkel, Ambros, and the Forces behind the Ockeghem Reception during the Late 18th and early 19th Centuries," *The Journal of Musicology*, 23 (2006), 7.

[3] August Wilhelm Ambros, *Die Grenzen der Musik und Poesie: Eine Studie zur Aesthetik der Tonkunst* (Leipzig: H. Matthes, 1855).

[4] Wilhelm August Ambros, *The Boundaries of Music and Poetry: A Study in Musical Aesthetics*, trans. J. H. Cornell (New York: G. Schirmer, 1893), xii. It is through Bernstein's article that I was made aware of Ambros's book on music aesthetics, and of the English translation. (I have no idea why the order of given names of the author is different in the English translation from what it is in the original German.)

particular, we can see how early in the history of musical formalism as a philosophical position, the theme of the antithetical arts began to play itself out. So, in light now, of Ambros's critique of Hanslick, I want to go over yet again what Hanslick had to say.

The Negative Thesis

The most well-known, most influential, and certainly the most frequently misunderstood of Hanslick's conclusions in his little book is what he himself called "the one main thesis, a negative one," which "first and foremost opposes the widespread view that music is supposed to 'represent feelings.'"[5] But the negative thesis extends as well to the view that music is supposed to "arouse feelings." "Thus the earlier writers," Hanslick averred, "have been of the opinion that music should arouse our feelings [*Gefühl*] and fill us with piety, love, rejoicing, and woe. In fact, however," he insisted, "to induce these feelings is not the task of music or of any other art."[6]

In sum, then, the negative thesis is a two-pronged attack on musical expression theories as they were then understood: the theory that music's artistic essence is the arousal of the garden-variety emotions, and the theory that it is the representation of them.

Of music in the first of these two roles, it is claimed that to arouse the delicate feelings is the defining purpose of music. In the second, the feelings are designated as the content of music, that which musical art presents in its works.

The two are similar in that both are false.[7]

Hanslick's strategy for supporting this two-pronged negative thesis is simple and direct. The argument is, abstractly formulated, that it cannot be the essential purpose of music to arouse or represent

---

[5] Hanslick, *On the Musically Beautiful*, trans. Payzant, xxii. For my previous attempts to get straight what Hanslick was saying, see: Peter Kivy, "Something I've always wanted to know about Hanslick," and "What was Hanslick denying?," reprinted in Kivy, *The Fine Art of Repetition: Essays in the Philosophy of Music* (Cambridge and New York: Cambridge University Press, 1993); and Peter Kivy, "On Hanslick's Inconsistency," reprinted in Kivy, *New Essays on Musical Understanding*.

[6] Hanslick, *On the Musically Beautiful*, 4.   [7] Ibid., 3.

the garden-variety emotions because, as a matter of fact, it *cannot* arouse or represent them. And since the arousal of emotions or the representation of them seem to be the *only* ways Hanslick envisioned for music to be expressive of the emotions, which is to say, to be describable in terms of the garden-variety emotions in an art-relevant way, he must be seen as entirely ruling out the relevance of emotive descriptions to our characterization of absolute music as an art.

There *are*, as a matter of fact, two places where Hanslick *seems* to deviate from this austere emotionless formalism. And I will get to them later on. But for now it is our task to understand how Hanslick defends the negative thesis; that is to say, how he undertakes to show that it is impossible for music, *absolute music*, that is, to either arouse or represent the garden-variety emotions.

The argument of Hanslick's against the possibility of emotive expressiveness in music that is most remembered, and has had, I think, a baleful influence on music aesthetics over the years, is what might be called the "argument from disagreement." The argument is used against the claim that music can "represent" the garden-variety emotions. But it is clear that if it is good—which it is not—it is good against the claim that music can "arouse" the garden-variety emotions as well. Thus Hanslick writes:

Can we call it the representation of a specific feeling when nobody knows what feeling was actually represented? . . . [C]oncerning the content of music everyone differs. To represent, however, is to produce a clear and distinct content. . . . How, then, can we designate something as what an art represents, when the very dubious and ambiguous elements of that art themselves are perpetually subject to debate?[8]

The point here is that the utter lack of agreement among qualified listeners, in any given case, as to what emotive predicate correctly describes the music, argues conclusively against the thesis that music represents the emotions. It is as if one person were to say that the *Mona Lisa* represents a woman, another that it represents a tiger, a third that it represents a cowboy boot. (Recall Hamlet, Polonius, and the cloud!) Yet that is exactly the case with regard to how music is described

---

[8] Hanslick, *On the Musically Beautiful*, 14.

emotionally, according to Hanslick. And the best explanation, the obvious explanation for why this is the case, is that music is *not* in the emotive representation business at all.

Furthermore, the same argument, if good, will show that music cannot be in the business of consistently *arousing* the garden-variety emotions either. Because if it were, then there would be general agreement about what emotive term describes what passage of music. It would be the term that correctly describes the emotion that that passage has aroused in you, and regularly arouses in most competent listeners. Hanslick does not explicitly state that the argument from disagreement applies as well to the arousal thesis. But it seems clear that he assumes that is the case. And we shall assume he so assumes.

However, the argument from disagreement is a very bad argument, as I have already said. And it is very bad just because the initial premise of chaotic disagreement over what emotive description applies correctly to what musical passage is palpably false. We know this most directly through our group experience of musical listening as well as through formal and informal "experiments" in which it has been shown time and again that within reasonable limits listeners *do, pace* Hanslick, agree on which emotive predicates apply to which expressive passages. And we know it by simple inference from the practice of text setting since the beginning of the seventeenth century, in which even the lay listener can perceive the consistent way in which the emotive expression of the text is reflected in the emotive expressiveness of the music: a practice which would not be possible if there were not general agreement both among composers and among their audiences as to what "correct" emotive fit is.

Another of Hanslick's three arguments for the negative thesis is far more interesting, as well as *effective* against the only two ways of understanding the emotive description of absolute music that Hanslick seems to envisage: emotive arousal and emotive representation. In an apparent anticipation of what has come to be called since its inception in the 1960s the "cognitive" theory of the emotions, Hanslick writes that

Only on the basis of a number of ideas and judgments (perhaps unconsciously at moments of strong feeling) can our state of mind congeal into this or that specific feeling. The feeling of hope cannot be separated from the representation of a future happy state which we compare with the present; melancholy compares past happiness with the present. These are entirely specific representations or concepts. Without them, without this cognitive apparatus, we cannot call the actual feeling 'hope' or 'melancholy'. . . .

But it is just this conceptual apparatus that absolute music cannot provide; and "the definiteness of feelings lies precisely in their conceptual essence."[9]

The thrust of this argument, like that of the argument from disagreement, is twofold, although it might not be quite so obvious at first glance. To understand this, let us take Hanslick's example of melancholy. I come to know that a friend of mine has suffered a misfortune and this causes me to become melancholy: a standard case of emotive arousal "in the real world." Obviously nothing like this happens in my experience with absolute music.

More relevant is a case in which I read in a novel of the heroine's misfortune and this causes me to become melancholy: a standard case of emotive arousal in art. But, again, nothing like this happens in my experience of absolute music because, as Hanslick is arguing, absolute music does not have the conceptual apparatus to represent the kinds of things that could cause me to be melancholic, as the novel does. Thus the argument for the negative thesis that we are presently considering is good against the arousal theory.

But it is good, *eo ipso*, against the representation theory too. For if music lacks the conceptual apparatus to represent fictionally the things that, in literary fiction, can arouse our emotions, it lacks the conceptual apparatus to "represent" the emotions themselves (although what it would even *mean* to "represent" the emotions is mighty unclear). Thus, given the assumption, which I will question in a moment, but in the event re-affirm, that in the only two ways Hanslick thought it made sense to describe music emotively, as arousing the emotions or as representing them, the present argument, if good, is good against both. And in my view, unlike the argument from disagreement, it *is* good.

[9] Hanslick, *On the Musically Beautiful*, 9.

The remaining argument in support of the negative thesis, which is, essentially, an implication of the argument from disagreement, is Hanslick's claim, already canvassed in the first chapter, that "one size fits all"; the claim, that Salieri and his librettist quite rightly thought of as a joke; that the same music is expressively appropriate to any text whatever, no matter what the text expresses. For if true, which it is not, it would be further evidence that music is not expressive, either through arousal or through representation of any emotion whatever, since if it were, it could *not* be the case that one might fit a given piece of music to any given text, no matter what the text's emotive character.

Having dealt with this extraordinary argument previously, we can give it short shrift now. Suffice it to say, just as our ordinary musical experience, and the history of text setting since the beginning of the seventeenth century, make it quite clear that, the argument from disagreement to the contrary notwithstanding, there is general agreement as to what garden-variety emotion a passage of music is expressive of (if it is expressive of any), there is general agreement among composers, since the beginning of the seventeenth century, about what music is expressively appropriate to what text, and general agreement among competent listeners about when composers have gotten the expressive "fit" right, and when they have gotten it wrong—witness, for example, the almost universally felt expressive incongruity between music and text in many of Haydn's nonetheless great settings of the Mass.

In sum, then, this is the way it stands with Hanslick's negative thesis and his arguments in its favor. Hanslick understood there to be but two ways on offer for how absolute music could be expressive of the garden-variety emotions: by arousing them or by representing them. His negative thesis was that since absolute music could neither arouse nor represent the garden-variety emotions, it could not be expressive of them, which is to say, could not be correctly described in emotive terms. That being the case, it could not be the primary function (or any function at all) of absolute music to be expressive of the garden-variety emotions, either as a stimulation to them or a simulation of them.

A Misunderstanding

The negative thesis was Hanslick's "Humean skepticism." And like Hume's skepticism (so-called) Hanslick's has been greeted with strong opposition, if not downright hostility, right from the get go. In his own day, as we shall soon see later on in this chapter, the opposition consisted in opposing, or at least amplifying his position so as to re-enfranchise genuine emotive descriptions of the absolute music canon. In our day, the opposition has been twofold. On the one hand there have been those, like myself, who accept Hanslick's negative thesis, *as stated*, right down the line, which is to say we acquiesce in the conclusion that absolute music neither represents the garden-variety emotions, nor arouses them (in any *artistically relevant* way). However, we believe that first of all the argument from disagreement is a bad argument and, in addition, that there is another way, besides arousal or representation, in which absolute music can be expressive of the garden-variety emotions: can be correctly described in emotive terms. If Hanslick's formalism, in denying that absolute music can ever be correctly, and in an art-relevant way, described in terms of the garden-variety emotions, is appropriately labeled "extreme formalism," then my own view should bear the label "enhanced formalism," which is to say, formalism enhanced by the inclusion, in the musical fabric, of expressive qualities. It shall be so-called in this book, and alluded to on numerous occasions.

But, on the other hand, there has been reaction to Hanslick's negative thesis in our own times along with a renewed interest in his "little book," aroused, no doubt, by the late Geoffrey Payzant's excellent new English translation: a reaction of *disbelief* to the effect that that *couldn't* really be his position. It is just too totally wrong, these objectors insist. No one of Hanslick's philosophical intelligence and musical sensibility could possibly be saying that music can't be melancholy, joyful, angry, and the like. So the search is initiated for an interpretation of Hanslick that can save him from complete emotive skepticism.

A passage that just about jumps off the page, if you are looking for a concession to emotivism on Hanslick's part, is the following, which occurs immediately after one of his spirited denials of music's power to *represent* the emotions, as a seeming concession to *arousal*, so to speak, a substitute. Hanslick writes: "How it happens that music can nevertheless excite such feelings as melancholy, gaiety, and the like (can, not must) we shall investigate later, when we discuss the subjective impressions made by music."[10]

Given this apparent concession to emotivism, the following "compromise" formalism can now be extracted from Hanslick's text, more in the bounds of musical "common sense." (1) Absolute music *never* has as whole or part of its artistic purpose the representation of the garden-variety emotions for the very simple reason that it *cannot* represent them. (2) Absolute music *can*, not must *sometimes* have as part of its purpose the *arousal* of the garden-variety emotions.

But there is trouble from the start with this concessionist interpretation of Hanslick. For proposition (2) seems plainly inconsistent with the negative thesis, which denies to absolute music *both* representation *and* arousal of the garden-variety emotions. What can be going on here?

Even before one turns to that part of Hanslick's book, chapter IV, where Hanslick promises to investigate how absolute music can arouse the garden-variety emotions, we have a broad hint in the present passage as to how we are to smooth over this apparent contradiction, which is, indeed, apparent only. For note well that what Hanslick promises to "investigate later" is "the *subjective* impressions made by music." "*Subjective* as opposed to *what*?" we are compelled to ask. And the answer that immediately comes to mind, which, in light of chapter IV, turns out to be correct, is: as opposed to the genuine, artistically relevant, "objective."

In chapter IV Hanslick refers to the propensity of absolute music to arouse the garden-variety emotions as "so well known that we need not tarry over it." Obviously he thought it was no big deal, and certainly not inconsistent with the negative thesis of *On Musical Beauty*. He wrote of this "well known" phenomenon: "We often see the listener deeply stirred by a piece of music, moved to joy or melancholy, transported in his innermost being far beyond *purely*

---

[10] Hanslick, *On the Musically Beautiful*, 9–10.

aesthetical pleasure, or disturbed." The italics are mine and are meant to underscore the crucial point that Hanslick is making, which he again reiterates immediately afterwards, that he is concerned here with the question: "to what extent this [emotive] effect is *aesthetical*."[11]

Let us first get a handle on Hanslick's use of the much disputed term "aesthetic" (or "aesthetical"). He writes in one place, just before the passages we have been examining: "Aesthetical contemplation cannot be based upon any features which are outside the artwork itself."[12]

One cannot tell which of two common senses of the word "aesthetical" Hanslick is assuming here. In one sense, the word has approximately the meaning of "having to do with art" or "art-relevant." On this usage, those properties or effects of an artwork that are not "aesthetical" are irrelevant to it *qua* artwork. I, and others, prefer to use the word "artistic" to convey this meaning because we want to say that although all aesthetic properties or effects of artworks are art-relevant, there are other properties or effects that properly belong to artworks, and are art-relevant, besides the aesthetic ones. I shall assume that Hanslick is using "aesthetical" in the latter sense, to mean "artistic" or "art-relevant." But what I have to say will be quite consistent with his using the word in the former sense too.

With this business out of the way, the first thing we can say about the passage under discussion is that Hanslick is, quite sensibly, confining the aesthetical properties relevant to its appreciation to properties *of the artwork itself*, not properties that may, one way or another, be transported to it from, as it were, "outside."

To what, then, are we to contrast the "aesthetic" effects of music? Well, one class of non-aesthetical effects, we are justified in concluding, are what Hanslick has called, earlier, "the subjective impressions made by music." And the "subjective impressions" he mainly has in

[11] Hanslick, *On the Musically Beautiful*, 49–50. Italics mine. See, also, *The Beautiful in Music*, trans. Cohen, 77. I have changed Payzant's translation slightly here, and followed Cohen, to better capture what I take to be Hanslick's meaning. For the German, see: Eduard Hanslick, *Vom Musikalisch Schönen: Ein Beitrag zur Revision der Aesthetik der Tonkunst* (Zwanzigste Auflage; Wiesbaden: Breitkopf & Härtel, 1980), 102.

[12] Hanslick, *On the Musically Beautiful*, 48. My italics.

mind, as we have seen, are the garden-variety emotions that absolute music arouses. In chapter IV he calls these emotive effects of absolute music "pathological." Here is what he says about them and how they come to be:

> in musical effects upon feeling, often an extraneous, not purely aesthetical element may be involved. A purely aesthetical effect addresses itself to a healthy nervous system and does not rely upon any degree of psychological abnormality.[13]

A reasonable picture now begins to emerge of how the negative thesis can be compatible with the admission that absolute music is able to, and indeed at times *does* arouse the garden-variety emotions. It does so in an aesthetically, which is to say an artistically *irrelevant*, way due to the psychological quirks of individual listeners, which Hanslick describes as "subjective" or "pathological." And if one takes "pathological" not in the more current sense of psychologically abnormal or even diseased, but in a more benign sense closer to "subjective," the picture makes perfect sense. If, for whatever personal, subjective reasons, I am in an emotionally overwrought state, or have some personal associations with a musical composition, then it might well move me to melancholy, or joy, or anger, depending on the circumstances, while leaving you completely unmoved to any of the garden-variety emotions. But my reaction, real though it may be, is aesthetically, artistically irrelevant. It has nothing to do with the musical composition *qua* artwork: it is, as Hanslick would say, "based upon...features which are outside the artwork itself."

We can now sum up Hanslick's extreme formalism in the following propositions.

(1) Absolute music cannot have as part or all of its artistic function the representation of the garden-variety emotions because it does not have the capability of representing them.

(2) Absolute music cannot have as part or all of its artistic purpose the arousal of the garden-variety emotions because it does not have the capability of arousing them in any art-relevant way, although

---

[13] Ibid., 50.

(3) it can and does arouse them in ways that are not art-relevant.

(4) Arousal and representation are the only even seemingly possible ways to work the garden-variety emotions into the musical fabric; and since neither can do the job, the garden-variety emotions must be seen to have no place at all in music's artistic function.

(5) Absolute music's artistic reason for being is "a specifically musical kind of beauty" which "is self-contained and in no need of [emotive] content from outside itself...."

Or, in other words: "The content of music is tonally moving forms,"[14] empty of any other content, emotive content in particular.

A Missed Opportunity

Enhanced formalism, at least of the kind that I espouse, is much indebted to Hanslick's extreme formalism, and embodies many of his conclusions (as we shall see in later chapters). But its launching pad, so to speak, is a denial of proposition (4) above. And what is remarkable is that Hanslick himself held enhanced formalism, and the denial of proposition (4) in the palm of his hand and failed to recognize the possibilities for a more successful formalism than his own, for reasons I will get to in a moment. First, though, the missed opportunity.

The passage I have in mind, in this regard, occurs not in the body of Hanslick's text but in the Foreword to the eighth edition of the "little book". Here Hanslick writes of the negative thesis:

The thesis first and foremost opposes the widespread view that music is supposed to "represent feelings." It is incomprehensible to me the way some people insist that this implies an absolute lack of feeling in music. The rose is fragrant, but we do not say that its content is the representation of fragrance....[15]

What is so intriguing and suggestive about this passage, the significance of which, I confess, I have failed to notice over years of reading and re-reading, thinking and re-thinking Hanslick's "little book," is that,

---

[14] Hanslick, *On the Musically Beautiful*, 28–29.   [15] Ibid., xxii.

in the rose analogy, Hanslick has exactly the property-ontology of modern enhanced formalism staring him in the face. The garden-variety emotions are to music neither as the burp to the cider (to appropriate O. K. Bouwsma's *bon mot*[16]) nor as object to representation but as fragrance to flower. They are phenomenological properties of the music that we hear in it as we see the redness of the apple and smell the fragrance of the rose. Hanslick had it right there, but failed to recognize the potential of the model or, therefore, avail himself of it. Why so?

Well, to begin with it must be kept in mind that the fragrance analogy does not occur in the body of Hanslick's book, as I have said, but in the Foreword to the eighth edition, published many years later—1891 to be precise. So it is reasonable to assume that when he wrote the book he had no such model in mind. The fragrance analogy was an afterthought—a *long* afterthought, at that.

Furthermore, it was an afterthought clearly inconsistent with the main text of *On the Musically Beautiful*. For it was just as vulnerable to the argument from disagreement, in which Hanslick put such great confidence, as the arousal or representation models of musical expressiveness. And were Hanslick to become a convert to the fragrance model, he would have had to completely revise his book to bring it into conformity. That, he was not inclined to do, as is made altogether clear by his republication of the main text, unaltered, in the eighth edition of 1891, and all ten editions published during his lifetime (with the exception of two passages to be discussed in the next section). The original text of *On the Musically Beautiful*, we must assume, still expressed its author's settled views, in 1891, or he would not, surely, have reprinted it almost without revision. So the passage in the new Foreword, which seems to presage what I have been calling enhanced formalism, that is, a formalism that countenances perceived emotive properties of musical form and fabric, remained an interesting anomaly, a missed opportunity, perhaps, and nothing more.

---

[16] O. K. Bouwsma, "The Expression Theory of Art," reprinted in Bouwsma, *Philosophical Essays* (Lincoln: University of Nebraska Press, 1969), 49: "For the sadness is to the music rather like the redness to the apple, than it is like the burp to the cider."

Birth Pangs

I said in the previous section that Hanslick's main text remained substantially unchanged throughout the numerous editions of his little book that appeared in his lifetime, but with the exception of two passages. These passages, excised from the text after the first edition, turn out to be crucial to the development of formalism; and I want to examine them briefly now; for they illustrate that the birth of musical formalism Hanslick was midwife to was by no means an easy one.

It has been noticed, by Mark Evan Bonds, in his intriguing account of how Beethoven's symphonies were understood in the nineteenth century, that the ending to the first edition of *On the Musically Beautiful* was completely excised in all subsequent editions. And he quite rightly observes that "In canceling the peroration of his argument, Hanslick would in effect change the nature of the argument itself."[17]

The excised peroration reads as follows (in Bonds' translation):

It is not merely and absolutely through its own intrinsic beauty that music affects the listener, but rather at the same time as a sounding image of the great motions of the universe. Through preformed and secret connections to nature, the meaning of tones is elevated high above the tones themselves, allowing us to perceive at the same time the infinite in works of human talent. Because the elements of music—sound, tone, rhythm, loudness, softness—are to be found throughout the entire universe, so does one find anew in music the entire universe.[18]

And in addition, Hanslick excised the passage which avers that in its possession of beauty, music "is capable of possessing, at the same time, a high degree of symbolic significance in its reflection of the great laws of the world, which is something we find in all artistic beauty."[19] So much, then, for formalism: music has representational content after all.

The lesson we must learn from these remarkable passages, so retrograde to Hanslick's formalist project, as we have come to know

---

[17] Mark Evan Bonds, *Music as Thought: Listening to the Symphony in the Age of Beethoven* (Princeton: Princeton University Press, 2006), 109.
[18] Ibid.   [19] Ibid., 110.

it, is how difficult the birth of musical formalism really was. For after so carefully developing the formalist argument, in the end Hanslick could not convince even himself to fully accept it. And so we get this last-minute recantation, completely inconsistent, plainly, with the argument that precedes it. As Bonds remarks, the peroration "might easily have been written half a century before by Schelling, yet it provides the climax of his entire 'revision' of the aesthetics of music."[20]

But like Galileo according to the well-known story, Hanslick recants his recantation, by omission, as it were, in all future editions of the little book. And so we have in the end, the first mature musical formalism, rescued, not without difficulty, by its founder, from his own initial failure of nerve.

Hanslick, then, seems to have remained steady to his skeptical, formalist text to the end, in spite of an intriguing but momentary lapse in the Foreword to the eighth edition, and the suppressed passages just discussed. However, his skeptical formalism did not go unanswered in his lifetime, as was pointed out at the beginning of this chapter. And to that answer we now must turn.

In Quest of Boundaries

No student of the Enlightenment can possibly miss the allusion, in the title of Ambros's little book on musical aesthetics, to Lessing's celebrated *Laocoon*, which bears as its sub-title: *On the Limits [Grenzen] of Painting and Poetry*.[21] Nor does Ambros leave the allusion in his title, *The Boundaries [Grenzen] of Music and Poetry*, for the astute reader to make out. For in the Preface to his book he explicitly likens his own project to Lessing's, when he writes that "a musical Lessing would seem to be needed."[22] And he leaves no doubt that it is *Laocoon* and the search for limits that he has in mind when, a bit later on, he mentions the work specifically, and compares

---

[20] Ibid., 109.
[21] Gotthold Ephraim Lessing, *Laocoon: An Essay upon the Limits of Painting and Poetry*, trans. Ellin Frothingham (New York: Noonday Press, 1957).
[22] Ambros, *The Boundaries of Poetry and Music*, ix.

Lessing's project of plotting the boundaries of poetry and sculpture to his own "investigation as to the point where poetry and music separate."[23] It would be useful, therefore, to remind ourselves of what Lessing was doing in *Laocoon*, before we go on to what Ambros was doing, which he understood, apparently, as the musical analogue of Lessing's project.

Lessing presents, in *Laocoon*, what has been called a "medium-specific" argument, in which one essentially tries to show that some given kind or genre of art, because of its *specific medium*, is best (or only) suited to a specific kind of subject matter.[24] Thus, for example, so it has sometimes been argued, cinema, because of its basically visual and action-oriented, temporal medium, is best suited to story-telling through action and event rather than through speech, which is why, Rudolph Arnheim once famously claimed, silent cinema is superior to the sound film, in that it must eschew speech and sound for action and event. It is more "cinematic."[25]

Lessing was by no means the inventor of the medium-specific argument, although he presented one of the most ingenious instances of the thing. The "ranking" of the arts and the specification of their (supposed) proper subject matter was a popular eighteenth-century philosophical and art-critical pastime. What Lessing claimed in *Laocoon*, is that, to put it one way, poetry is well suited to the representation of actions and events, because poetry is a temporal art, an event art if you like, whereas sculpture and painting are not well suited to the representation of actions and events, because they are static, non-temporal arts and can only capture the pregnant moment.

The argument, at this point, is not particularly noteworthy; but it becomes so when Lessing broaches the subject of poetic *description*, and introduces the famous example of Homer "describing" Achilles' shield in the *Iliad*. "The rule is this," Lessing tells us: "that succession in time is the province of the poet, co-existence in space that of the artist." And so: "To try to present a complete picture to the reader by

[23] Ambros, *The Boundaries of Poetry and Music*, 12.

[24] See, Noel Carroll, *Theorizing the Moving Image* (Cambridge: Cambridge University Press, 1996), Part I.

[25] See, Rudolph Arnheim, *Film as Art* (Berkeley: University of California Press, 1957).

enumerating in succession several parts or things which in nature the eye necessarily takes in at a glance, is an encroachment of the poet on the domain of the painter, involving a great effort of the imagination to very little purpose."[26]

Homer, apparently, understood the limits of poetic description, at least intuitively, or so, anyway, Lessing thinks. For when he came to describe the shield of Achilles, Lessing points out, he chose to describe the *process* of its *making*, an action, a temporal event, to which poetry, a temporal art, is well suited, rather than to give it a static, tedious, item-by-item accounting. "Homer does not paint the shield finished, but in the process of creation. Here again he has made use of the happy device of substituting progression for coexistence, and thus converted the tiresome description of an object into a graphic picture of an action."[27]

It should be observed that when Lessing puts these "limits" on poetry, and painting and sculpture, they do not appear to be limits in a factual but in a normative sense; which is to say, it is not that poetry *can't* describe the present appearance of an object or that sculpture *can't* represent an action or event. It is that when they do so they are working *against* the nature of their respective mediums: they *can* do it but they *shouldn't*, because when they do, they are the worse for it as artistic products.

But when we come to Hanslick's skeptical arguments against the emotivists, the issue is no longer a normative one: it is about what absolute music *cannot* do; it *cannot* arouse or represent the garden-variety emotions, so there is no normative question to consider. Ought implies can. It is otherwise, however, with the "musical Lessing." And with the necessary preliminaries in place, it is now time to turn to him.

Ambros's quest for the limits or boundaries of absolute music starts with a rather pedestrian and, for the mid-nineteenth century, an already outmoded canvass of the fine arts, and their "appropriate" subject matter, much indebted obviously to the familiar Enlightenment project, as well as to the more recent effort along similar lines but, needless to say, of far greater philosophical depth, by

---

[26] Lessing, *Laocoon*, 109.   [27] Ibid., 114.

Schopenhauer in Book III of *The World as Will and Idea*. It is through this catalogue that Ambros plots his musical boundaries; so we had best run through it briefly. He begins, like Schopenhauer, with architecture.

"Architecture," Ambros tells us, "is the art most dependent upon matter."[28] It has no subject: "it represents *nothing* . . . Matter in this case requires from the artist only that he should give it *beautiful forms*, wherein the *architectural* idea may clearly express itself."[29] "Next to it comes the plastic art," which is to say, statuary.[30]

Not surprisingly, it is the human form that Ambros identifies as *the* proper subject matter of the sculptor. Matter *matters*: "This [art] also has to do with the overcoming of crude matter, though considerably less so than architecture."[31] It is the subject matter, however, that dominates: which is to say, humanity and what lies beneath. "In plastic art we are confronted with the form of man, rendered visible to us by statues on every hand—but we also recognize the spiritual and moral nature of his [i.e. the sculptor's] conceptions as expressed in forms of ideal beauty."[32]

Painting follows hard by. And as matter matters less in sculpture than in architecture, matter matters still less in painting than in sculpture. "Thus, beautiful bodily form now yields to the moral and intellectual nature." In painting, the "given material," which is to say, the subject matter, "now advances still further into the foreground, and the altogether natural question when looking at a picture (and the most usual one) is: 'What does it represent?'"[33]

We then come, in this step-by-step decline in importance of matter to art, to poetry. "While, in painting, the material element is kept far in the background, and the intellectually moral nature of man advances to occupy the foreground fully, in *poetry* matter at last vanishes altogether."[34] And we are now ready for the appearance of absolute music in Ambros's scheme. Is *it*, as Hanslick would have it, "a mere sounding play with forms?"[35] In describing absolute music in formal terms, as "sounding play with forms,"

28 Ambros, *The Boundaries of Music and Poetry*, 13.   29 Ibid., 14.
30 Ibid.   31 Ibid.   32 Ibid., 16.
33 Ibid., 17.   34 Ibid., 19.   35 Ibid., 23.

Ambros avers, in answering his own question, "we have described the *body* of the piece of music. The body, however, requires a soul."[36]

It is more than somewhat disconcerting to the contemporary sensibility to realize that Ambros was not speaking altogether metaphorically in his invocation of the soul–body distinction, but actually seemed to believe that the issue between Hanslick's musical formalism and his own musical "expressionism" (if that is the right word) *literally* turned on the broader issue of scientific materialism versus *some* kind of mind–body dualism (with religious overtones?), although one would be hard put to say what Ambros's alternative to scientific materialism might have been. Thus he writes, in unveiled derision of "physiologists" such as Carl Vogt who "will laugh scornfully over the spirit sought for by us, and assure us that the whole witchery is based upon the excitement of our nervous system by means of sound-waves—as it can notoriously also be excited by means of spirituous liquors, opium, and the like."[37]

Whatever "metaphysics," beyond "aesthetic metaphysics," Ambros may have thought was at issue between him and Hanslick I think we can safely put aside as irrelevant to present concerns. For I think it will become clear, as we proceed, that what Ambros meant, in practice, as the "soul" of music can be well understood in terms quite free of any extraneous metaphysical baggage of the mind–body variety.

As we saw, the progression of the fine arts, for Ambros, goes from architecture to sculpture to painting to poetry to absolute music. Poetry and absolute music are, then, "contiguous" arts, as it were. And it is at the intersection of these two arts that Ambros looks for the "soul" of absolute music. As he puts this point: "And as we before spoke of the body of music, and said that it demanded a soul, we feel that we are led to the conviction that poetry alone is able to breathe this soul into it. We are right in calling music a poetic art."[38] How music gains its soul, through the spirit of poetry, and what exactly that means, we must now inquire.

---

[36] Ibid., 31.   [37] Ibid., 33–4.   [38] Ibid., 51.

Ambros's Answer

Ambros writes: "Where a *boundary* is to be drawn between two domains, a *point of contact* between them must, in general, first be ascertained. The point of contact between poetry and music lies in the *excitement of moods* [*Stimmungen*]."[39] Ambros continues: "The effect of music likewise consists essentially in this, that it awakens moods in the hearer, and, indeed, moods of a very determinate coloring."[40]

Ambros's "answer" to Hanslick is, then, a very simple one, but, as we shall see in the next chapter, startling in its anticipation of a contemporary response to Hanslick's, and to the enhanced formalist's denial that absolute music can relevantly arouse the garden-variety *emotions.* The answer is, put baldly, to grant the point and offer *different* feeling states from emotions that music *can,* and *does* (so it is claimed) arouse, which is to say "moods": in the German, *Stimmungen,* as opposed to *Gefül.*

Contemporary advocates of absolute music as mood-arousing rather than emotion-arousing, as we shall see in Chapter 4, tout the former view as providing an explanation for how absolute music can arouse mood-states, where it cannot, they tend to agree, the garden-variety emotions. Ambros, clearly, has the same intuition, although he fails to provide any clearly discernible account of *how* absolute music really does the job. He does, however, have a fairly clear idea of what the problem is, namely, *how to do it without words.* Thus he writes: "Now, music conveys moods of finished expression; it, as it were, forces them upon the hearer. It conveys them in *finished* form, because it possesses no means for expressing the previous series of ideas which *speech* can clearly and definitely express."[41]

The thought, here, as I perceive it, is this. Language can arouse a mood, either in speech or writing, by presenting to the hearer or reader a sequence of ideas, say, the events and characters in a story, that eventually give rise to a mood in listener or reader: a somber mood if the story is a sad one, an upbeat mood if the story is upbeat, and so

---

[39] Ambros, *The Boundaries of Music and Poetry,* 51.
[40] Ibid., 52.   [41] Ibid., 53.

on. But absolute music cannot do that; it does not have the words. So it must, *somehow*, arouse the mood in a *fait accompli*, without the "previous series of ideas" that language can project. It must, *somehow*, convey the mood "in *finished* form." Unfortunately, Ambros never, as far as I can see, cashes out the *somehow*. We never do find out *how* music can do this—which is not surprising, since, as I shall argue in the next chapter, absolute music *cannot* do this, any more than it can arouse the garden-variety *emotions*. Nonetheless, that Ambros was able to formulate the "mood response" to Hanslick's emotive skepticism so early in the game, is remarkable enough. And another remarkable insight follows directly.

What Ambros goes on to say is that the experience of a mood in listening to absolute music does not stop with the mood's arousal in the listener. Rather, the listener goes on, then, to *project* the mood onto the music, as it were, as a perceived quality *of the music*. "Now, *the state of mind which the hearer receives from the music he transfers back to it*; he says: 'It expresses this or that mood.' "[42]

The notion of projecting onto the world as a quality of *it* what is, in fact, only a felt response *to* the world, is not a notion that Ambros was, by any means, the first to entertain. It is the operative principle, for example (although I think Ambros is unlikely to have known this) whereby, on Hume's account, the *feeling* of "necessary connection" between events is *perceived as* an actual relation between events: "as we *feel* a customary connexion between the ideas, we transfer that feeling to the objects; as nothing is more usual than to apply to external bodies every internal sensation, which they occasion."[43]

Perhaps more relevant to present concerns, Ambros's idea of the projection of felt mood states *onto* music is an anticipation of the doctrine of "fusion," that played a prominent role in philosophical aesthetics, during the early years of the twentieth century, and had it that aesthetic qualities in general, beauty in particular, were feeling states that the perceiver "fused" onto the world as perceived qualities. The view was famously stated, for beauty, by George Santayana, in his

---

[42] Ibid.

[43] See, David Hume, *Inquiry Concerning Human Understanding*, ed. Eric Steinberg (2nd edn.; Indianapolis and Cambridge: Hackett, 1993), 52n.

widely read book, *The Sense of Beauty*, where he wrote, for example, that: "Beauty is an emotional element, a pleasure of ours, which nevertheless we regard as a quality of things."[44]

But far more important I think, than Ambros's discovery, or re-discovery of the "fusion" principle, doubtful anyway, at best, is what his invocation of it *implies*: namely, that whatever the "ontological" status of moods in music might finally be, they are in the event, *perceived in the music* as phenomenological properties *of it*. Hanslick, as we have seen, had a glimmering of this fruitful possibility for the emotions, when he wrote the Foreword to the eighth edition of his book, in 1891. But Ambros already had more than a glimmering in his "answer" to Hanslick, in 1855, although his "mechanism" for getting mood *into* music may be highly suspect.

The State of Play: 1855

There has been no more vigorous opponent of the literary analogy, in musical aesthetics, than Eduard Hanslick; no past thinker more likely than he to be in sympathy with my characterization of literature and music as "antithetical arts." But that he went too far, in his rejection of the literary model for music, in completely exiling emotive descriptions of music, was already obvious to Ambros and is the thought behind what I have been calling "enhanced formalism," which is to say, a formalism that recognizes emotive properties of music as perceptual, phenomenological properties, not semantic or representational ones. It is something like this insight that Ambros had, when he substituted "mood" for "emotion" as the feeling content of absolute music, and suggested that by a kind of "fusion" the mood is perceived as "in" the music.

It was the strange fate of musical formalism, in the first half of the twentieth century, and perhaps before, to have made itself, almost as part of its definition, the view that emotive descriptions of music are strictly *de classe*: talk about music engaged in only by the musically unwashed, who just don't know any better. Ambros's insight was

---

[44] George Santayana, *The Sense of Beauty* (New York: Random House, 1955), 50.

lost, if ever it was noticed in the first place: the insight that you can have formalism *and* the emotions, or moods (if you prefer) just so long as you put them where they properly belong: in the formal structure that formalism is all about. I am not saying that Ambros was always steady to this text. On the contrary, in the later parts of his book, the emotive and literary descriptions of the absolute music canon begin to exceed what even enhanced formalism would continence. But the germ of enhanced formalism was there, in the early, "theoretical" part.

Ambros did have the wrong "mechanism" for getting moods "into" music, which is to say, by way of their first being aroused in the listener. (Why it is the wrong mechanism we will have occasion to see in the next chapter.) But he *did* have the right idea, in recognizing that we experience moods, in the event, as "in" the music. And that is the insight present-day enhanced formalism is fashioned to preserve.

The emotive austerity of Hanslick's formalism eventually led, late in the twentieth century, to dissatisfaction with it. And, not surprisingly, the reaction of the unsatisfied was to aim at the opposite extreme: to make of absolute music a "literary" art. It is that attempt to combine what are antithetical arts, that this book is all about. It is an extended argument against the attempt (with a few digressions along the way). And with the historical background now in place, it is time to get on with it.

PART II:

The Fortunes of Formalism

4

Mood and Music

Introduction

In the previous chapter we saw musical formalism come into full flower in Hanslick's "little book," along with the denial that absolute music could, or, therefore was meant to, arouse or "represent" what I have been calling the "garden-variety emotions." We saw as well that this denial of the emotive connection drew an immediate reply from Ambros to the effect that the loss of emotion could be made up for by the substitution of "mood." This move on Ambrose's part presaged a similar move in contemporary philosophy. And it is the purpose of the present chapter to explore that move in one of its contemporary manifestations.

The idea that there is a very special connection between music and the affective life goes back, in philosophy, to Plato and before philosophy to Pythagoras and the Orphic mysteries. When I speak of "a very special and intimate connection" I mean, I should add, a connection beyond even the special connection that has been thought to exist, since time out of mind, between the affective life and *all* of what we have known since the eighteenth century as the fine arts. Music has been thought special, in this regard, even among those human practices, that is to say the fine arts, which have been thought special, as a group, among all *other* human practices.

It is important to remind ourselves that since the beginning, and until late in the eighteenth century, these claims about music had always been, as far as we can tell, claims about *sung* music: musical settings of texts. But with the emergence of pure, textless, instrumental music as a major art form, in the works of Haydn, Mozart, Beethoven, and many distinguished "underlaborers," the special claim of music on the affective life became *both* more problematic *and*, ironically, more *insistent*. It indeed became a "philosophical problem."

The reason appears to me to be clear. Without a text, music lost its conceptual, representational, and narrative content. What seemed left to it, for "content," was its *affective* content alone. And so it became an urgent priority to insist on its presence above all else.

Furthermore, the affective content of instrumental music was normally cashed out in terms of its disposition to arouse in listeners affective states it was described as "having," since it was agreed, on all hands, that listening to instrumental music can be, at its best, a deeply moving experience. But in the absence of a text—that is, in the absence of conceptual, representational, and narrative content—pure instrumental music seems to lack all of those components that give the other arts their power over the affective life. It thus became, and remains a philosophical as well as music-theoretical problem to provide an explanation for how pure instrumental music, *sans* conceptual, representational, and narrative content *can*, nevertheless, arouse affective states in its audiences.

It has not, I suspect, evaded the reader's vigilance that until now I have been describing music's effect on the listener in a somewhat archaic as well as non-specific way. I have referred to its connection with our *affective* lives and its supposed capacity to arouse in us *affective* states. And, of course, the "affect" language has a distinctly eighteenth-century cast to it, in addition to covering a wide range of possible subjective manifestations. This has been done on purpose, and it is now time to make that purpose clear.

The traditional way of representing the special connection music is supposed to have with what I have been calling the "affective life" is to say that music has the power of arousing the human emotions, which are, of course, a sub-set of the human "affective states." And the reason I have preferred until now to say "affective states" instead of "emotions" is to leave open the possibility that even though it turns out that music cannot arouse emotions in listeners, for reasons already suggested, it might, nevertheless, arouse other affective states.

It is a familiar move in the debate over whether or not pure instrumental music can arouse what I like to call the "garden-variety" emotions—sadness, fear, happiness, anger, and a few others—to agree that it *cannot* arouse them in their full-blooded form, but can in a kind of diluted, weakened, yet still recognizable simulacrum.[1] The next step from here is to give up on the garden-variety emotions altogether and move on to other affective states that might satisfy the craving for a special connection between music and affective states, while avoiding the suspect notion of "weakened" emotions and the well-known skepticism with regard to the power of music to arouse emotions in the first place.

It is precisely this latter strategy that Ambrose employed, as we have just seen. And now Noel Carroll has resorted to this very strategy, anticipated by Ambros some one-hundred-and-fifty years ago, in his insightful and searching paper, "Art and Mood: Preliminary Notes and Conjectures," where he writes:

Formalists argue that it is nonsense to maintain that instrumental music arouses emotions. Music lacks the logical machinery to represent the kinds of objects that such emotional states require . . . Maybe the resolution to this dispute is to grant the formalist the concession that music does not arouse emotions properly so called, for the reasons he gives, but add that in many cases what music does arouse are moods—affective states that are objectless, global, diffuse, often ambiguous . . . The proposal gives the formalist his point, while also acknowledging the opposing faction's estimation of the importance of the affective side of music.[2]

It is Carroll's suggestion, as it was Ambros's, that moods rather than emotions are what pure instrumental music arouses, that I want to critically examine here. I think it is wrong, and for some of the same reasons I have given in the past for thinking that it is wrong to think music arouses the garden-variety emotions. But Carroll's argument is powerful, subtle, thorough, and complex, and it merits serious consideration.

---

[1] On this see, for example, Stephen Davies, *Musical Meaning and Expression* (Ithaca, New York: Cornell University Press, 1994), 307; and Jerrold Levinson, "Music and Negative Emotions," in *Music, Art and Metaphysics: Essays in Philosophical Aesthetics* (Ithaca, New York: Cornell University Press, 1990), 313.

[2] Noel Carroll, "Art and Mood: Preliminary Notes and Conjectures," *Monist*, 86 (2003), 551.

Let me just add, before I get on with it, that Carroll's paper, as the title implies, is not just a paper on *music* and moods but a preliminary investigation into the role moods play in *all* of the fine arts. And with most of what Carroll says about moods with regard to arts other than pure instrumental music I am in total agreement, as I usually am with *anything* he has to say about the arts. It is only about moods in *music* that we disagree. I will now get on to that disagreement without further delay.

Moods

What *are* moods, as opposed to emotions? That in itself is a philosophical and psychological question of some difficulty. But as this chapter concerns Noel Carroll's idea about how absolute music can engender moods in listeners, it is, of course, *his* idea about what moods are, as opposed to emotions, that I will accept here for the sake of the argument.

The most telling characteristic of moods, in contrast with emotions, and perhaps the one from which most of the others follow, is that moods, unlike emotions, do not take intentional objects, which is to say, unlike emotions, they are not directed at anything. As Carroll puts it, "whereas emotions are directed toward particular objects or have intentionality, moods do not."[3] Or another way of putting it: "Moods are global rather than focal; moods pervade perception, rather than focusing it."[4]

Carroll goes on, after making this basic and crucial distinction between moods and emotions, to enumerate other ways in which moods and emotions are to be distinguished, all, or almost all, related I think, as I have said, to this basic and crucial one. I do not propose to canvass the lot, as I think it is neither necessary nor useful to do so for present purposes. But two or three of them might help to fill in the picture.

"Related to the objectlessness or lack of the relevant sense of directedness of moods," Carroll suggests, "is a second feature of moods, as

---

[3] Carroll, "Art and Mood," 526.   [4] Ibid., 528.

distinct from emotions. Emotions are selective and exclusive. Moods are incorporative and inclusive."[5] Furthermore, since "Moods are objectless and global," they "pervade the area within the perimeters of perception, rather than carving out or shaping its contour, as an emotion does."[6] But "moods, like the emotions, are not disengaged from cognition"; "they bias the subject toward making certain kinds of judgments instead of others," although they are not, as emotions are on some accounts, judgments themselves.[7] And, finally, "Moods probably give the organism information about the subject's levels of energy and tension relative to its preparedness for responding to situations and challenges."[8]

Given, then, this general characterization of what moods are like, as opposed to emotions, the question must be broached of how *works of art* can possibly engender them in us. "For on our account, the cognitive biases that moods enjoin are, in large measure, dependent upon the coping resources of the organism, including, importantly, its level of energy relative to environmental challenges." So it seems as if "the overall mood state is intimately connected to factors over which artists have virtually no control."[9]

"My strategy," Carroll states, in dissolving what he calls the "mystery" of how art can elicit moods, "involves acknowledging that artists elicit mood states indirectly rather than directly." And, he continues: "They can do this in two ways; 1) by arousing emotional states in audiences which then linger on and metamorphose into mood states, and 2) by arousing certain feeling states (somatic, phenomenological ones) in audiences, which feelings are associated with the overall mood states of which they are components or constituents; these feelings, in turn, contribute to the elicitation of the cognitive biases of the mood states in question."[10]

The first indirect method by which artists can impart moods to their audiences, that is to say, by first arousing emotions "whose undertow, figuratively speaking, is a mood,"[11] assumes that works of art *can*, in the first place, arouse emotions. And although there is a good deal of philosophical controversy surrounding that assumption, there is

---

[5] Ibid., 527.   [6] Ibid., 528.   [7] Ibid., 528–9.   [8] Ibid., 530.
[9] Ibid., 539.   [10] Ibid.   [11] Ibid., 541.

also a good deal of agreement among philosophers of art that arts with narrative, conceptual, and representational content do, indeed, through this content, arouse *at least* the garden-variety emotions, and, in their more sophisticated incarnations, perhaps more subtle emotions as well.

But it is that very content that pure instrumental music lacks; and it is that very lack that has fueled skepticism about the ability of such music to arouse the garden-variety emotions, from the writings of the first modern musical formalist, Eduard Hanslick, to the present day. Indeed, it is the whole point of moving from emotions, with their necessary concepts and intentional objects, to "objectless" moods, to evade the need for the conceptual apparatus that absolute music, as Hanslick had already convincingly argued, cannot provide. So to fall back on emotive arousal to facilitate mood arousal is simply to give up the game. It is the second, then, of Carroll's two proposals for how the arts engender moods, to which he must resort in the case of absolute music. And as he himself is forced to concede, "Of these two hypotheses, the latter is surely the more speculative."[12]

It has always been thus with conjectures about how absolute music might engender affective states: "speculative" at best. Nevertheless, given his track record, Carroll's speculation merits serious consideration. And to that I now turn.

Mood–Musical Machinery

Carroll begins his argument for the power of absolute music to induce moods in listeners by pointing out that "The connection between mood and music is explicit in our culture where beloved tunes bear titles like 'In the Mood' and 'Mood Indigo.'" He continues: "People often say that they select music according to their mood."[13]

When we do select music according to our mood, Carroll goes on to say, we do not do so "simply to boost those [moods] already in place," but "apparently, we also use music to change our moods . . . Feeling low, for example, I may listen to the scherzo from Beethoven's *Ninth*

---

[12] Carroll, "Art and Mood," 539.   [13] Ibid., 545.

Symphony, whereas feeling wired, I might listen to the adagio from Bach's *Violin Concerto in E*." And, furthermore, "If music has the capacity to change our moods, it must have the capacity to induce moods."[14] The question now is *How?*, given that it cannot do so by arousing the garden-variety emotions, as the arts with conceptual, narrative, and representational content can.

Carroll offers two hypotheses for mood-arousal in music. The first, only briefly mentioned, is actually a hypothesis that *does* rely on the arousal of emotions by absolute music—an option that we would have thought closed. The second, more elaborately worked out and steady to his previous text, is an attempt to do the business, as one would have been led to expect, without the discredited option of emotive arousal.

Here is the first hypothesis, in Carroll's words:

Indeed, there may be ways in which even pure instrumental music can sometimes evoke emotional states. Some instrumental music is modeled on the sound of the human voice. Perhaps when a musical interlude sounds like an emotional exchange, maybe one fraught with angry conflict, there is enough information to enlist the listener in an emotional response. And in virtue of its structural organization, pure instrumental music may surprise and possibly startle us, and, as well, engender certain varieties of suspense and frustration. To the extent that we are willing to call these formally induced states emotions—emotions whose objects are the music—instrumental music can be said to elicit emotional responses and, subsequently, emotional spillover [in the form of moods].[15]

The second hypothesis is more leisurely in its laying out. Carroll begins with the "uncontroversial" premise that "while conceding that much of the relevant instrumental music lacks the means to engender emotional states, properly so called, it nevertheless has the capacity to elicit or arouse feelings, i.e., affectively charged, phenomenologically sensed states." Given, then, that absolute music can arouse "feelings," it seems possible that some of these "phenomenologically sensed states" might be "the component or constituent feeling elements of moods . . ."; and by "activating" these, "music can induce in the audience the cognitive predilections that typify various mood states."[16]

---

[14] Ibid., 546.   [15] Ibid., 546–7.   [16] Ibid., 547.

But the question remains of *how* absolute music can activate these feeling components of moods. Carroll conjectures: "In all likelihood, a major musical lever for the provocation of affectively charged sensations is the impression music gives of movement."[17] However, that cannot be the entire answer, for the further question must immediately arise of what the *connection* might be between the "impression" of motion absolute music might give to the listener, and the feeling components of moods that, on Carroll's hypothesis, the impression of movement is supposed to arouse. To *what* does the lever connect? What does it push?

The answer Carroll wants to give is that perceiving motion *in* the music gives us the "urge"—I suppose that is the right word—to move in the way we perceive the music as moving: "almost everyone," as Carroll points out, "has experienced an inner impulse to move when listening to music...." And when we feel this urge to move the *way* the music is moving, we experience the feelings that may be associated with the urge to move in those ways, or with those ways of moving themselves. Thus the terms by which we describe musical motion, "speeding up and slowing down, rising and falling, pushing, plodding, going against the tide...," and so forth, "may not only describe the musical text, but also how the music sounds or feels to us."[18]

This cannot be the whole story, though. "We have advanced the claim that pure instrumental music can induce mood states by triggering certain feelings, namely sensations that make us *feel* like moving certain ways. But how does that get us to the sorts of cognitive biases that crucially comprise mood states?"[19] For, it must be remembered, moods are not completely divorced from cognitive states: "cognitive biases," as Carroll calls them. Where do they come from in the art that, by hypothesis, is barren of conceptual, representational, and narrative content?

Here is Carroll's answer: "the same feelings that prompt us to move in response to the music also prompt us to imagine how someone or something would move to the music."[20] To amplify the point: "the bodily feelings, both somatic and phenomenological,

---

[17] Carroll, "Art and Mood," 547.   [18] Ibid., 548.   [19] Ibid.
[20] Ibid.

stirred by the impression of movement in instrumental music, not only inspires certain ranges of overt movement, but also cognitive biases, notably a tendency to *imagine*, imagistically or otherwise, or to recollect, or to attend to the kinds of movement, and perhaps associated activities and habits of mind, suggested viscerally by the movement in the music." Or, put in a nutshell, "it seems fair to say that the impression of movement in music, with non-random frequency, engenders feelings that in one way or another *bring to mind* certain kinds of movement."[21]

Carroll, apparently apprehensive that some of his readers might find the emphasis on detecting motion in music somewhat suspect, rounds off his account with an evolutionary explanation of how and why we should have the proposed propensity to perceive motion in music. "Motion detection," Carroll writes, "as well as ascertaining the possible general significance of the movement would have been of the utmost importance to our ancestors, as it is to other animals." And, he suggests: "That is perhaps why we are able to derive the impression of movement in something as 'unrealistic' as music in the first place. We come equipped, in a manner of speaking, with innate motion detectors keyed to sound and vibration; it is an alerting system—sometimes an early-warning system, as when a herd of herbivores starts moving at the sound of a distant stampede."[22]

At this point the reader has a fair idea of Carroll's views on how pure instrumental music might engender moods in listeners. Many of the niceties of the account I have had to omit. But I think a general outline, sufficient to my critical purposes, is now in place. Before I get down to that business, however, I think it would be well to lay out, very briefly, the conditions that, I think, a successful account of how absolute music might arouse moods in listeners must satisfy.

Rules of Engagement

(i) To start with, I think there should be convincing evidence adduced that absolute music does indeed engender moods in

---

[21] Ibid., 549.   [22] Ibid.

listeners before we are offered an explanation for *how* absolute music might do it. There is no purpose, obviously, in trying to elaborate the possible musical machinery for curing warts, when there is absolutely no evidence that music has such curative powers.

(ii) The explanation, obviously, must be a plausible one.

(iii) The explanation must be one for how absolute music engenders moods in musical listeners in what I shall call the *canonical cases*: that is to say, the cases in which people are listening to music the way it is supposed to be listened to in its status *as a fine art*.

(iv) And, closely related to (iii), the moods that the theory is concerned with must be moods relevant to our appreciation and enjoyment of absolute music as *music*; that is, as *art*.

All of these conditions will become clearer as my critique of Carroll's position unfolds. And before I start with it I need only add that they are the very same conditions that must be satisfied by a successful theory of how absolute music can arouse *any* affective states, including those I call the "garden-variety" emotions. I have argued in the past that all the theories with which I am acquainted, as regards how absolute music can arouse the garden-variety emotions fail to satisfy *at least* one of the above conditions. I am afraid that I am of the same mind concerning Carroll's theory of how absolute music might engender moods, sophisticated and well thought out though it may be,

The Skeptical Avenger Strikes Again

To begin with the *prima facie* evidence *for* absolute music's actually arousing or engendering moods in musical listeners seems to me, at best, very thin. Indeed, everything that Carroll adduces in this regard is perfectly compatible with the claim which I do not deny, but, in fact, heartily endorse, that absolute music can be *expressive of* various moods, which is to say, it can "possess" them as properties we "perceive in" the music, along with its other musical features. I have endorsed a similar view with regard to musical emotions, on numerous occasions, and what arguments I have advanced for it over the years apply, in many, if not all respects to moods as well.[23] It is the essence of "enhanced formalism."

Carroll says that the connection between mood and music is explicit in our culture, and this is certainly true. But that is adequately explained by the hypothesis that Western music has been, since time immemorial, *expressive of* moods. We do not need the hypothesis that it arouses them. Moods are in the music, not the man.

I am sure Carroll is also correct in averring that people often claim to select music *according to their mood*. But when they select music that is in the same mood as they are, I do not think it has anything to do with arousing or sustaining moods. I think rather that there is some kind of implicit "aesthetic" or "moral" sense of appropriateness at work here that makes it seem aesthetically or morally fitting that we hear somber music when somber, upbeat music when upbeat. Somber music for funerals is a case in point. Clearly it is chosen as appropriate or fitting for the somber mood of funerals. However, I scarcely think it is intended to make mourners somber; they already are. And upbeat music is *not* played, not because it is morally inappropriate to try to lift people from grief; rather, I suggest it is because it is just aesthetically, or in some related way felt to be inappropriate, jarring, or not fit for the occasion.

Finally, Carroll adduces as evidence that absolute music is mood arousing that we apparently do, and say we do use absolute music with specific moods to change our moods; to cheer us up when we are feeling low, and so forth. And on first reflection this perhaps seems like solid evidence. Why would we say that absolute music can change our moods if we didn't experience it so? Why would we continue to use it that way if it didn't work?

Let me suggest an analogous case that presents, I think, an even deeper analogy than might first appear. Clearly astrology works. Clearly the stars and planets must affect our lives and can predict our futures. Why else would so many of us say that it can? Why else would we resort to astrology and astrologers, sometimes at considerable expense, if astrology didn't work?

---

[23] On this see, for example, Peter Kivy, *The Corded Shell: Reflections on Musical Expression* (Princeton: Princeton University Press, 1980); reissued with extensive additions as, *Sound Sentiment: An Essay on the Musical Emotions* (Philadelphia: Temple University Press, 1989).

The fact is that, to no one's real surprise anymore, we do not form our beliefs or conduct our behavior rationally; we do not perform controlled experiments to find out if all of the daily rituals we go through to ward off the evil eye really work or not. (We still think getting wet will cause us to catch "our death of cold" and still take vitamin C to ward it off long after the negative results are in.)

No doubt many people think that pure instrumental music can change their moods in virtue of *its* moods, as they also think that astrology works—evidence to the contrary notwithstanding. And, interestingly enough, I think the musical and astrological beliefs have been with us just as long, as well as having the same or similar sources: numerology, number mysticism, and the Pythagorean conviction that the universe is governed by number and musical harmony (itself based on the arithmetical division of the octave). These convictions about the effects of music and the heavenly bodies on our lives are of ancient origin, and deeply embedded in our psyches. I take none of them as evidence of anything but human credulity.

But a word of caution here. In arguing that there is no evidence absolute music can alter or engender moods, I am arguing for the *specific* thesis that there is no evidence somber music can engender a somber mood in virtue of its being *somber*, upbeat music an upbeat mood in virtue of its being *upbeat*, and so on: in other words, there is no evidence absolute music has specific magic bullets for specific mood arousals. However, I am certainly *not* arguing that there is no evidence great music can lift me, for example, from a depressed mood. It can and frequently does, by taking my mind off my troubles and immersing me in a great work of the musical art. And, by the way, I choose a great work of music even though somber, over a trivial work of music, even though cheerful, because it is the *music*, not its specific *mood* that is the *modus operandi*.

But now moving on to the second of our conditions for a successful defense of absolute music's power over our moods. The best evidence, really, it might be argued, for the belief that absolute music engenders moods in listeners would be a satisfactory account of *how* it *can*. For if it *can*, then it *will*. And that being the case, we can forget about the lack of direct evidence that it does: in other words, we can forget about condition (i).

It will be recalled that Carroll has *two* explanations for how absolute music might engender moods in listeners: the first relying on its power to arouse emotions that leave moods in their wake, the second eschewing the highly suspect notion that absolute music can arouse the garden-variety emotions and relying on other means of doing the business.

Carroll suggests, it will be recalled, two ways that absolute music might arouse emotions. Some instrumental music, Carroll observes, is "modeled on the sound of the human voice"; and, he further observes, music that, for example, sounds like an angry emotional exchange might contain "enough information to enlist the listener in an emotional response." Alternatively, musical structure, in its unfolding, "may surprise us, startle us, and . . . engender certain varieties of suspense and frustration."

The first suggestion, that music arouses emotions through resemblance to the sound of the human voice, is as old as Plato's *Republic* (when read with a bit of hindsight), and has been with us in modern times since the end of the sixteenth century (at least). I have little doubt that Carroll well knows the major problem with this suggestion; for the assertion that "there is enough information" in a passage of "angry music" to make us (say) angry is meant to anticipate that problem. The fact is, however, as I have argued in other places, there *isn't* "enough information" in absolute music expressive of anger to arouse anger or any other garden-variety emotions. The hearing of an angry voice will not arouse a garden-variety emotion in me *unless* I know *who* is angry, *what* she is angry about, *who* she is angry with, and so forth. When I have *that* "information," I may get angry, if I think the anger is unjustified, or I may become afraid, if the anger is directed at me, or I may be overjoyed if the anger is directed at someone who I think deserves it, and so on. This is precisely why fictional characters expressing anger may make me angry, if I think the anger is unjustified, or cause me to become afraid, if the anger is directed at me, overjoyed if the anger is directed at someone who I think deserves it, and so on. This is precisely why fictional characters expressing anger can arouse the garden-variety emotions: there *is* "enough information" in novels and plays and movies. And it is precisely why "angry voices" heard in absolute music cannot: there is not "enough information" in absolute music to do the job.

The suggestion that the "suspense and frustration" the unfolding of musical structure may arouse in the perceptive listener are "emotions" capable of "emotional spillover" into moods (even if we accept the possibility) would have the following unsatisfactory consequence. *All* "suspenseful" passages would draw in their wake the *same* mood—whatever mood suspense tends to engender. And the same would be true, *pari passu*, of "frustrating" passages. But surely this is an intolerable conclusion. For passages in absolute music that engender suspense in listeners, and passages in absolute music that frustrate listeners' musical expectations, occur in passages of music that are expressive of a wide range of moods: sad music, somber music, gay music, exuberant music, upbeat music, angry music, and so on. That *all* of these passages, if they also engender suspense, elicit the *same* mood in listeners (whatever it would be), and ditto for frustration, seems to me to be very hard to credit.

Indeed, I do not think Carroll has much faith in this strategy anyway. For his argument is brief and quite perfunctory. In fact I have taken more time refuting it than he has spent propounding it. It is the second strategy that really bears the weight. And to that strategy I now turn.

Carroll's second hypothesis for mood arousal by absolute music, it will be recalled, is that absolute music arouses "feelings, i.e., affectively charged, phenomenologically sensed states," that lead to the eliciting of moods. I actually think that, *in general terms*, Carroll is right about this, and will explain in the concluding section of this chapter what kinds of feelings and moods I have in mind. But with regard to the kinds of feelings and moods that Carroll has in mind I am in disagreement. And the nature of that disagreement now needs to be spelled out.

Carroll thinks that the "feelings" absolute music arouses are what he calls "component or constituent feeling elements of moods." And he thinks absolute music arouses them through the impression of motion that absolute music presents the listener. The listener perceives the apparent motion, feels the urge to move the way the music moves, and this, so to speak, makes her feel the way the music is described as moving. Finally, "the same feelings that prompt us to move in response to the music also prompt us to imagine how someone or something would move to the music." For example—and the example is of utmost importance—"Stately music may dispose us to imagine moving in a stately fashion ourselves, to imagine others doing so, or to remember people moving in a regal procession, or to construct mental images of such pomp and ceremony . . . ," and so on.[24] Thus the conceptual "content," if that is the right word, necessary for moods to be engendered by absolute music, the "cognitive biases" of moods, as Carroll puts it, are provided—and I will not soften the blow here with euphemisms—by our using absolute music as a springboard to our imaginings of people moving to the music in ways we deem appropriate. We are, so to speak, providing a "program" in the imagination to give the moods the leg up that they need.

Now there are many questions one might want to raise with regard to the psychological conjectures Carroll makes prior to this point in the argument; conjectures that, essentially, prepare us for it. But I shall leave those conjectures alone, mainly because I am at a loss to know quite how, exactly, they are to be evaluated. (By experiment? By argument? By intuition?) Rather, I shall concentrate on the present claim because it is a very familiar one in the "philosophy of music" and I think I *do* know how to deal with *it*.

To begin with, Carroll, of course, is *absolutely right* that pure instrumental music *can*, and no doubt frequently *does*, give rise to the kinds of mental images he is talking about in musical listeners, and in the way he suggests: picturing in the mind's eye characters or personages moving in regal processions, pompous ceremonies, and the like, to the accompaniment of the music. Thus he has satisfied condition (ii): he has given at least *part* of a *plausible* explanation for how the affective states in question, namely moods, can be engendered in listeners by absolute music. But this, as it stands, is a hollow victory, *unless* condition (iii) can be satisfied as well: unless, that is to say, the process of picturing to ourselves characters or personages moving to the music can be construed as part of what I called a *canonical* case of music listening.

---

[24] Carroll, "Art and Mood," 548–9.

Now I do not want to deny that there may be more than one *canonical* way of listening to absolute music. But the *canonical* way that Carroll has explicitly stated he has in mind, my way, as a matter of fact, is the way of *formalist* listening. For recall that Carroll sees his project here as "negotiating a truce" between musical formalists and those who maintain that absolute music can arouse emotions, by substituting moods for emotions, and presenting a plausible musical machinery the formalists can accept for the arousal of *moods*, since "Formalists argue that it is nonsense to maintain that instrumental music arouses emotions," music lacking "the logical machinery" for doing so.

But that project of "negotiating a truce" between formalism and the "arousalists" (if I may so call them) must fail if what is offered to the formalists as a crucial part of the arousal machinery is the imagining process Carroll proposes. For that is just the kind of "mind wandering" that, according to the formalist account, is destructive of his *canonical* listening mode. To quote, on this point, a well-known formalist of impeccable credentials, whom I quoted earlier on: "at moments I do appreciate music as pure aesthetic form, . . . as pure art . . . with no relation at all to the significance of life . . . Tired or perplexed, I let slip my sense of form . . . and I begin weaving into the harmonies . . . the ideas of life . . . ."[25]

It is important to emphasize, here, that, unlike Clive Bell, the author quoted above, I am making no normative claim: rather, a purely descriptive or, if you like, a definitional one. I do not claim that formalist listening is the only *canonical* listening, nor do I claim that if there *are* other *canonical* ways of listening to absolute music, it is the best of them. What I claim, simply, is that listening to absolute music the way Noel Carroll suggest we would have to, to have moods engendered in us, *cannot be* part of the kind of *canonical* listening to absolute music that is the *formalist's* way of listening. And so even though Carroll may be right about how absolute music can engender moods in listeners, he has not managed to negotiate a truce between formalists and arousalists. For formalism cannot countenance as *canonical* formalist listening the listening

---

[25]   Clive Bell, *Art*, 30.

Carroll describes. As formalism construes it, Carroll has not satisfied condition (iii).

And, to conclude, the same holds for condition (iv). Carroll's way of listening does not satisfy it. For the moods that, on Carroll's view, absolute music engenders, are engendered by means of features, the listener's images, that are not part of the music, *qua* music, or *qua* art; and so the moods themselves, that these images help to engender, are not artistically, musically relevant to the formalist's listening experience. They may be relevant to some *other* kind of *canonical* listening; but that is for others to spell out, for whom that other kind of listening is *canonical*.

The major reasons for my rejecting Carroll's account of how absolute music might engender moods, rather than emotions, in listeners are now on the table. But before I depart from my critique, I would like to mention, briefly, three further, if minor, difficulties with his view.

Carroll adduces, as part of his argument that the ability of absolute music to engender moods is just acknowledged "common sense," as it were, the collections of musical excerpts usually referred to as "mood music." He writes: "indeed, collections of music are marketed with the promise of promoting certain moods, like relaxation, nostalgia, and romance." He adds, tellingly I think: "And though this use of music strikes some connoisseurs as tacky, it does not appear, in principle, impossible."[26]

The telling part of the addendum is where Carroll acknowledges that "connoisseurs" will find such uses of music "tacky." For the reason they will is, clearly, that that kind of music listening not only fails to be *canonical* listening in the formalist mode but fails to be *canonical* listening in any other mode that might be considered *canonical* by the serious listener to the classical music repertory. So even if listening to a whole record or disc of "mood music" could put one in a nostalgic mood, or "in the mood for romance," it would fail to satisfy condition (iii) of the "rules of engagement," and would not, therefore, count as a serious example for the aesthetics of music; nor, by the way, would Carroll's choosing a Beethoven scherzo to

---

[26] Carroll, "Art and Mood," 538.

cheer him up, or a Bach adagio to calm him down, since any kind of *canonical* listening would require listening to whole compositions, not merely excerpts for mood-enhancing purposes.

Furthermore, I think to simply entertain as a *Gedankenexperiment*, the listener to (say) a major symphony in the classical music canon experiencing the mood-swings, from one end of the affective spectrum to the other, that the symphony might musically exhibit, as, literally, *felt affective states*, would amount to a *reductio* of Carroll's claim. I ask the reader to listen, for example, to one of the well-known Romantic symphonies of Schumann, or Brahms, or Tchaikovsky, lay his hand upon his heart, and swear to me that he has "felt" his way through it, "mood-wise." A person susceptible to mood swings like that in listening to absolute music is not just an unusually "sensitive" listener—he is a man with a problem. I cannot credit this kind of listening, if indeed there is anyone who does or can do it, as *canonical* listening, at least in the formalist mode. And so if there are, indeed, listeners of this stripe, I would say their mode of listening does not satisfy condition (iii) any more than does the listener to "mood music" who "gets in the mood."

Finally, I do not find Carroll's "evolutionary" explanation for our perception of "motion" in music plausible, but should point out, before I give my reason, that the evolutionary explanation is certainly not crucial to Carroll's project, and its failure not by any means fatal to it.

I think we must be very circumspect in our description of music as "giving the impression" of motion, which is the phenomenon Carroll's evolutionary explanation is supposed to account for. Of course we all know that music isn't *literally* in motion. But nor does it "give the impression of motion" in the sense of producing the "illusion" of motion, as do the blinking lights on a neon sign or the rapid appearance of dots on a television screen, which are actually used by biologists and psychologists to perform experiments in "motion" perception in primates. I think the best we can say is that motion words seem appropriate descriptions of music in some figurative, attenuated sense. Music is, to be sure, as Carroll describes it, "unrealistic" in this regard. There is neither motion in it, nor even the illusion of motion. That being the case, I think it unlikely that we owe our hearing of "motion" in music to the same evolutionary process that gave us our tendency to perceive motion visually for survival purposes.[27]

For the reasons stated above, then, I do not see the move from emotions to moods as a promising way of satisfying the formalists—myself included—and the "arousalists" both. But that leaves us with some unfinished business still since, as I stated early on, I certainly agree with Carroll that moods *do* play a part in the formalist's experience of absolute music, and with the arousalist's in general, that listening to the masterpieces of the Western classical music canon can be, in the best of times anyway, a deeply moving experience. I have argued at length about the compatibility of formalism both with the view that absolute music can be described in emotive terms and with the view that absolute music arouses emotion. My view, as I have said, has been called "enhanced formalism,"[28] and has been given a good run for the money in previous articles and books.[29] This is not the place to go over that yet again. But a word, perhaps, is necessary.

When Hanslick launched modern musical formalism, in his "little book," he never meant to deny that music could be described as having all sorts of "qualities," describable in ordinary, non-musical language. Thus, absolute music can be "clumsy," "dramatic," "turbulent," "tranquil," and so on. It can be described, in other words, in terms of what Frank Sibley famously called "aesthetic concepts."[30] How music comes to have such aesthetic properties is, of course, a philosophical problem in its own right, but not one I intend to grapple with here. Suffice it to say, however philosophers differ on the matter, most would agree that it makes sense to ascribe these aesthetic properties to music and that we "perceive" them in it in some proper sense of the word.

---

[27] I should point out that years ago I presented an evolutionary argument, not unlike Carroll's, for the perception of the "animate," which is to say, living forms, in musical sound. (See *The Corded Shell*, 57–9.) I do not think that my explanation is open to the same objection I have made to Carroll's. But here is not the place to go into it. In any case, it is all too easy to come up with such evolutionary accounts, in the armchair, as it were, which is why Stephen Jay Gould called them, derisively, "Just So Stories."

[28] By my good friend Phillip Alperson.

[29] See Peter Kivy, *Music Alone: Philosophical Reflections on the Purely Musical Experience* (Ithaca: Cornell University Press, 1990).

[30] Frank Sibley, "Aesthetic Concepts," *Philosophical Review*, 67 (1959).

What Hanslick denied in his formalism is that music could be described in terms of the garden-variety emotions, and that, as we have seen, because he saw no alternative to construing emotive terms as either ascribing to music the power to arouse the garden-variety emotions or to represent them, both of which powers he denied to it. What "enhanced formalism" is, then, is an enhancement of Hanslick's formalism, allowing it to include emotive properties as perceptual properties *of the music*: in other words, aesthetic properties in Sibley's sense.

I have nothing more to say on the subject of enhanced formalism here. Rather, I would like to conclude merely with some brief remarks suggesting why, the above criticism to the contrary notwithstanding, I can still agree with Carroll on two points: that moods are rightly considered as part of the absolute music experience and that the absolute music experience can be as deeply moving as the experience of any of the other arts, and, yes, even mood inducing in a sense I will specify below. All depends, however, on placing the moods where they really are, and understanding what is aroused for what it really is.

A Non-skeptical Conclusion

What role do the "garden-variety moods," as I shall now call them, play in absolute music? Very simply: the same role that the garden-variety emotions play in enhanced formalism. Absolute music is (sometimes) expressive of them. They are part of the musical fabric and we perceive them *in* it, as Ambrose first suggested, and as I have already suggested above. They are aesthetic properties of the music, in Frank Sibley's sense. It is in that role that it is perfectly correct to say of them, as Noel Carroll does, that "The connection between mood and music is explicit in our culture . . . ."

But if, as I claim, absolute music in the *canonical* formalist setting arouses neither garden-variety emotions *nor* garden-variety moods, *wherein* lies its power to move us affectively, and *what* affect does it move us to? Again, I have written a good deal elsewhere about "how music moves," and have no wish to repeat myself unnecessarily here.[31]

---

[31] On this see, for example, *Music Alone*, chapter 8.

Suffice it to say that, on my view, great music, in the Western absolute music canon, moves us to a kind of enthusiasm, or excitement, or ecstasy, directed at the music as its intentional object. This account of how music moves us emotionally has, among its distinct advantages, on my view, not only that it provides the sought for intentional object of the musical emotion, as well as the necessary beliefs and concepts, but implies that only music the listener experiences as great or beautiful or outstanding music moves the listener emotionally, at least in the formalist's *canonical* case, which, indeed, has been *my* experience, anyway.

Finally, it bears pointing out, before I conclude, that this account of how absolute music moves us emotionally *also* provides for the possibility that absolute music can engender at least one *mood* in listeners in just the way Carroll suggests artworks usually engender moods, namely, by arousing "emotions whose undertow, figuratively speaking, is a mood." For if absolute music can arouse the *emotion* of enthusiasm, or excitement, or ecstasy, in the way described above, that emotion can perhaps also leave in its wake a general mood of upliftedness, or exaltation as *its* "undertow," as Carroll would have it. And so it turns out that, at least in this particular case, Carroll's account of how absolute music engenders moods—*a* mood, anyway—is right on the money, as I will argue more fully in Part III. And on that positive note I will close this chapter. For it is time now to dive into the main argument of the book: the ancient quarrel between literature and music, for which the previous chapters have now prepared us.

5

Persona Non Grata

Introduction

Literary interpreters of the absolute music canon tend to fall into two distinct groups. There are those, I think in the minority, who throw caution to the winds, sometimes more, sometimes less, and impute to pure instrumental music narratives in startling detail, even to the extent of naming names, and there are those, of a more circumspect disposition, who put narrations to the music that are vague or sketchy enough to slip by without striking the average music lover as wildly implausible or "off the wall." The most popular and most frequently resorted to artifice, for those narrative interpreters of the more moderate stripe, to underwrite their readings of the absolute music canon, is a shadowy figure that has become known as the musical "persona." This character is the subject of the present chapter.

The musical persona performs, really, two functions for the narrativist: to give absolute music a fictional content that is supposed to account for its artistic substance and interest, at least in part; and to explain how absolute music is capable, which such theorists claim it is, of arousing what I have been calling the "garden-variety" emotions—love, happiness, fear, melancholy, anger, and a few other such. I shall critically examine both of its functions in what follows. But first we must know the animal we are stalking. I turn to that now.

The Musical Persona

It appears that the character of the musical persona first stepped upon the stage in the pages of Edward T. Cone's justly admired monograph, *The Composer's Voice* (1974). An accomplished composer, performer, and theorist, Cone also possessed a fine philosophical sensibility; and *The Composer's Voice*—The Ernest Bloch Lectures for 1972—had a lasting influence on those philosophers concerned with the conceptual issues surrounding the nature and effects of absolute music, in particular, those philosophers who were searching for a *moderate* alternative to the musical formalism that was regnant at the time.

The gist of Cone's thesis is that "any instrumental composition, like the instrumental component of a song, can be interpreted as the symbolic utterance of a virtual persona."[1] And Jerrold Levinson, although neither citing Cone, nor calling his musical character "persona," utilizes what I take to be the persona concept to explain how absolute music arouses the garden-variety emotions. Thus he writes:

> Usually what happens is of an *empathetic* or *mirroring* nature. When we identify with music that we are perceiving—or perhaps better, with the person we imagine owns the emotions or emotional gestures we hear in the music—we share in and adopt those emotions as our own, for the course of the audition. And so we end up feeling as, in imagination, the music does.[2]

I shall not pursue Cone's version of the musical persona any further here beyond paying the respects due to him. Nor will I say anything more right now about Levinson's imagined musical persona, although I will return later on to his notion of "empathetic" or "mirroring" listening. Rather, I want to concentrate, in some detail, on the most recent version, to date, of the musical persona, in Jenefer Robinson's important book, *Deeper than Reason*. It displays in a small, concentrated conceptual space, almost the whole array of problems such theories must encounter.

Robinson's launching pad for her attempt to attribute personae to works of pure instrumental music is an interpretation of a song by Brahms, "Immer leiser wird mein Schlummer" (Op. 105, No. 2). She writes of the song: "To my mind 'Immer leiser' is a paradigm of Romantic expression. It is a short lyrical piece in which the

---

[1] Edward T. Cone, *The Composer's Voice* (Berkeley, Los Angeles, London: University of California Press, 1974), 94.

[2] Jerrold Levinson, "Music and Negative Emotion," in Levinson, *Music, Art, and Metaphysics: Essays in Philosophical Aesthetics*, 320–1.

protagonist is explicitly articulating in a number of different ways what her emotions are and how they change and develop."[3] In short, Robinson reads "Immer leiser" as the utterance of a "dramatic speaker," embodied, obviously, *in the text*. And she then tries to work her passage from this completely non-controversial claim to the highly controversial one that pieces of pure instrumental music are expressions of a dramatic speaker, in the absence of any text to give substance to the claim. As she puts her point, "it is eminently reasonable to interpret at least some Romantic instrumental music as expressions of emotions in characters or personae in the music."[4]

The imputation of a dramatic speaker, or persona, to a song is, of course, non-controversial because the text supplies the speaker or persona in a non-controversial manner. But where there is no text to do the job, the imputation of a dramatic speaker or persona becomes highly controversial indeed, as we shall see.

Robinson's poster boy for her persona interpretations is another work of Brahms': the Intermezzo in B-flat minor, Op. 117, No. 2. It is, not surprisingly, in ABA form—not surprisingly because this musical form has been, throughout the history of Western art music, one of the major and most satisfying organizational principles in the composer's tool box. That being the case, the "story" attributed to the Intermezzo must be one in which it makes sense for the persona to repeat at the end what he or she said or experienced in the beginning. And the frequency with which ABA form occurs in the absolute music repertoire makes persona a very repetitious character—a point I shall return to later on.

Thus, on Robinson's view, the return of the A theme, which she describes as a theme with a "yearning" quality, betokens "the character has accepted that yearning is to be his fate, has recognized that he will not achieve his desire, and sorrowfully, reluctantly, has resolved himself to the realization."[5] Robinson, by the way, refers to the persona of the Intermezzo as "he" without giving us any explanation for how she can sex personae, another point to which I shall return.

---

[3] Jenefer Robinson, *Deeper than Reason: Emotion and its Role in Literature, Music, and Art* (Oxford: Clarendon Press, 2005), 320.
[4] Ibid., 335–6.   [5] Ibid., 343.

Robinson's "literary" analysis of the Intermezzo goes into considerably more detail than the above synopsis suggests. But the remarks which follow, about the plausibility or necessity of such an interpretation of the absolute music canon, are of a general nature, meant to argue the implausibility of the persona interpretation *tout court*, not merely Robinson's persona interpretation of this particular work. Her interpretation will serve as a convenient reference point for what follows, which is, indeed, an argument to the effect that the failure of the persona interpretation is one of many cases in point to come, of the claim that literature and absolute music are indeed *antithetical arts*.

Persona Passions

Robinson writes of the Brahms Intermezzo that "if we do not interpret the piece as a [persona's] psychological drama in which powerful emotions are tracked and experienced, we cannot understand why the piece is so powerfully moving."[6] And Levinson, as we have already seen, also uses the musical persona as the major operator in explaining how absolute music moves the listener emotionally, which is to say, arouses the garden-variety emotions. I shall examine both of these claims critically in this section, beginning with Robinson, and then going on to Levinson, briefly, at the close.

There are really two claims that Robinson is making here, that it would be well to prise apart, although they are obviously dependent one upon the other. Robinson is claiming that: (1) the existence of a musical persona in the Brahms Intermezzo can account for "why the piece is so powerfully moving"; and (2) without postulating the existence of a musical persona in the piece "we cannot understand why the piece is so powerfully moving," which is to say, the only possible explanation for the fact that "the piece is so powerfully moving" is that it depicts a musical persona's "psychological drama."

It is, I think, very easy to defeat both of these claims. Let us look at the second first.

The second claim, it appears to me, is a claim in search of a transcendental argument. In order to make the second claim good

---

[6] Robinson, *Deeper than Reason*, 346.

Robinson would have to provide an argument to the effect that the *only* condition under which it would be possible for the Intermezzo to be "so powerfully moving," which it *is*, would be that it contained a musical persona involved in a psychological drama. Robinson gives us no such argument, and in a moment I shall suggest why no such argument could be in the offing. So as it stands claim (2) argues that the Brahms Intermezzo is "powerfully moving"; the only possible explanation for its being "powerfully moving" is the persona explanation; therefore, the persona explanation is true. That there *must* be one (at least) other explanation and that, therefore, a transcendental argument for Robinson's claim is not in the offing I shall now go on (quite easily) to show.

Formalists of my stripe, which is to say, enhanced formalists, formalists who hear emotions *in* the music, find the Brahms Intermezzo, and many other masterpieces of the absolute music canon, "powerfully moving." Yet, being formalists, we do *not* hear musical personae in the music we emote over. Indeed, I was being powerfully moved by pure instrumental music long before I ever even *heard* of the musical persona, or that such a creature might inhabit the works which so powerfully moved me. So there *must* be another explanation, besides the persona theory, for how absolute music is "so powerfully moving." And it must be a *formalist* explanation that does not appeal to any purported literary content of absolute music, since the listeners whose emotive experience it is supposed to explain are formalist listeners, albeit, at least in some instances, enhanced formalists like myself.[7]

So much, then, for Robinson's claim that the *only* way to explain how the Brahms Intermezzo, and other works like it, move us, emotionally, is that they embody musical personae enacting psychological dramas, or the notion that a transcendental argument to sustain it might be forthcoming. Nevertheless, the defender of the musical persona might respond that even though the musical persona may not be the only mechanism for the arousal of emotions by absolute music, it is *one* of such mechanisms among others. This response brings us to the first of Robinson's claims about the musical persona, namely, that the

[7] I have provided such an explanation in my book, *Music Alone: Philosophical Reflections on the Purely Musical Experience* (Ithaca, New York: Cornell University Press, 1990), chapter 8.

presence of the musical persona *can* make absolute music powerfully moving. I turn now to that claim. Its *failure*, it appears to me, lies at the heart of the thesis of this book, that literature and absolute music are *antithetical arts*.

Those who place literary interpretations on the absolute music canon are between a rock and a hard place. Make your interpretation too elaborate and detailed and you do so on pain of offending common sense and eschewing authorial intention in a performing art where the composer's performance intentions are important to all, and holy writ to most. The unhappy consequences of the other alternative we are about to confront.

The musical persona is a fictional "character" that is supposed to inhabit *some* works of absolute music. This character in his or her adventures is supposed to have the power to sustain our artistic interest, as characters in literary fiction do, and deeply move us emotionally, as do the characters and plots of the great literary works of the canon. To test this claim let us begin by reminding ourselves just what it is about the memorable characters of fiction that interests and moves us.

What makes the characters in the novels of Jane Austen, say, or Dickens, and their adventures, so profoundly interesting to us, as well as so deeply moving? Obviously, without getting specific, we are enthralled and moved by such as inhabit these works because they are persons of flesh and blood, with names (!), clothed in humanity by literary geniuses. They "live," because all of the resources of literary language have been marshaled to paint them and their adventures for us in depth and detail. They are not just nameless, featureless "personae." We are deeply interested in them because there is *so much* to be deeply interested in; we are deeply moved emotionally by them because there is *so much* about them to deeply move us emotionally. These are such familiar truths, such utter platitudes, that it is embarrassing to have to state them. And yet I cannot but think that defenders of the musical persona must have forgotten them entirely, or the musical persona could never have gotten a foothold in the philosophy of art.

For if we ask what makes the musical persona and "his" adventures in the Brahms Intermezzo, as described by Robinson, so profoundly interesting to us, and so profoundly moving, the answer is: *absolutely nothing.* Robinson's musical persona, and his or her completely empty skeleton of a story—a plot outline, merely, not yet a plot—give us no such fictional materials as can be got from the novels of Austen and Dickens, and must, therefore, leave us profoundly *uninterested* and profoundly *unmoved.* We do not even know the sex, unless we take Robinson's word for it, of the character with which we are supposed to be so intellectually and emotionally enthralled.

The conclusion of these considerations must be that the musical persona in the Brahms Intermezzo, as described by Robinson, has the literary resources neither to interest us nor to move us. And this conclusion can be generalized for *any* musical persona hypothesized for *any* work in the absolute music canon. It can certainly be seen as valid against Levinson's use of the persona to explain how absolute music might arouse the garden-variety emotions. But there is *another* problem, as well, which Levinson's appeal to the musical persona lays bare, and which requires our scrutiny. So I return, now, to Levinson, in concluding this section.

How, precisely, does our recognition of the musical persona in a musical composition arouse the garden-variety emotions in us, on Levinson's view? In answering this question Levinson resorts to the oldest philosophical account we possess of how fictional characters arouse emotions in their audiences, Plato's, in *Republic* X (606b−608c), which is to say, empathy, or "mirroring" (as Levinson also calls it). Thus, the theory goes, we perceive the music as the emotive expression of a musical persona and, by empathy or mirroring, *we* come to feel the emotions that we perceive the musical persona as expressing.

But, as has been pointed out by previous critics, the empathy or mirroring account of how fictional narratives arouse our emotions does not in many, if not most cases, track the right emotions. Of course I may, when appropriate, be caused to have the same emotion as the fictional character. *I* am happy when the characters who deserve it "live happily ever after." However, as Noel Carroll puts the point: "In the standard case, when we are emotionally engaged by fictions, we do not identify emotionally with characters by, so to say, taking on their emotions."[8] On the contrary, we react to *their* emotions with

[8] Noel Carroll, *A Philosophy of Mass Art* (Oxford: Clarendon Press, 1998), 260.

different emotions. I am made angry, or fearful by Iago's jealousy; I am not made jealous. And I rejoice in his discomfiture.

On Levinson's account, however, we *always* feel the same emotion as the musical persona is supposed to be expressing. And that should set off alarm bells. Why should the musical persona always arouse in me the same emotion he or she is experiencing, whereas fictional characters in literary works do not? I suggest it is because the persona theorist can find no fictional circumstances in the music to tell us *what* emotion to feel, and so naturally latches on to the only thing we do know: that the persona is sad, or angry, or cheerful, or whatever.

However, a moment's reflection should convince us that for the *same reason* we cannot be aroused to any *other* emotion than the emotion the persona is expressing, we cannot be aroused to *that* one either. Whether we feel *with* a fictional character or feel *at* a fictional character, whether we are sorrowed by Anna Karenina's sorrow, or moved to some *other* emotion by it depends on what circumstances she is in, and the kind of person she is. But as we have seen, the musical persona and his or her musical "surroundings" can give us no such information. The musical persona no more has the power to make you angry by his or her anger, than the power to arouse in you any other emotional state.

The conclusion, then, that forces itself on us, appears to be that the musical persona, as regards the power to engage our interest or move our emotions, is, as they say, an "empty suit." But that is not where this shadowy character's troubles end. There is more to come.

Da Capo

Nearly every symphonic first movement, from Haydn through Brahms, is in sonata form, with, in very many cases, the exposition literally repeated. The same goes for the first movements of string quartets, sonatas of all kinds, and the various other chamber music genres. As well, in many cases, particularly in the Classical period, the development-cum-recapitulation is literally repeated as well. If the finale is in sonata form, as frequently is the case, the same pattern of repetition will be in evidence. Theme-and-variation movements, which abound in the absolute music repertoire, usually are constructed on a theme in two sections, each of which is repeated, and variations with the same structure and same pattern of literal repeats. And the rondo, Haydn's favorite form for symphonic finales, has its own pattern of literal repeats.

Furthermore, the minuet in the Classical symphony, and the scherzo in Beethoven's and the Romantic's symphonic works, exhibit even more literal repeats. And literal repetition abounds as well in the Baroque dance forms, concerto grosso, French overture—the staples of the Baroque instrumental repertoire.

The repeats that I have so far mentioned are what might be called "external" repeats: literal repeats of whole discrete sections of a musical movement. But the repetitiousness of absolute music does not end with external repeats: it is "internally" repetitious as well. Thus, to take perhaps the most famous case of internal repetition in absolute music, the first movement of Beethoven's Fifth Symphony, the well-known "fate" motive on which the movement is constructed, occurs, on my reckoning, approximately 45 times, in the 124 measures of the exposition alone; and the exposition, by the way, is *repeated*.

Finally, sonata form itself is based on the principle of repetition. For the recapitulation of a sonata movement is, of course, the return of the material already heard in the exposition. And although the recapitulation is not, as a whole, a literal repeat of the exposition, large sections of it *are*. It is for this very reason that the third Leonore Overture, which is supposed to be a "preview," as it were, of the plot of the opera, but is also in sonata form, was seen as an artistic failure, since the recapitulation "tells the story" all over again.

Considering, then, how ubiquitous both external and internal repetition are in absolute music, it seems no exaggeration to say that the art of absolute has been, from Bach through Brahms, "the fine art of repetition."[9] And that conclusion, it seems to me, is a *reductio ad absurdum* of the view that absolute music can be understood as a persona's psycho-drama (or any other kind of drama, for that matter). Let me spell this out.

[9] See Peter Kivy, "The Fine Art of Repetition," in Kivy, *The Fine Art of Repetition: Essays in the Philosophy of Music*, 327–59.

Let's begin with the external repeat. If Beethoven's Fifth Symphony is a musical persona's psycho-drama—and surely it is, for the literary crowd, the paradigm case—it is a very strange drama indeed. The first "scene" of the first "act" is performed *twice*! The *Eroica*, another of the literary crowd's darlings, also has a first scene repeat; and the first scene is 155 measures long (as compared with the Fifth's 124). Furthermore, the third act of the *Eroica*, which is to say, the scherzo, has numerous "scene" repeats. Not to mention that both first movements are in sonata form, with, therefore, much repeated material in the recapitulation. Imagine, if you will, going to see *Hamlet* and finding various of its scenes enacted two or more times. Weird! But what would be weird in a literary work is *de rigueur* in absolute music.

But going on from external repeats to internal repeats, the latter are equally damaging to persona interpretations. For if the motives and themes of instrumental forms are the "utterances" of musical personae, these personae are very odd characters, to be sure. For they repeat the same utterances over and over again in the same "speech," as if Hamlet were to say "To be, or not to be," 45 times in one soliloquy. How *can* that make sense as a way of interpreting the absolute music canon?

That the literary and the purely musical are, in this regard, at odds, are *antithetical*, should be no news to anyone in the musical world. It was long ago remarked on by Heinrich Schenker, who wrote that "language . . . prefers exactly the opposite strategy [to absolute music]—that is, a continuous flow, without repetition."[10] And the musical persona is just a special case of the literary, which is to say, the linguistic arts, misapplied to absolute music.

Robinson at one point brings up the fugue for mention as a hard case for the persona theory, averring that "Even in Peter Kivy's favourite example of 'music alone', the fugue, the different strands of the fugue are often described as voices or as characters."[11] Of course the parts of a fugue, as in other cases of "part writing," are called

---

[10] Heinrich Schenker, "The Spirit of Musical Technique," trans. William Pastille, *Theoria*, 3 (1988), 88.
[11] Robinson, *Deeper than Reason*, 335.

"voices" for no other reason than that they derive their names from the ranges of the singers in four-voiced choral polyphony (the standard form of part-writing since the beginning of the seventeenth century): soprano, alto, tenor, bass. There is no "programmatic" significance at all to the nomenclature. But never mind that. Let's see how the fugue fares.

Fugue XVI of the Well-tempered Clavier, Book I, in G minor, begins with the statement of the subject in the tenor voice. The soprano voice then answers with the subject while the tenor continues with the counter-subject. And so on. It is a four-part fugue.

Is the fugue the utterance of one persona, who speaks in four voices, or the utterances of four personae, who each speak in his or her own voice? Thinking of the fugue as the utterance of one voice boggles the mind. Whatever the persona "says" he or she says over and over again, and, not only that, says different things simultaneously, sometimes four things at once, it being a four-part fugue. Therein interpretational madness lies.

Not to worry, though, defenders of the musical persona are likely to reply. We never thought for a moment that a four-part fugue is the utterance of a single musical persona. Rather, of course, it is a "conversation" between, in this case, four "voices": four musical personae. However, not much reflection will reveal that this suggestion is equally implausible.

So the G-minor Fugue, of the Well-tempered Clavier, Book I, is a "conversation" between four musical personae. But, truth to tell, it is a very strange conversation. When soprano "answers" tenor, who begins the conversation, she dos not respond to what tenor "says"; she *repeats* what tenor says. And nor does tenor listen to what soprano says; rather, he goes on to say something else (the countersubject) all the while soprano is saying what tenor has already said. At times *all* four of the personae are speaking at once; and at no time, except for the first statement of the subject, do any of the conversationalists have the floor to him- or herself. Imagine, if you will, a spoken drama in which such a "conversation" takes place. Yet we are to believe that the conversation model makes sense of the fugue. It does not. It makes *nonsense* of the fugue. (It is theater of the absurd two-and-a-half centuries before its time.) If an interpretation is supposed to make sense of what it interprets, the persona interpretation of a fugue is an abject failure.

What must strike anyone acquainted with the history of opera as an art form, and the aesthetic disputes that were at its heart, as truly bizarre, is that if the persona theory *were* true, there needn't have been a "problem of opera" in the first place; because the "problem" of opera, or more generally, music drama, has always been seen as the problem of combining in one artwork two antithetical arts, the literary (or dramatic) and the musical, which, as Schenker put it, pursue two different strategies, the one "a continuous flow, without repetition," the other the strategy of external and internal repetition. The history of opera is the history of attempts to reconcile music with drama. Hanslick put it well: "As everyone knows, to satisfy in due proportion the musical and dramatic requirements is considered to be the ideal of opera; this ideal itself is nevertheless for this very reason a constant struggle between the principle of dramatic realism and that of musical beauty . . . ."[12] Absolute music is free of the problem because it has no "text" to be reconciled with. The persona interpretation gives it a problem it does not have by trying to give it a text it does not have, with predictable results. The fine art of repetition resists the attempt to make drama of music, as every opera composer has discovered.

One might, to be sure, in response to the argument from repetition as stated above, severely restrict persona interpretations to those works in which there is no external repetition, and internal repetition is at a minimum. Robinson, indeed, makes a very modest claim, at least to begin with, for the musical persona (although she is not consistent), maintaining merely that "it is eminently reasonable to interpret at least some Romantic instrumental music as expressions of emotions in characters or personae in the music."[13] But making *such* a modest claim seems to me cold comfort.

To begin with, even if one restricted the personae claim just to those intimate miniatures of the Romantic piano repertoire, such as the Brahms Intermezzo, and other works of that kind, one would

[12] Eduard Hanslick, *On the Musically Beautiful*, trans. Geoffrey Payzant, 23.

[13] Robinson, *Deeper than Reason*, 336.

still run up against *both* external and internal repeats, as well as the ubiquitous ABA song form. And those pieces with programmatic titles, which, of course, abound in the Romantic era, would be ruled out immediately as not being absolute music at all, by definition. Thus the number of works that qualify for persona interpretation, even in the period most favored for such interpretations, would be almost vanishingly small.

Furthermore, the overwhelming preponderance (and *dominance*) in the absolute music canon of works, for reasons stated above, recalcitrant to persona or other narrative interpretations, the instrumental music of Bach, Haydn, Mozart, and Beethoven, to mention only the most obvious cases, strongly suggests, on theoretical grounds, that we resist the thesis that *any* "absolute music" *at all* can possess personae or other narrative content. The more reasonable thesis, which I shall defend later on, is that *some* of the music—not very much, indeed—now included in the absolute music canon might be "discovered" to be "program" music after all. What the criteria for such "discoveries" may be remains for us to see (and more of that anon).

Pleasure *sans* Persona

I have raised the next objection to the persona theory before, in response to other theories, both of the narrative and of the representational kind, but it is relevant to the persona theory as well, and must be raised yet again.

If absolute music were a narrative art form, as the persona theory makes it out to be, it would be in yet another respect a very bizarre one indeed. For it would be a narrative art form from which large numbers of musically sophisticated listeners derive deep satisfaction, and concerning which they profess to have deep understanding and appreciation, even though they are completely unaware of the purported narrative content of the works they enjoy and appreciate, or even that anyone thinks that they have such content at all.

If a person professed to enjoy listening to recitations of German narrative fiction, professed to deeply appreciate such fiction, without understanding a word of German, but insisted that he did so because he "liked the sounds and their structure," he would be taken for weird or mad. If a person professed to enjoy listening to the Brahms Intermezzo, and other works like it, professed to deeply appreciate and enjoy them, completely unaware that some people heard personae and their stories in them, did not hear personae or stories in them herself, but said she listened because she "liked the sounds and their structure," she not only would *not* be thought weird or mad; she would be thought to belong to a rather large group of musical listeners, among whom could be counted distinguished musicians, music theorists, and others of deep musical sophistication. Something is amiss here that demands explanation; and it is the persona theorist's burden to provide it.

Of course the liberal-minded might like to say that, no doubt, there is more than one way of listening to absolute music: as *absolute* music and as narrative music. But is there any other major art form that exhibits this odd trait? How can an art work *both* be richly rewarding as pure form and richly rewarding to others as fiction. A puzzle certainly remains. I think this puzzle is powerful prima facie evidence against the persona theory, and narrative interpretations in general of the absolute music canon. And, of course, as we have seen, and will see, it is not, by any means, the only evidence.

Charity

My own philosophical misgivings anent the whole persona project for absolute music are amply supported by the repetition argument, and, as far as I am concerned, it alone should close the book on the idea. But perhaps there are those who feel otherwise. And since Robinson, for one, has more strings to her bow, it behooves us to pursue the persona issue a bit further.

There is in artistic interpretation what might be termed a "principle of charity" to the effect that, *ceteris paribus*, the interpretation of an art work to be preferred is the one that renders the art work being interpreted a better work of art than it would be under any of the other interpretations on offer. Assume, then, for the sake of argument, that there is a completely formalist interpretation of a given work of absolute music, in the present case the Brahms Intermezzo, that accounts for as many of the musical events as the persona interpretation does, which is to be preferred? I gather from the tenor of Robinson's remarks that *she* would prefer *her* interpretation of the work as a persona's psycho-drama, for it makes of the piece more than a "mere" sound structure but a piece of fictional narrative that "records and expresses a poignant and profound psychological experience."[14] In other words, the persona interpretation adds to the work a dimension that the formalist interpretation cannot impart. And this, one assumes, can be generalized for any persona theorist's interpretation of any work in the absolute music canon.

To the contrary, however, I would argue that the principle of interpretational charity implies rejection of the persona interpretation in favor of the formalist one. For, as I have argued in (3) above, the proponent of the persona theory is committed to very spare, abstract descriptions of the persona and his or her travails, empty of detail and nuance, on pain of the accusation of over-interpreting: of reading into works of absolute music fictional narratives that are the product of the interpreter's fantasy, that could not possibly have been intended by the works' creators; and that common sense tells us could not possibly be contained therein. To instance a case in point, the persona in the Brahms Intermezzo is, as I have pointed out, a completely empty abstraction, the psycho-drama he or she inhabits an utter banality, a plan in need of a plot. Accepting Robinson's persona interpretation of the Intermezzo would make of a perfect gem in miniature of absolute music a shabby, poverty-stricken narrative, indeed completely barren of the things that make fictional narratives interesting and valuable to their audiences. This is a clear example of adding Y to X and ending up with less than X.

Of course the above remarks assume that the works we are talking about are those in the absolute music canon, which is to say, the masterpieces, or, at least, the best the genre has to offer. And perhaps it might be argued that a very poor example of absolute music, by a mediocre practitioner of the art, *would* be improved by a persona interpretation over a formalist one, *ceteris paribus*. So the principle of

---

[14] Robinson, *Deeper than Reason*, 346.

charity might apply to such works, where it does not to the works in the canon. But aside from the fact that it *is* the works of the canon that we are primarily interested in, there are, as we have seen, and will see, *other* reasons to reject persona, and other narrative interpretations besides the failure of the principle of interpretational charity, that would rule out such interpretations of mediocre works of absolute music as well.

But there is yet another tactic that the persona theorist might employ at this point in the argument. It might be objected that *no* formal analysis of the Intermezzo could possibly account for as many musical events as a persona-based narrative analysis does, and hence the *ceteris paribus* condition cannot obtain. That *seems*, at least, to be the moment of Robinson's remark that "If we hear the Intermezzo as a psychological mini-drama, then we can detect qualities in the music that we otherwise might miss . . . ."[15] And this response to the specific case of the Brahms Intermezzo might well be made into a general claim that a persona or other "literary" interpretation of a work of absolute music is always to be preferred because it always will be able to account for more of the musical events than a formalist interpretation can. Or, to put the claim in a somewhat weaker version, a persona or other narrative interpretation of a piece of absolute music is to be preferred *if* it can account for more musical events than any formalist interpretation.

There is no reason to think, at least on first reflection, that, in *every* case, a persona or narrative interpretation will account for more musical events than a purely formalist one could do. But the issue is a non-trivial one. And the whole question of *when*, if ever, a persona or narrative interpretation of a piece of absolute music is mandated or justified, when that is, we might want to say, as I put it previously, that we have "discovered" a piece of absolute music to *really* be, instead, program music, requires a separate hearing. That separate hearing is to come. For the nonce I propose the conclusion, though, from what has been already said, that the persona theory of absolute music exemplifies the thesis of this book, that the literary arts and music are antithetical arts. It exemplifies

---

[15] Robinson, *Deeper than Reason*, 346.

the ancient quarrel between literature and music in each of the difficulties we have encountered in attempts to apply persona interpretations to the absolute music canon. In short, I believe we have adequate justification already for declaring the musical persona *persona non grata*.

6

Action and Agency

Introduction

If I wanted to explain to someone, innocent of musical speculation, either by philosophers or by musicologists, what the "problem" of "absolute music" is, I would first, of course, tell the unenlightened one what is meant by "absolute music" in the first place. I would say something like: "By absolute music we mean instrumental music without text, program, extra-musical title, bereft of either literary or representational content. In other words, an art of purely abstract but perhaps expressive sound."

I would then go on to say that if absolute music, so defined, is thought of as one of the fine arts, then it presents the following problem. All of the *other* fine arts are, for the most part, arts *with* literary or representational content. And that content plays a major role in accounting for what it is in these arts that gives us such deep and abiding satisfaction. But absolute music does not possess such content. So it is a puzzle as to what it is in or about absolute music that gives what *appears*, at least, to be the same *kind* of deep satisfaction that the other arts, the arts with content, give. That, in brief, is the "problem" of absolute music.

The problem thus being stated, the unenlightened one would then be ready to hear that a proposed solution to the problem of absolute music, popular both in philosophical and music-theoretical circles, is to deny that absolute music does indeed want for literary content. It does have it, after all, and so our appreciation of it is very like our appreciation of novels or plays. It is another of the narrative arts, and pleasures us in just the way those other arts do.

But here the unenlightened one becomes puzzled. "Didn't you begin," he says, "by telling me that you mean by absolute music, music *without* narrative content? So how can you *explain* the appeal of absolute music by appeal to its *narrative content*? If it *has* narrative content, then it *isn't* absolute music, so defined."[1]

The simplicity of this response, it appears to me, disguises an insight worth pursuing. And it is my purpose to pursue it in this, and the following chapter.

Strategies

Suppose I were to "explain" the appeal of absolute music by showing that, appearances to the contrary notwithstanding, absolute music has narrative content. Would I *really* have explained the appeal of absolute music? I don't think so. What I would have shown is that there is no such thing as "absolute music," so defined. I would have shown that "absolute music" is an empty set.

Of course, to have shown that there is in the Western musical canon no absolute music, as defined, is to have shown no small thing. And in a way it really is to have explained the appeal of absolute music, if, that is, the narrative content is equal to the task (which I will argue is not the case). The explanation is that we were just mistaken about what it is that is appealing to us. It is not absolute music but "absolute music" so-called. Furthermore, since "absolute music" so-called turns out to be a form of narrative art, there is no "problem" of its appeal, if, that is, there is no problem of what appeal the paradigm narrative arts such as novels and plays have for us. However, if there *is* a problem with the narrative arts *tout court*, then at least there is no *special* problem with "absolute music" so-called, since it is just a special case of narrative art. One problem—which turns out, in the end to be a pseudo-problem, has been dispatched. There *is* no absolute music, so no special problem about *its* appeal. It is the null class.

---

[1] This is not a made-up story. A conversation of just this kind took place between me and a very clever graduate student with little knowledge of music. I can't remember who the student was.

The attempt to prove, from above as it were, that there is in the Western musical canon no such thing as absolute music, so defined, I call the "extreme" claim. But there is a more moderate approach to the problem of absolute music, which I shall call the "modest" claim. It is the subject of this chapter, and the next.

The modest claim goes something like this. The formalist claims that absolute music—*all* absolute music—is empty of narrative (or other) content. But it can be shown, according to the modest claim, that some works of absolute music *do* have a narrative, "literary" content. So the formalist's claim is false.

In the present chapter and the following one, I want to critically examine three "narrative" interpretations of works in the absolute music canon; one from the nineteenth, two from the twentieth century. About each I want to ask two questions: Is the interpretation valid? If it is valid, what does it prove? My source for these interpretations is the collection of essays, *Music and Meaning*, edited by Jenefer Robinson, the title of which pretty much speaks for itself. They are contained in Part II of the book, *Music and Story-Telling: Literary Analogy*. Again, the title tells the tale.

Quarteto Serioso

In his essay, "Music as Drama," Fred Everett Maus presents an analysis of the passage that opens Beethoven's String Quartet in F Minor, Op. 95, in distinctively dramatic terms, "comparing the Beethoven passage to a stage play."[2]

To be sure, this composition invites such strategies. It was given the title *Quarteto serioso* by the composer, and as Joseph Kerman remarks: "The F-minor Quartet is not a pretty piece, but it is terribly strong—and perhaps rather terrible."[3] That it, at least the first movement, is "dramatic," the enhanced formalist will readily agree to. That it is a "drama," of course, is another matter.

---

[2] Paul Everett Maus, "Music as Drama," in *Music and Meaning*, ed. Jenefer Robinson (Ithaca, New York, and London: Cornell University Press, 1997), 126.

[3] Joseph Kerman, *The Beethoven Quartets* (New York: Alfred A. Knopf, 1967), 169.

For Maus, however, the epithet "dramatic" is not enough. It is clearly a "drama" that he is looking for in the opening of Op. 95. "It would be natural to call the quartet a conspicuously *dramatic* composition, and the analysis [of the opening] makes the sense of drama concrete by narrating a succession of dramatic *actions*: an abrupt inconclusive outburst; a second outburst in response, abrupt and course in its attempt to compensate for the first; a response to the first two actions, calmer and more careful, in many ways more satisfactory."[4]

As the above quotation makes quite clear, the leading idea of Maus's analysis is "action." And Maus does not hesitate to dot the "i" in the very next sentence: "I suggest that the notion of action is crucial in understanding the Beethoven passage." And by "action," of course, is meant, principally, "human action." "A listener follows the music by drawing on skills that allow of commonplace action in everyday life."[5] And as far as what, essentially, a human action is, "it is a necessary condition for an action that it can be explained by citing the agent's reasons, by ascribing an appropriate configuration of psychological states."[6]

I will return, in a little while, to the concept of human action. But before I do it would be a good idea to have before us Maus's "action analysis" of the Beethoven passage in question, at least in general terms. In general, then, "the events of this piece are a rough, abrupt initial outburst, and a second outburst that responds to many peculiar features of the opening but also ignores some of its salient aspects, matching the roughness and abruptness of the opening and combining urgent response to the first passage with a strained disjunction."[7]

Now taken in isolation, as a description of the opening musical events of Op. 95, the above would raise no formalist eyebrows, certainly not mine, unless one were a formalist of the most extreme kind, who insisted that the only language admissible in describing absolute music is technical, music-theoretic language. Maus makes it a point, initially, to emphasize that his analysis is couched in language that is *not* music-theoretic. "These are not technical terms in music theory. Nor do they name emotional qualities, though they do anthropomorphize

---

the passage somewhat, describing it as one might describe a person or a human action."[8] But the enhanced formalist does not deny that extra-musical language, other than emotive language, is sometimes appropriate to the description of absolute music, "action language" included, just so long as it sticks to describing the "phenomenology" of musical surface and structure, and does not go on to impute semantic or representational properties to it. All of the resources of language, including the metaphorical and figurative, are open to the enhanced formalist, in describing his world. Indeed, *like everyone else*, he cannot do without them.

But it is very clear that Maus, in his action descriptions, means to go beyond what even the enhanced formalist is willing to say. This begins to emerge when Maus writes of his analysis, "the explanations the analysis gives for events in the piece . . . cite reasons consisting of psychological states, explaining the events of the piece just as actions are explained." Thus, "many features of the second outburst are explained by ascribing an intention to respond to the first outburst and beliefs about the precise points of unclarity in the opening gesture." And again, the analysis "ascribes *thoughts* that refer to the opening, that is, thoughts that the opening had certain features that make a compensating action appropriate."[9] We are now deep into action-intention language, and, it begins to appear, well beyond where the enhanced formalist is prepared to go. Just how deep in we really are, we are about to see.

"In general," then, Maus tells us, "the description of the Beethoven passage *explains* events by regarding them as *actions* and suggesting *motivation*, *reasons* why those actions are performed, and the reasons consist of combinations of psychological states." The natural question, therefore, must arise: "But to whom are these ascriptions of action and thought made?"[10] One can't, after all, have actions without actors. Freely floating actions are as metaphysically suspect as freely floating properties in general.

Maus is distressingly "flexable" about specifying agency. He simply rounds up the usual suspects and leaves it at that. "For instance," he writes, "if I follow musical actions as though they are currently

---

[8] Ibid., 114.   [9] Ibid., 120.   [10] Ibid., 121. Author's italics.

taking place, I could be following the actions of imaginary agents, but I could rather be *imagining* that the *composer* is currently performing these actions. Or," Maus continues, "if I follow actions of which the future is open, I could be following the actions of imaginary agents, or I could be imagining that the *performers* are *improvising*." Furthermore, curiously enough, he is not the least bit troubled by these "evasions," as he calls them. They simply "record an aspect of musical experience"; they "reflect a pervasive *indeterminacy* in the identification of musical agents."[11]

But not only is agency indeterminate in musical works, it is not even clear that there is a distinction between the agent and the action at all: "in musical thought, agents and actions sometimes collapse into one another." Thus: "An F-minor triad or the opening motive of the Beethoven might be regarded as actions, perhaps typical actions of some recurring character; but they might instead be regarded as agents, as characters within the composition." And, finally: "This indeterminacy between sounds as agents and as actions is possible because musical texture does not provide any recognizable objects, apart from the sounds, that can be agents."[12]

At this point Maus is ready to complete the argument that the opening passage of Op. 95 can be understood as something very like a "stage play." And to do that he first gives us a four-point analysis of just what at least some of a stage play's identifying characteristics are, in his view: what he calls "a somewhat simplified, idealized notion of a 'normal stage play.'"

Four properties will be relevant: (1) a play presents a series of actions; (2) the actions are performed by fictional characters (or fictionalized representations of mythical or historic figures); (3) for the audience, it is as though the actions are performed at the same time as the audience's perception of the actions; and (4) the series of actions forms a *plot* that holds the actions together in a unified structure.[13]

Maus concludes with, I have to say, *surprising confidence*, that: "The analogy between the opening of the quartet and the 'normal stage

---

[11] Maus, "Music as Drama," *Music and Meaning*, 121–2. Author's italics.
[12] Ibid., 125.   [13] Ibid., 126.

play' holds up fairly well."[14] It is a conclusion which seems to me, far from holding up fairly well, to be far from the truth, as I will now try to show.

Dramatis Personae

In spite of Maus's enthusiasm for, and confidence in the analogy he is drawing between the "normal stage play" and the opening of Op. 95, I think it must be rejected. It may look good to the already committed. But to the skeptical formalist, even of the enhanced persuasion, it looks highly suspect. And to show this I want to imagine, in what directly follows, a conversation between someone I will call the "true believer," and his adversary, the "formalist skeptic," in which the former tries to convert the latter to his dramatic interpretation of absolute music.

The true believer will begin, as Maus has done, by pointing out that the opening of Op. 95 is well described as an "outburst" and the following passage as another "outburst" that is "an attempt to *respond* to the first [outburst] and *compensate* for it."[15] He will then go on to maintain that in doing so he is "describing and evaluating the [musical] events *as* actions."[16] And so the passage in question satisfies the first necessary condition for being a "normal stage play," namely, that it "presents a series of actions."

But we cannot have actions without agents to perform them, which is why Maus's second necessary condition for the "normal stage play" is that "the actions are performed by fictional characters . . . ." And here the trouble starts. For the formalist skeptic will be quick to point out that there are no discernible "fictional characters" in Op. 95.

The true believer is ready for this skeptical response. Maus remarks that "a stage play normally involves a definite number of fictional characters at different points in the play . . . But the agents in the Beethoven passage are indeterminate." And, he adds, quite rightly, in something of an understatement: "It may seem strange at first to think of music as a kind of drama that lacks determinate characters."

---

[14] Ibid., 127.   [15] Ibid.   [16] Ibid., 125.

However, Maus calls out attention to Aristotle's well-known claim, in the *Poetics*, that in tragedy it is plot that is paramount, character of secondary importance. "Perhaps," he concludes, "Aristotle's remarks can help one grasp the suggestion that music can be dramatic without imitating or representing determinate characters *at all*."[17] There is, truth to tell, no help to be got from Aristotle.

Oddly enough, the old Butcher translation *seems* to lend support to Maus, in a passage he does not quote, where Aristotle is represented as saying that "without action there cannot be a tragedy; but there may be without character."[18]

But it would be a very careless reader indeed who construed Aristotle to be saying here that, literally, we can have a tragedy with a plot, which is to say, a sequence of human actions without agents to perform the actions. For one thing, he does not say a tragedy without characters (plural); rather a tragedy without character. And what he means by absence of character (as opposed to absence of characters) is made very clear in the next sentence. "The tragedies of most of our modern poets fail in the rendering of character...."[19] In other words, you can't do without a good plot in a tragedy; you can do without good, *well-drawn* characters: characters without *character*. So a better translation of the problematic assertion about what a tragedy can do without is the following: "you could not have a tragedy without action, but you can have one without character-study."[20]

Furthermore, it is not only clear that Aristotle was not endorsing the utterly absurd concept of tragedy without characters, it is clear that he thought you cannot even know what the plot *is* without knowing *who* and *what* the characters are. Thus, although "tragedy is not a representation of men but of a piece of action...," and agents in tragedy "do not therefore act to represent character...," nevertheless, "character-study is included for the sake of the action,"[21] which is to

[17] Maus, "Music as Drama," *Music and Meaning*, 128. Author's italics.

[18] Aristotle, *On Poetry and Music*, trans. S. H. Butcher (Indianapolis and New York: Bobbs-Merrill, 1956), 10 (vi).

[19] Ibid.

[20] Aristotle, *The Poetics*, trans. W. Hamilton Fyfe (Cambridge, Mass.: Harvard University Press; London: William Heinemann, The Loeb Classical Library, 1953), 27 (vi).

[21] Ibid., 25 (vi).

say, characters act to represent action, and without characters to act there would be no actions, hence no plot. As well, what the action is is a function of who the character is and what the character intends the action to be, which is true both of real and of fictional human actions.

So much, then, for the false hope that Aristotle's remarks on tragedy can give any aid or comfort to the view that there can be drama "without imitating or representing determinate characters at all." On Aristotle's view, there cannot be tragedy without plot; and there cannot be plot without determinate characters, although they may be characters not particularly well drawn. Furthermore, what Aristotle says is clearly right; and it is right not just for tragedy but for drama *tout court*—and that includes musical drama as well.

If someone were to propose to you that an object before you is a duck, but a duck that clucks instead of quacks, lacks webbed feet, and cannot swim, you would have good reason, I think, to suggest that he consider revising his hypothesis about what in fact the object is. Likewise, the formalist skeptic is well within the bounds of reason and good sense to suggest that, in the absence of identifiable, determinate characters or agency, or even a clear way of telling the action from the actor (who can't be identified anyway), the true believer should seriously consider revising his hypothesis that the opening of Op. 95 is a "drama." It doesn't quack; and it is of little help to call a chicken a "special kind of duck."

But at this point it behooves us to ask just what, really, Maus's claim is. Is he really saying that the opening of Op. 95 *is* literally a *play*?

Hedging

Compare the following two claims that Maus makes in his discussion of the Beethoven passage. (1) "[M]usic can be dramatic without imitating or representing determinate characters at all." (2) "[T]he Beethoven passage is connected to everyday life by action, belief, desire, mood, and so on."[22]

---

[22] Maus, "Music as Drama," *Music and Meaning*, 128–9.

Which of these two claims is Maus making? Or is he making both?

The word "dramatic" can rightfully be applied *both* to things that are dramas and things that are not. One might, for example, say that the tragedies of Shakespeare are very "dramatic" whereas Ibsen's plays generally are not. Or one might say that Alpine scenery is very "dramatic" whereas the English countryside is not. So when Maus says that "music can be dramatic without imitating or representing determinate characters *at all*," he may be saying something completely uncontroversial, as I would be if I said that some natural scenery can be "dramatic," where, *obviously*, no characters are imitated or represented. In that sense of "dramatic," as I have said, the enhanced formalist has no problem: in that sense of "dramatic," the enhanced formalist is perfectly willing to admit that the opening of Op. 95 is "dramatic," which is to say, it has "dramatic qualities" about it.

Claim (2), however, seems like an entirely different animal. For it sounds more like what I would be saying if I said that "*Hamlet* is connected to everyday life by action, belief, desire, mood, and so on." As a claim about *Hamlet* it is plainly true. As a claim about Op. 95, however, it is palpably false. For without identifiable, or determinate characters, one *cannot* have action, belief, or desire. One cannot have an action, or know *what* the action is without a determinate *actor*. One cannot, a fortiori, have a belief or a desire, both *states of mind*, without a determinate character who is in such a state of mind. Furthermore, it requires the full resources of language or dramatic action to reveal that characters are in such states of mind and to delineate just what particular instances of those states of mind the characters are experiencing. None of these resources is available in Op. 95, or any other work of absolute music. And to argue that one can have a *drama* without them is to argue that you can have the duck without the quack.

As for "mood," the enhanced formalist has no inclination to deny it to absolute music as an "expressive" property, any more than he wishes to deny to it the garden-variety emotions as expressive properties. But before I close the book on Maus's theorizing over "action" in Op. 95, there is one further of his claims that requires critical examination.

Action as Explanation

Early on, it will be recalled, Maus suggests that construing the musical events in Op. 95 as action-events can provide an understanding of those events, which is to say, why they are as they are and why they occur as they occur. "The scheme works," for the music, as for human beings, Maus tells us, "by identifying certain *events* as *actions* and offering a distinctive kind of *explanation* for those events," which explanation involves ascribing "sets of psychological states to an agent, states that make the action appear reasonable to the agent and that cause the action."[23]

Maus continues, "it is a *necessary condition* for an action that it can be explained by citing the agent's reasons, by ascribing an appropriate configuration of psychological states." And with regard to the case in question, Op. 95, Maus avers: "The Beethoven analysis includes some terms that always indicate actions. An abrupt outburst, for instance, is always an action, as is a reasoned response."[24]

Problems abound. To begin with, it is clearly true that a necessary condition for human action is "that it can be explained by citing the agent's reasons...," at least in part. Indeed, what *action* an item of human behavior *is*, is defined by the agent's reasons or intentions. However, it is plainly false that "An abrupt outburst... is always an action...," witness the "abrupt outburst" of radiation that characterizes supernovas. And witness too the "abrupt outburst" that opens Op. 95. There is absolutely nothing in our so describing this musical event to necessitate our denoting it a human action, and, by consequence, ascribing it to a rational agent.

Maus describes the musical event that follows the opening outburst as a "response" to it. But, again, there is nothing in that to necessitate calling the response an action, or attributing agency to it. My cactus responds to light; it is hardly, on that account, an agent or its response an action. Thus, neither the description of the opening as an "outburst," nor the immediately succeeding musical event as a

---

[23] Maus, "Music as Drama," *Music and Meaning*, 119. Author's italics.
[24] Ibid., 120. My italics.

"response," goes beyond purely "phenomenological" description of music that the enhanced formalist can fully endorse.

However, Maus is not content with the description of the event following the outburst as a mere "response." It is, he says, a "rational response." And *that* description clearly implies action and agency.

The reason, of course, why Maus wants to go beyond mere phenomenological description of the music in terms of outburst and response, to description in terms of outburst and response *as human actions*, is that, as we have seen, he wants to tap into the explanatory resources of human action discourse to explain the sequence of musical events in Op. 95. But these resources are not available, and because of something we are already well aware of: *indeterminacy of character*. To explain the outbursts and responses in *Hamlet*, say, we would, as in "the real world," have to know who, in some detail, the characters are who are making these outbursts, and responding to them, and what in some detail is on their minds. We must know their motives, reasons, desires, emotions, moods. The "indeterminate" characters of Op. 95, however, just because of their "indeterminacy," do not *have* any determinate motives, reasons, desires, emotions, moods. They are *characterless*. They are not just badly drawn characters. They are characters *not drawn at all*.

If ever there were evidence for the thesis that literary fiction and absolute music are antithetical arts, here it is, in Maus's attempt to make a drama of the musical events that open Op. 95. A real human being must be determinate in every respect relevant to human beings. A fictional human being may be indeterminate in some respects, as can a dramatic figure. (What was Hamlet's shoe size?) But a fictional human being cannot be indeterminate *tout court* without vanishing into non-existence, along with the drama he (or she?) is supposed to inhabit.

For the reasons stated above I think Maus's action-driven dramatic interpretation of Op. 95 comes to naught. But surely, the true believer will respond, it does not follow from Maus's failure to produce a successful action analysis of Op. 95 that another kind of action analysis of a different musical composition might not succeed. And we do have another such waiting in the wings. So let's bring it into the footlights and see if it is any more successful.

Some Principles of Interpretation

It is very clear, from the title of his essay, "Action and Agency in Mahler's Ninth Symphony, Second Movement," that Anthony Newcomb is pursuing a project very similar to that of Maus, and, indeed, he expresses approval of the essay by Maus we have just considered. For as in the case of Maus's analysis, the operative concepts of Newcomb's are "action" and "agent." So, not surprisingly, similar problems arise. Nevertheless, similarities notwithstanding, it will be useful to critically examine Newcomb's analysis if for no other reason than at least to assure ourselves that what won't work for Beethoven won't work for Mahler either. And, in any case, there *are* differences between the two approaches as well, which invite separate consideration.

Newcomb's essay conveniently divides itself into two (unequal) parts. In the first, briefer part, he outlines what might be described as some principles of interpretational strategy on which his interpretation of the Mahler movement is based, and the long second section which is devoted to the interpretation itself. We therefore will look critically, to begin with, at the interpretational strategy and then go on to the interpretation proper to take a look at that.

Newcomb begins with what, I suppose, might be called some "first principles," not so much argued for as more or less enumerated in the manner of axioms. Here they are.

(1) "A large component of most [absolute] music lies in its power . . . to delight with its patterns in sound . . . But in some [absolute] music these patterns seem to force upon some of us recognition of meaning connected to other aspects of our life . . . ."[25]

(2) "[I]n music as in the other arts (verbal, filmic, literary, painterly) *aspects of agency are not continuously displayed, nor are aspects of narration. Both are intermittently operative.* Even the most 'expressive' music . . . at times simply swirls or dreams or chugs along in decorative fashion. But in this it is essentially no different from painting

[25] Anthony Newcomb, "Action and Agency in Mahler's Ninth Symphony, Second Movement," Robinson, *Music and Meaning*, 132.

and literature. It may differ from them only in the balance of these functions.''[26]

(3) "I claim that in [absolute] music we understand...behavior patterns which we associate with separable agencies...In stage drama we also see and hear patterns of behavior, but there the separate (fictional) entities are physically presented to us. In [absolute] music they are not. In [absolute] music we must go about isolating and identifying the characteristic or expressive elements in the behavior patterns (as we must also in drama). Then we must in addition decide how to group them into agencies, as we need not in drama.''[27]

(4) "[H]uman agency is represented [in absolute music] in a distinctive fashion in these unattached, in that sense abstract attributes—unattached, that is, to any specific human simulacrum... The composer's activity of combining musical attributes, and the listener's activity of isolating and interpreting to construct plausible agencies, is a distinctive part of the musical representation of agency...[Absolute] music can present shifting constellations of attributes that do not *have* to be attached to specific (fictional human) figures.''[28]

These four claims can be seen as a step-by-step progression from what might be thought the obvious and self-evident to something less so but, nevertheless, offered without much, if any argument. However, each of them is problematic, when put under skeptical scrutiny, which I aim to do now.

Some Principle Doubts

Claim (1) begins with what surely is the completely uncontroversial proposition that absolute music has the "power...to delight with its patterns in sound." But what immediately follows this innocuous proposition is by no means itself innocuous, although it may appear so on the surface.

---

[26] Newcomb, "Mahler's Ninth Symphony," *Music and Meaning*, 133. Author's italics.
[27] Ibid., 134.   [28] Ibid., 135–6.

We are told that the patterns of sound of *some* absolute music "seem to force upon some of us the *recognition* of *meaning* connected to other [non-musical] aspects of our life . . . ." *Something* may indeed be forced upon some people in listening to absolute music. That surely we can grant Newcomb. The question is *what*?

The first thing to notice is that, according to Newcomb, "recognition" is what is forced upon some people; and the second thing to notice is that it is recognition of "meaning." Now, I take it, if I "recognize" p in S, it follows that p really *is* in S. So in choosing "recognize" as the operative verb here, Newcomb has begged the question at issue. In stating that "recognition" of "meaning" in some absolute music is forced upon some people when listening to it, Newcomb is, *eo ipso*, asserting that that music *has* meaning. But that is exactly what the formalist and, for that matter, many a "man on the street" denies. Newcomb has simply assumed in his description, without argument, that some absolute music has meaning, which is exactly the point at issue. What claim (1) *should* be, what the formalist is quite willing to accept is that some people, in listening to some absolute music, may have forced upon them the "impression" that that music has "meaning." Whether that "impression" is "recognition," whether, in other words, the impression is a *correct* impression, depends upon whether or not it can be shown by rational argument that the music does indeed have meaning. One cannot have it on the cheap.

Claim (2) fares no better than claim (1), particularly so as the failure of claim (1) means that it can provide no support for claim (2), if that is what was intended for it to do.

As far as I can make out, claim (2) seems to be some kind of slippery slope argument, if it is an argument at all and not just another begging of the question. It begins by pointing out the obvious fact that in the representational arts of drama, literature, film, and painting, their aspects of agency and of narration are not "continuously displayed," by which Newcomb means, I presume, that not every aspect of these genres is meant to contribute to its representational or narrative content; some are there for, shall we say, merely decorative or other "aesthetic" purposes. Likewise, even the most apparently "expressive" music, as Newcomb puts it, "at times simply swirls or dreams or chugs along in decorative fashion." Music may have more of the decorative in it, and less of the narrative, as compared with the more obviously representational arts. But in the end "it is essentially no different from painting and literature in this regard." It is simply a matter of degree; it differs "from them only in the balance of these functions."

Now there seem to me to be two possible ways of construing the argument here. If Newcomb is simply assuming that some absolute music has agents and a narrative, then the argument is that its rather long and frequent passages of pure decorative pattern should not give us pause. Absolute music is not different in kind from the (other) representational and narrative arts, only different in balance, in degree. It just has *less* narrative and agency, *more* pure decoration.

But, again, if this is what is going on, the question has been begged. An explanation is being offered for the preponderance of pure decoration over narrative and agency in absolute music, without first establishing that it possess any agency or narrative at all.

Perhaps, then, claim (2) is supposed to present an argument for the existence of agency and narrative in absolute music. It does say that the difference between absolute music and the arts of content is one of degree, of "balance," in regard to the quantity of pure decoration as opposed to agency and narrative content. But if it is a matter of degree, not a difference in kind, then it would seem that absolute music must possess agency and narrative content, even though it may be in a low degree compared with representational painting, and narrative or dramatic fiction. However, unless one simply *assumes* that absolute music has agents and narrative content, the very point at issue, one cannot argue about the *degree* to which it has them.

Of course there is the logically trivial point that a bald man differs merely in *degree* from a man with hair, since one can go bald by degrees, one hair at a time. But, nevertheless, a bald man *is* a man with no hair, different in kind, in that respect, from a man who is hirsute. And if one wants to play the same logical game with absolute music, claiming that it differs in degree, merely, from painting, narrative fiction, and drama, with regard to how *much* agent content and narrative content it possesses, then that is perfectly consistent with its having, as the formalist insists, none at all, just as the bald man possesses zero degree of hair. That is a game I am certain Newcomb did not intend to play.

The third claim is that "in [absolute] music we understand...
behavior patterns, which we associate with separable agencies." We
do this in stage plays too, Newcomb says. But the big difference is that
in drama "the separate (fictional) entities are physically presented to
us. In [absolute] music they are not." In *both* stage plays and absolute
music, "we must go about isolating and identifying the characteristic
and expressive elements in the behavior patterns...." However, in
absolute music, since the characters are not physically present, we
must, on the basis of the "behavior patterns," "decide how to group
them [the behavior patterns] into agencies...."

Let us take the case of the dramatic stage play first; for example, the
murder of Polonius in *Hamlet*. Of course I see, as Newcomb puts it, a
pattern of behavior. But I also see it straightaway as a human action:
the action of Hamlet murdering Polonius. I see a whole: I see Hamlet
murder Polonius (under the impression that he is killing the king).
Indeed, without knowledge of the agent and his intentions, I would
not know *what* the action is that I am observing in the motion of the
human body. For the same motion may be a very different action,
depending upon circumstances and intentions. Is the raised hand and
arm a request to be recognized at a meeting, a blessing, a command
to stop my car, or the Nazi salute?[29] In the play, as in human life
in general, there is no problem knowing what the meaning is of the
human action I am observing, because I know who the agents are,
and what is on their minds.

But absolute music is a different matter entirely. For since, in
absolute music, as Newcomb puts, it, "the separate (fictional) entities
[i.e. the characters] are [not] physically presented to us," they must be
inferred from "the behavior patterns." Or, in Newcomb's words: "we
must in addition decide how to group them [the behavior patterns]
into agencies, as we need not in drama."

There is, however, something conceptually amiss here. Let us
grant, for the sake of argument, that there are "behavior patterns"
to be perceived in absolute music. (In a moment I will contest that.)
What exactly *is* a behavior pattern? Well I suppose it is, as I just

[29] On this see, Arthur C. Danto, *Analytical Philosophy of Action* (Cambridge: Cambridge
University Press, 1973), ix–xi.

suggested, an item of behavior, an arm-raising, say, that might be any one of a number of different human *actions*, depending upon *who* is doing the arm-raising, and in what circumstances. To repeat the possibilities, it might be a request to be recognized at a meeting, a blessing, a command to stop your car, or the Nazi salute. But you don't, you *can't* infer from the arm-raising *who* the arm-raiser is. The inference goes in the opposite direction: you infer what human action the arm-raising is from who the arm-raiser is, and what his or her intention-in-action is. So Newcomb has it conceptually backwards. Even if one could recognize behavior patterns in absolute music, one could *not*, as Newcomb claims, "decide how to group them into agencies...," which is to say, infer the agent from the behavior pattern. It has to go the other way round. Once you know the identity of the agent, then you can identify the behavior pattern in the music as a human action of a certain kind. Barring that, the behavior pattern would be consistent with numerous different agents.

Furthermore, however, to call what we recognize in absolute music as *behavior* patterns already begs the question at issue. It is agreed on all hands, to be sure, that we hear *patterns* in absolute music. Who would deny that? And enhanced formalism certainly embraces the view that at least *some* of these patterns are *expressive* patterns: that is, successions of musical passages that possess expressive properties describable with the terms we customarily use to describe the garden-variety emotions. But that they are patterns of *behavior* we can only know by the presence of identifiable agents doing the behaving. Such agents, however, are exactly what we do *not* have, according to Newcomb; such agents, on the contrary, are what we are supposed to infer *from* the behavior patterns. So we are in the logically unfortunate position of needing the behavior patterns to infer the agents and needing the agents to infer the behavior patterns: a circle from which there seems no escape.

By the time we get to the fourth claim, it seems to me, the difficulties of Newcomb's position have become overwhelming. And so claim (4) seems to back away from the analogy between absolute music and staged drama to such a degree that one wonders why one should not, at this point, reach the conclusion that it fails altogether.

Newcomb says that "human agency," in absolute music, "is represented in a distinctive fashion . . . ." And what makes the fashion of representation so "distinctive" is that the representation is "unattached . . . to any human simulacrum . . . ."

Now what kind of representation of a human agent is unattached to any human simulacrum? Let us say it is a representation of the kind, to use Richard Wollheim's well-known concept, where we cannot "see in," or in this case, "hear in" the representation the character or agent represented. For example, I might use pins stuck on a map to represent agents in a spy network, each agent with a pin of a different color. Each pin "represents" a human being, but none of them is a "human simulacrum." I can't "see in" that blue pin, stuck in Cairo on my map, agent 007.

But surely this is not the kind of representation that can serve the purposes of representational art, at least in the traditional sense. It is a non-starter. *That* cannot be what representation of agents without a human simulacrum could be and still be counted as artistic representation of the kind that concerns us here.

Newcomb goes on to assert that "The composer's activity of combining musical attributes, and the listener's activity of isolating and interpreting them to construct plausible agencies, is a distinctive part of the musical representation of agency." What are we to make of this?

To start with, it is extremely odd to call what Newcomb is describing here as "representation." In ordinary cases of artistic representation there is neither "interpretation" nor "construction." If a person with the proper background and education sees Part I of Goethe's *Faust*, she sees and hears, directly, what is happening, and can give you a "plot summary" when it is over. Of course she may not know what Goethe was trying to "say" through his representation of the Faust story. That indeed is where "interpretation," properly so-called—the construction, if you will, of a plausible philosophical or psychological or moral thesis—comes in. And there may here, of course, be conflicting interpretations, and irreconcilable disagreements concerning them.

But with absolute music we are, apparently, faced with "interpretation" and "construction" right from the get-go on Newcomb's view.

It is as if it required a complex process of inference to determine whether Part I of *Faust* is about a man who makes a compact with the devil and seduces an innocent girl named Margarita, or whether it is about a king who decides to divide up his kingdom among his three daughters. If that is the situation we are in when listening to absolute music, then it is very strong evidence that the composer did not intend to represent human agencies and actions in his music in the first place or that (far less plausibly) he intended and failed. You may call that, as Newcomb does, representation in a "distinctive fashion," peculiar to absolute music. But I think the proper description of it is "no representation at all."

Newcomb concludes what I have characterized as Claim (4) by averring that absolute music "can present shifting constellations of attributes that do not *have* to be attached to specific (fictional human) figures." Taken alone, and at face value, this is a statement that the enhanced formalist can happily acquiesce in. *Certainly* absolute music can correctly be described, the enhanced formalist would agree—who would not?—as a display of "shifting constellations of [musical] attributes," among which, but by no means the only ones, are constellations of *expressive* attributes, which is to say, the garden-variety emotions. And the enhanced formalist would furthermore agree whole-heartedly that these musical attributes "do not *have* to be attached to specific (fictional human) figures." They not only do not have to be, they *cannot* be, because there are no fictional human agents in absolute music, on the enhanced formalist's view. There are merely the constellations, which is to say, patterns of musical attributes, among which are the expressive ones. *That is what absolute music is*, according to the enhanced formalist.

But it is clear that Newcomb does *not* mean what the enhanced formalist would *like* him to mean. What he means, rather, taken in context, is that the constellations of musical attributes do not have to attach to *specific* fictional characters, like a Gretchen or a Faust, a Lear or a Cordelia; rather, they attach to what I suppose might be called "abstract character types."

We are confronted, then, with something very like the "indeterminate characters" that Maus descries in Beethoven's Op. 95. And they are no more palatable in Newcomb's version than they are in Maus's.

Indeed, a narrative populated by character types rather than characters seems a metaphysical monstrosity or a narrative so void of human interest or emotional content as to be worse than no narrative at all, if it is any narrative at all.

At this point it seems inevitable to conclude that Newcomb's principles of interpretation for absolute music, if that indeed is what they are, provide little hope, if any, for an understanding of absolute music as a narrative or dramatic art. But I would not want to rest the case against it on purely theoretical grounds. It behooves us, therefore, to determine what practical use Newcomb makes of these principles, by considering his specific interpretation of a specific work, for which these abstract principles were supposed to prepare us. To that I now turn.

Etwas täppisch und sehr derb

The second movement of Mahler's Ninth Symphony, the subject of Newcomb's interpretation, has the following, somewhat elaborate tempo indication, in the usual location for such things, the upper left-hand corner of the first brace. It reads: *Im tempo eines gemächlichen Ländlers*; which is to say, "in the tempo of an easy-going Ländler." And Mahler adds to this the further performance instruction, *Etwas täpisch und sehr derb*, which Newcomb translates as: "somewhat clumsy and very sturdy, earthy, coarse."[30]

I emphasize the obvious, here, but as we progress it will become clear why this has been necessary. And the obvious is this. What is put in the left-hand corner of the first brace of a modern score is not a title, or any other kind of "invitation" to place a programmatic interpretation on the work. It is the composer's instructions as to how he or she wants the performer or performers to perform the piece, the most common instruction, of course, being a tempo indication, with, at times as in the present case, indications that go well beyond that to more subtle aspects of performance, which, beginning with Beethoven (I think), become more and more elaborate and exacting.

---

[30] Newcomb, "Mahler's Ninth Symphony," *Music and Meaning*, 137.

With this out of the way, let us get on with Newcomb's interpretation of the movement.

Newcomb begins: "I ... propose that the opening musical idea projects a characteristic way of behavior that one might call 'clumsy' or perhaps 'rustic.' " He continues: "I claim that the immanent musical attributes of this [first] section will lead the attentive and culturally attuned listener to begin imagining an agency that is 'clumsy.' " Newcomb then goes on to reinforce this claim with reference to Mahler's performance instructions, adduced above, and concludes his thought here: "But I maintain that, even were the words to fall away, the meaning would be there for the culturally prepared and attentive performer or listener."[31]

So far, then, we have a "clumsy agency." What more can we say? Newcomb goes on: "The contrast between, on the one hand, initial assertiveness and brusque interruptions [in the music] and, on the other hand, inability to conclude—this contrast [in the music] evokes something of insecurity, bombast, even bluster to add to this rustic clamorousness." But who or what is this clumsy, bombastic, agency? Newcomb concludes "that it is the protagonist of the piece, that acts this way."[32]

But is there only one character in this drama? Is it a monologue? Well, there is, at least, another "agency," but whether it is a new character remains an open question. "Even in its first appearance," Newcomb writes, "one cannot mistake the new vigor with which the new agency rushes, so to speak, onto the stage—the energy of its interruption." However, the puzzling thing about this new agency is that, as Newcomb puts it, "Whether this action-force comes from within a single protagonist or from a separate agency coming from outside is, I believe, finally indeterminate."[33]

But the indeterminacy goes even further and deeper than this. The first agency, the protagonist, the "clumsy" and "rustic" one, is represented by a Ländler, a "clumsy" and "rustic" country dance. Newcomb locates the entrance of the new agency at the place where the Ländler gives way to a waltz, the ultra-civilized, erotic dance of the

---

[31] Newcomb, "Mahler's Ninth Symphony," *Music and Meaning*, 137.
[32] Ibid., 138.   [33] Ibid., 139–40.

nobility and sophisticated city-dweller. And he distinguishes not one, not two, but three possible musical agencies—an ambiguity that is not a sign of weakness in absolute music but "a distinctive aspect—and a possible strength—of musical agency...." Here are the three possibilities. "The action-force can be simultaneously understood as

(1) an *external* agency—for example, urbanness, or a particular social group of which urbanness is a large generalization;
(2) as *another person* (as in Charpentier's *Louise*, a wildly successful new opera that Mahler conducted repeatedly in Vienna in the years leading up to the Ninth and that uses the waltz as the sounding symbol of the corrupting forces of the city that bring down the simple lass of the title role); or
(3) as *an element within the protagonist's own personality*—this last a particularly powerful possibility in a culture fascinated with multiple personality manifestations and disorders."[34]

I do not think that, for my purposes, we need go through the rest of Newcomb's analysis in detail. Rather, I want to cover just a few more of the crucial steps and Newcomb's general summary of what the content of this musical narrative is, as he sees (or rather hears) it. And we can then go on to some critical remarks.

The Ländler with which the movement opens Newcomb designates Dance A, the ensuing waltz Dance B. Dance C, "the last of the distinctive characters/agencies/ways of behavior in this movement..." is another, (slow) Ländler, which gives an "impression of willful intervention to stop the headlong rush of Dance B...."[35]

Newcomb then asks: "Who or what did this?" He gives the answer, with which we have now grown familiar, that there is no answer: "In music, the answer to this question *must*—or, I would say from the positive side, *can*—remain indeterminate," as opposed to "prose drama, or film [where] the author could—would probably need to—answer this question, with something such as a visit of a childhood sweetheart or the chance turning up of a photograph, or

<hr />

[34] Ibid., 141.   [35] Ibid., 147.

the unexpected wiffing of a smell touching off this reaction of our protagonist."[36]

Towards the close of his analysis Newcomb seems to have plumped for the interpretation of Dances A, B, and C as the actions or psychological states—it is very difficult to say which he intends—of a single individual. Thus: "In defense of understanding the agency of Dance C as coming from the same personality as that of Dance A (the connection between Dances A and B has already been point out) I would point out not only the appearance of A as counterpoint then midsection to C in its own tempo but also the pastoral color of the instrumentation of both and the characteristic Ländler style common to both." And Newcomb then avers of this agency that "the agency thus found is a psychologically highly complex one . . . ."[37]

I press on now to Newcomb's extraordinary conclusion—extraordinary, I think, because of the rather startling psychological complexity he seems willing to ascribe to this admittedly sketchy, abstract, one is tempted to say empty, character, or "agency," as Newcomb prefers to call it, for obvious reasons, that he envisions striding through the second movement of Mahler's Ninth. (But I get ahead of myself.) It must be quoted at some length. Newcomb writes:

One could follow further the story and the evolution of this protagonist (which one might think of as a class rather than an individual). It is in my view one of the more powerful embodiments of one of the classic archetypal plots of the time, the corruption of the individual by modern urban society—again I cite Charpentier's *Loise*. There is a struggle in Mahler's movement, but it is not at all a heroic struggle. Foregrounded are issues of weakness of will, of lapses of attention, of addiction to external glitter, entertainment, and the racy life, of banalization and brutalization of the initial clumsy, rustic image, and of the realization only intermittently and too late of the need to resist.[38]

This gives us a pretty good idea of what Newcomb thinks the narrative content of the Mahler is. We must now go on to give it a closer, critical look.

---

[36] Newcomb, "Mahler's Ninth Symphony," *Music and Meaning*, 149–50.
[37] Ibid., 151.   [38] Ibid., 153.

The Vague and the Vacuous

Let's begin at the beginning: *Etwas täppisch und sehr derb*. This is, to again belabor the obvious, neither a title nor a direct description of the movement's extra-musical "content." It is an instruction as to the *manner* in which the composer wishes to have his music performed. Nevertheless, it is not the usual laconic tempo indication but an instruction from which I think one would be justified in inferring something about the musical character of the piece: *it* is somewhat clumsy and very coarse, and so forth. In other words, the instruction to play the piece in a somewhat clumsy and very coarse manner doesn't make much sense really, if it is not intended to get the performers to *bring out* something that is in the piece, namely, its clumsy, coarse musical character. This far the enhanced formalist is more than willing to go with Newcomb.

Now there are three obvious things (I will not speak of the unobvious things) one might mean in calling a work of music "clumsy." One might, of course, mean to *criticize* it for its ineptness; as "clumsy," in the sense of badly, awkwardly composed. Many works of second-rate composers are "clumsy" in that sense. I will call this "literal clumsiness."

One might be saying that music is clumsy in that it is a *representation* of something or someone clumsy. I call this "representational clumsiness." The first movement of Mozart's *Musical Joke* (K. 522), for example, and, particularly, the fugato, is a representation of clumsy, badly brought off music: it is a good musical representation of bad music. And the music for Baron Ochs, in *Rosenkavalier*, is clumsy music, in that it is part of the dramatic representation of a clumsy man. (There is a complication which I will get to in a moment.)

Finally, there is music which is "clumsy," I will say, in an "aesthetic" sense. It is *expressive of* clumsiness, the way it might be expressive of joy, or melancholy. Or, to put it differently, it is clumsy the way it might be tranquil or turbulent. Clumsiness is its musical character, *qua* music. It is "aesthetically clumsy."

Now aesthetically clumsy music might also be clumsy music in the sense of being incompetent in a certain way, as might melancholy music, or turbulent music. But if it *were* clumsy in both senses, it would still be two *different* things, both true of it: that it was aesthetically clumsy, and that it was clumsy, which is to say, incompetent music in a certain way.

Furthermore, and this is the complication I mentioned above, music might represent clumsiness through its aesthetic clumsiness *or* through its literal clumsiness. I think that Mozart's *Musical Joke* does so in the latter way, Baron Ochs's aesthetically clumsy music in the former way. For Baron Ochs's music is not literally clumsy; it is not, that is to say, incompetent music—far from it. But my take on the *Musical Joke* is that we have here *literally* clumsy music. I think Mozart deliberately set out to write literally clumsy, *bad* music, to represent literally clumsy, *bad* music. That he was a genius, however, enabled him to write bad music that is ingenious in its badness. It is clumsily bad in a way that only a musical genius could make it bad.

Newcomb, I believe, although his essay is far from clear in this respect (as in others), wants to claim that the clumsiness of Mahler's music, in the second movement of the Ninth Symphony, is what I have been calling aesthetic clumsiness, *and* that this aesthetic clumsiness is being used by Mahler to *represent* clumsiness—the clumsiness of the protagonist Newcomb hears in the music. So he is claiming that the clumsiness of the movement is aesthetic clumsiness serving as representational clumsiness. And I shall be arguing, in what follows, that although he is perfectly justified in ascribing aesthetic clumsiness to the Mahler movement, there is no convincing evidence at all for his claim that the aesthetic clumsiness is representational clumsiness. Indeed all the evidence points in the opposite direction. The fact is, I shall argue, that all of the evidence adduced for representational clumsiness is evidence for aesthetic clumsiness, and that alone.

The first, and really crucial claim of Newcomb's, from which the rest of his interpretation more or less follows, begins: "the opening musical idea [of the movement] projects a characteristic way of behavior that one might call 'clumsy' or perhaps 'rustic.'" And if we leave out the description of the clumsiness as "a characteristic way of behavior" then the claim is quite congenial to the enhanced formalist, who is quite willing to acquiesce in the description of the music as being clumsy in the aesthetic sense.

But the rest of this first claim immediately puts us in contested territory—indeed, on the face of it, is flat out false. "I claim that the immanent musical attributes of this [first] section will lead the attentive and culturally attuned listener to begin imagining an agency that is 'clumsy.'" It is, of course, an *empirical* claim that the musical passage in question will lead all competent listeners to imagine therein an *agency* that is clumsy, beyond the mere perception of aesthetic clumsiness (which the enhanced formalist grants). And empirical claims cannot be decided, one way or the other, a priori, in the armchair. However, even without extensive empirical investigation, it ought to be pretty much beyond doubt that this claim is false; it is contrary to the ordinary experience of people who listen to and give the least bit of thought to their experience of absolute music. And if it *were* true that all competent listeners are led to imagine agency in the Mahler passage, and passages like it, then all formalists would have to be declared either liars, or not competent: not "attentive and culturally attuned." For it is *their* claim that they do *not* hear or imagine such things in this kind of music.

It is important to dwell on this point, for it is absolutely crucial to Newcomb's argument. If it is *not* the case that, as Newcomb insists, "the meaning [of the passage and what follows] would be there for the culturally prepared and attentive performer or listener," then the rest of Newcomb's analysis cannot get off the ground. But Newcomb's claim, I would urge, is flat out false. If it were *true*, there would be no such thing as a formalist reading, as opposed to a narrative or dramatic one, of such passages. There would be no argument. It would be otiose to try to *convince* anyone that a formalist reading is wrong.

This point is so crucial to Newcomb's argument that we must belabor it yet further. Note well Newcomb's choice of words here. He first puts it that the competent listener would inevitably be stimulated "to begin *imagining* an agency that is 'clumsy.'" Would one say, of the *Mona Lisa*, that every competent viewer of it would "imagine" a woman in the picture? Of course not. I might be stimulated to "imagine" all sorts of things. But what makes it a picture of a woman is that every competent viewer *sees* a woman in the picture (which is not to assert, of course, is deluded into thinking there is a real woman there). By parity of reasoning, would one say, of *King Lear*, that every competent viewer would "imagine" that there was a king named Lear who was dividing up his kingdom among his daughters, and so on? Of course not. I might be stimulated to "imagine" all sorts of things. But what makes *King Lear* a dramatic narrative and not a pattern of meaningless sounds and motions is that every competent viewer *sees* and *hears* the king and his daughters do and say the things they do and say (which is not to assert, of course, is deluded into thinking there is a real king and daughters).

There is no mystery as to why "imagine" was Newcomb's word of choice. It is a "weaker" word than one of the "perceive" words. It seems more likely that the theoretically uncommitted might accept the notion of imagining an agent while listening to the Mahler than actually "hearing" one. Because if you hear one then you are committed to saying that you hear the agency *in* the music, as you see King Lear *in* the play. But if you (merely) "imagine" the agency, then it is "in" *you*, not necessarily in the music.

However, that is a far weaker claim than Newcomb is really trying to pull off. So it is not surprising that a little while later he is talking not about imagined content but about *meaning*, to wit, "the *meaning* would be there for the culturally prepared listener."

The choice of the much over-used word "meaning" in this regard is a bad one, I think. But there is no need to make heavy weather of that. Let us presume that, the way Newcomb is using the word, the "meaning" of *King Lear* is its narrative content, as it would be glossed in a plot summary, and ditto for the "meaning" of the second movement of Mahler's Ninth. And so, since the plot of *King Lear* is not just "imagined," it is *there*, as "meaning," for the culturally prepared and attentive viewer, so the plot likewise, the "agency," in this case, of the Mahler is there, as meaning, for any culturally prepared and attentive listener.

However, now Newcomb's claim is again in trouble. For it should be perfectly obvious that although the "meaning," as construed above, of *King Lear* is certainly there for the culturally prepared and attentive viewer, that is by no means the case for the "meaning" of the Mahler movement. For *whom*—for *how many*—of culturally prepared and attentive listeners is Newcomb's agency, and the rest of the story, *there*? The first person *I* have run across for whom it is there is

Newcomb himself. And it is no good to say that after Newcomb points it out, lots of people will hear it and it will be there for them. For one thing, lots of people who read Newcomb's message will continue, like me and other formalists, not to hear agents or agencies in the music. For another, if "meaning," as construed above, were really in the Mahler, we wouldn't need assistance in hearing it. It would be as apparent to us as the plot of *King Lear*. What *are* there for all culturally prepared and attentive listeners are the expressive and other phenomenological properties that the music possesses, the clumsiness among them, as the enhanced formalist admits. But to go from there to "meaning," as construed above, is an unjustified step. And if it be claimed that not hearing what Newcomb hears simply *eo ipso* disqualifies one as a culturally prepared and attentive listener, then the claim simply becomes true by fiat—what is sometimes called the "conventionalist sulk."

As for myself, I require no further argument to convince me that Newcomb's interpretation of the Mahler cannot get off the ground. Nevertheless, I do believe it will be instructive to critically examine the further claims Newcomb makes about the "meaning" of the Ninth's second movement. To that I now turn.

The Virtues of Ambiguity?

With the appearance of the second dance, the waltz, you will recall, Newcomb identifies the entrance of a new element. You will recall as well, that he describes it as an action, but is unable to say whether it is another action of a single protagonist, or the action of another protagonist newly entering the scene. Whether the one or the other is, he avers, "finally indeterminate," and indeterminate too whether, if it is a second agency, that agency is "a social group" or "another person."

Now I put it to the reader that given this degree of indeterminacy we cannot be dealing here with narrative fiction in any true sense of the concept. If an interpreter of what he claims to be a work of narrative fiction invokes the canonical dramatic texts as what he means by narrative fiction, and then admits that he cannot tell you who the characters in the narrative are, whether there is one character or there are many, whether we are confronted with agents or agencies or protagonists, whether there are in the narrative physical events or only mental events, and so on, you are justified in concluding that the interpreter is simply mistaken in his claim that he is dealing with a work of narrative fiction. Or, else he has redefined narrative fiction to accommodate a case that, given the customary definition, does not fall under it.

Newcomb gives every evidence of awareness that this indeterminacy constitutes a problem for his interpretation. For when, towards the end of his essay, the ambiguities multiply even further, and we are driven to ask, "Who or what did this?," he is driven to give something like a justification for his failure to answer the question that, it seems, tries to make a virtue of the apparent defect. In absolute music, Newcomb says, "this question *must*—or, I would say from the positive side, *can*—remain indeterminate."

Newcomb seems to be offering us two options here, one of which, he thinks, is a plus, a positive for absolute music, the other a negative. To take what seems to be the negative option first, it is that absolute music *must*, cannot be other than indeterminate with regard to the "who" and the "what" of its purported narrative content. It is compelled, in other words, by its nature, to lack the means for disambiguation. But if this is the situation, then we are justified, as before, in rejecting the claim in the first place that absolute music has dramatic or narrative content. If it cannot do this crucial thing that dramatic and narrative fiction can, if it cannot fulfill this necessary condition, then it cannot, for that reason alone, possess narrative or dramatic content.

But what are we to make of the second, "positive" option: that absolute music "*can*" remain indeterminate? What construction are we to put on "can" here, and what is "positive" about it?

One possibility would have it that in absolute music the composer *can* choose to leave his music indeterminate in the above matters, if he wishes, or can choose to make these matters completely determinate. This is a "plus" for absolute music because it leaves the composer two options rather than only one, as opposed to the writer of novels or the playwright. This however is not a viable way to read what Newcomb is saying, because it is clear that absolute music *can't* be determinate in these respects. It *must* remain indeterminate. And for this reason the formalist rejects the claim that absolute music has dramatic or narrative content.

The second option is to construe "can" in this wise. Because of its special nature as an art, as opposed to dramatic and narrative fiction, absolute music can, so to speak, "get away with it," which is to say, get away with this indeterminacy, while they cannot. And, furthermore, this indeterminacy is a positive feature, an artistic virtue.

But why should indeterminacy, ambiguity, be a virtue? After all, it is no virtue in philosophy or science or news-reporting or the other knowledge-seeking disciplines.

Well perhaps there is the suggestion here, although Newcomb certainly does not make it explicit, that we are talking about what is sometimes called "literary," or, more generally, "artistic ambiguity,"[39] which is an ambiguity that is agreed upon to be a virtue when employed in artworks to proper effect. To take a classic case: Was there a ghost, or was it "all in the mind," in *The Turn of the Screw*? It is, of course, not a defect in Henry James's story that this is "indeterminate," that it cannot be decided. It is part of the point of the story, and part of what makes it such a jolly good story. It is an artistic "plus."

Why could we not think of the kind of indeterminacy Newcomb hears in the Mahler as a form of artistic ambiguity, like the ambiguity in James's novella? Not only that, think of the *degree* of artistic ambiguity in the music, as opposed to that in the literary work. Whereas in *The Turn of the Screw* there is *one* ambiguity, the matter of the ghost, in the Mahler *everything* is up for grabs; it is ambiguity all the way down. And since artistic ambiguity is a positive aesthetic value, the sheer quantity of it in the music more than makes up for what it may lack in other positive features of fictional narrative that *The Turn of the Screw* possesses, most obviously, all of those particularities of plot and character that abound in literary works.

But, surely, anyone can see that this is utter nonsense. First, artistic ambiguity cannot be added up like money in an account; it is not the

---

[39] See, for example, William Empson, *Seven Types of Ambiguity* (2nd edn.; London: Windus, 1947).

more the merrier. It is the right ambiguity, in the right place, skillfully employed.

Second, and more to the present point, you cannot have artistic ambiguity *uberhaupt*. It must exist as a foil to the general rule of determinacy. The ghost question stands out in a context of clearly delineated characters and a clearly worked out plot. The ambiguity exists in virtue of the determinacy in which it is embedded. You can't use artistic ambiguity as an artistic device in the complete absence of the determined narrative in which it must have its being. Thus the superfluity of ambiguity in absolute music, if such music is treated as drama or narrative fiction, cannot save it from disaster by appealing to the positive aesthetic virtue of artistic ambiguity. With regard to artistic ambiguity, more is not necessarily or even normally better. And in absolute music, resorting to it as an answer to formalist skepticism is a counsel of despair. The skeptic's response is that absolute music is not an *indeterminate* narrative; *it is no narrative at all.*

A Remarkable Conclusion

Moving on, now, to the close of Newcomb's analysis, I want to call the reader's attention to the (to me) astounding conclusions that Newcomb reaches. These conclusions are: (1) The protagonist of the Mahler movement is "a class rather than an individual." (2) "Foregrounded" in the movement "are issues of weakness of will, of lapses of attention, of addiction to external glitter, entertainment, and the racy life, banalization and brutalization of the initial clumsy, rustic image, and of the realization only intermittently and too late the need to resist." They are astounding for separate reasons.

What is so astounding about the first conclusion is the bizarre notion of a protagonist in a fiction being a "class," not an individual. What in the world could that mean? How are we to understand a fictional narrative or drama whose main character is a complete abstraction: an "abstract object"? Who would care about such a "character"?

Of course we all know what it means when someone says of a character in a play, say, "This play is not just about Willie Loman. It is about a whole class of Americans of that period that we should notice, that we should think about", etc. and so forth. But, obviously, logically prior to symbolizing a class of individuals, a protagonist must *be* an individual. Maybe Willie Loman represents a class of Americans. Maybe Anna Karenina represents a class of women in loveless marriages who are hopelessly involved with other men. But before they are *that*, they are Willie Loman, salesman and father, and Anna Karenina, wife and mother. *They* are not abstractions (and thank God for that); they are flesh and blood human beings, with all of their particulars on display, which is why, of course, we *care* about them. A protagonist (who?) is a class, not an individual, is a metaphysical monstrosity no one wants to countenance in fiction.

What is so astonishing about the second conclusion, mind-boggling is not an exaggeration, is the *exactitude*, the *specificity*, the *complexity*, as regards what could, broadly speaking, be called expressive properties or "states of mind" purported to be in the music. There is a long-standing dispute over whether even the most basic, simple emotive states, the garden-variety emotions such as joy, sorrow, anger, can be expressive properties of music, it being agreed upon by most defenders of music's expressive capacity that the more complicated, "conceptual" emotions are ruled out. And now here is Newcomb asserting that Mahler's music can be expressive of "weakness of will," *akrasia*, surely one of the most complex as well as controversial of human states of mind, already recognized by the ancient Greeks as problematic and paradoxical. Furthermore, Newcomb not only says that weakness of will is a property of the music. He says it is "foregrounded" as an "issue"! In what is customarily described as a piece of absolute music, Mahler, Newcomb is telling us, has raised as an issue, weakness of will (along, by the way, with "lapses of attention, of addiction to external glitter, . . . banalization and brutalization . . ."). All of these "issues," according to Newcomb, every culturally prepared, competent listener is supposed to hear in the music. This, in a word, is *preposterous*.

Here is a work that someone might fairly claim "raises the issue" of weakness of will: *Hamlet*. Was the melancholy Dane suffering from *akrasia*? Or was he exercising understandable caution in undertaking the murder of his uncle, the king, on the word of what was taken to be a ghost? Or was his fabled "delay" merely the result of "circumstances beyond his control"? After all, he did murder Polonius, under the impression that he was murdering Claudius. Furthermore, if Shakespeare *was* "raising the issue" of weakness of will in his play, what was he saying about it?

The text of *Hamlet* is a rich repository of linguistic resources to appeal to in trying to answer these questions just because it *is* a *text*, which Mahler's Ninth Symphony is not, except in the attenuated sense writers on music customarily appeal to when talking about musical scores. And there is no need to give chapter and verse. You can go to the literary critics for that. We all know how they ply their trade; how they support their interpretations with references to the behavior of fictional characters, their psychology, their relationships with one another and to their world, the world itself that they inhabit, and so on, all embedded in elaborate literary language with complex and deep semantic content. If *any* work of art at all can raise such complex issues as weakness of will, and there is even some question about *that*, then they are literary works, like *Hamlet*, with all the above-named conceptual apparatus. There is no such apparatus in the Mahler, or in any other work of absolute music, that can conceivably represent to the culturally prepared and attentive listener the concept of weakness of will, let alone raise it as an issue. That it caused Newcomb to "imagine" (his term, you will recall) weakness of will and the rest I have no doubt. We have his essay to prove it. That, however, is of no particular concern to the vast number of other listeners who have heard the work with no such result. Nor does it constitute "raising the issue."

At this point one might well be wondering about the absence, so far, of a concept that many think essential to any discussion of artistic interpretation, namely, the concept of the artist's *intention*. In the case before us, it might be argued, the problem is *indeterminacy* of the musical "text"; and surely that indeterminacy can be decisively resolved by appeal to what Mahler *intended* his music to "represent," "mean," "convey" (or whatever the operative term might be). There is not much in Newcomb's interpretation about authorial intent. But there are two nods in that direction which ought to be looked at before we close the book on Mahler's Ninth.

Newcomb twice alludes to the fact that Mahler frequently conducted Gustave Charpentier's opera *Louise*, as relevant to his interpretation of the Ninth's second movement, which he takes to be a story of the corruption of innocence by urbane sophistication, the same story (roughly) of the operatic work. What could the relevance be of this fact? The obvious answer seems to be that it is supposed to provide evidence relevant to Mahler's *intention* with regard to the content of the music in question. But it is, after all, pretty slim evidence, if evidence at all. Mahler conducted many operas in his career, with many diverse plots. How many other of these fit the music? And what evidence of intention, anyway, is Mahler's familiarity with the plot of *Louise*, or any other opera? It looks like a drowning man grabbing at straws. If the plot Newcomb is attributing to the Mahler were an extremely *outré* plot, that we would find it hard to believe the composer would have come up with, then his familiarity with the plot through experience of an opera he had conducted would be evidence of *possible* intention. It would show that it was not impossible for Mahler to have come up with that *outré* plot. But the corruption of innocence is hardly a very original, outlandish, or little known theme. And that the intention to put it to music as a *possible* intention for Mahler, in the limited sense that he was acquainted with it as a plot theme, hardly needs evidence at all. His conducting *Louise*, given these considerations, seems a palpable red herring.

The second apparent allusion to authorial intent is, I suggest, in Newcomb's claim that there might be just *one* protagonist in the Ninth's second movement, with many conflicting psychological traits, "a particular powerful possibility," he adds, to support the claim, "in a culture fascinated with multiple personality manifestations and disorders." Obviously the fact, if it is one, that his age was fascinated by multi-personalities, is meant to bear upon the thesis that Mahler represented such a personality in his music. How so? Again, I think, by the attempt to establish his *intention* of doing so. And in this case, it is clear, the proving of *possible* intent is much to the point, since many listeners, including myself, would find the suggestion that the music in question represents or is about the very rare phenomenon of multiple personality wildly implausible, if not completely off the wall, and, in addition, that Mahler could not reasonably be thought as having any such intention in composing it.

Now the question of whether or not authorial intent is relevant to artistic interpretation at all, and if so what its relevance might be, is an extremely complex one, which I do not intend to go into in depth in this book, or in this place, although I will have *something* more to say about it in the next chapter. Suffice it to say, here and now, that even *if* the intention to put the plot of *Louise* into his music, or represent multiple personality in his music, were possible intentions for Mahler, it does not imply, obviously, that they were actual intentions. And, furthermore, even if one or the other were an actual intention of his, it does not imply that his music embodies either of those intended things, since, obviously, intention does not guarantee fulfillment, as many may intend to win the race, but only one succeeds. And in the case of pure instrumental music, it is not the composer's incapacity but the recalcitrance of the medium that results in failure of intention, if intention there is, of the sort in question. In a word, the formalist argues, it is just plainly *impossible* for pure instrumental music to tell the story of *Louise*, or represent a multiple personality, no matter how strong the composer's intention to do so.

What If?

I have been, throughout this chapter, highly critical of two attempts to show that two of the acknowledged masterpieces of the absolute music canon, Beethoven's String Quartet in F minor, Op. 95, and Mahler's Ninth Symphony, possess dramatic or narrative fictional content. My conclusion is that these attempts have failed. But before I close I want to consider, briefly, the hypothetical question of *what* would have really been established had these attempts succeeded. Two things, I think, would have been established: something quite specific and something quite general. Let us look at the specific thing first.

What would Maus and Newcomb have shown, specifically, if their interpretations were valid (which I claim they are not). The obvious answer—*one* obvious answer, anyway—is that two movements of absolute music, the first movement of Op. 95 and the second movement of Mahler's Ninth, have dramatic or narrative fictional content. They would have shown, to put it another more general way, that contrary to what formalists claim, *some* absolute music has extra-musical content.

But I do not think that that is the correct way of describing what Maus and Newcomb might have shown. I think the correct way of describing what their interpretations would have shown, had they been valid, is that the two works of music in question are *not*, as had previously been thought, *absolute music*, as absolute music is defined.

Imagine the following case. Someone accuses the little old lady who lives in the dilapidated house on the corner of being a witch, on the evidence of her "witch-like" appearance, the evil-smelling concoctions she brews at night, when the moon is full, and her uncanny ability to cure various diseases that the local physicians can do nothing with. She is burned at the stake in Salem, in the year 1610.

Subsequent investigation, however, reveals that there is nothing at all of black magic in the unfortunate lady's behavior or cures. She brews her obnoxious nostrums at night because she has other things to do during the day, when the moon is full because it provides light for her labors. And the curatives she brews turn out to be remedies well known to the medical profession outside of the provincial precincts of Salem Massachusetts. In short, there is nothing "supernatural" about her or her activities. All have a perfectly natural explanation.

What has this subsequent investigation shown? Suppose it were to be responded: It has been shown that the unfortunate lady was a "non-supernatural" witch. I imagine that would be thought a strange kind of answer, and that the correct response is: It has been shown that the lady in question was *not* a witch at all, as "witch" is customarily understood. And, by parity of reasoning, I suggest we should conclude that Maus and Newcomb have shown Beethoven's Op. 95 and Mahler's Ninth Symphony, respectively, *not* to be works of absolute music at all, as "absolute music" is customarily understood—if, that is, their interpretations are valid. That is the specific conclusion. Now on to the general one.

Many of those who put narrative or dramatic fictional interpretations on works of the absolute music canon make what I call the "modest claim" that not all such works have narrative or dramatic fictional content, only certain ones, from certain periods, perhaps. Thus Maus avers that "For at least *some music*, any satisfactory account of structure must already be an aesthetically oriented narration of dramatic action,"[40] and Newcomb that "in *some music* these patterns of sound seem to force upon some of us recognition of meaning connected to other aspects of our life...."[41] And Robinson too, as we saw, puts forth the modest claim that "it is eminently reasonable to interpret at least *some Romantic instrumental music* as expressions of emotions in characters or personae in the music."[42]

Well, the bad news for anyone who wants to put forth merely the *modest* claim is that if the interpretive methods of Maus and Newcomb and Robinson are held valid, the modest claim will not stand up. For their methods will produce the same results when applied to *any* piece of instrumental music in *any* period of music history, from the viol music of the Elizabethans, to the orchestral suites of Bach, to the symphonies of Haydn, Mozart, and Beethoven, to Mahler's Ninth. If these interpretive methods are held valid, there is *no* absolute music, as "absolute music" is customarily understood, in the Western musical canon.

To many, like myself, this conclusion amounts to a *reductio ad absurdum* of the interpretive methods of Maus, Newcomb, Robinson, and others in the musical community. But, of course, one man's *reductio* is another's welcome conclusion. And there are those in the musical community who defend the thesis that "absolute music," as customarily understood, is an empty set: the null class. For them the validity of the interpretive methods discussed in this chapter would be good news indeed. My own view, as I have argued at length here, is that they are not valid.

Does this mean I deny altogether the possibility of discovering that some work or other of the absolute music canon is *not* "absolute music," as customarily understood? By no means; and in the following chapter I want to examine just such a possible case.

---

[40] Maus, "Music as Drama," *Music and Meaning*, 129. My italics.
[41] Newcomb, "Mahler's Ninth Symphony," *Music and Meaning*, 132. My italics.
[42] Robinson, *Deeper than Reason*, 335–6.

7

Shostakovich's Secret?

Introduction

In the previous two chapters I examined some attempts to interpret works in the absolute music canon as narrative art works. And I argued that these attempts had failed in their purpose.

My way of characterizing these attempts, and my way of characterizing my conclusions is important for what directly follows. So it bears repeating.

It appears to me that the most perspicacious way of representing these matters is as follows. The concept of absolute music, pure instrumental music, "music alone," as I have sometimes described it, is quite clear and uncontentious. And if you don't agree with me about that, never mind. All I ask, at this point, is that you accept my concept of absolute music provisionally, and give me a chance to run with the ball. You can make up your own mind after I have had my downs.

"Absolute music," then, as defined, is pure instrumental music without text, title, program, dramatic setting, or any other extra-musical apparatus. It is music, as defined, without representational, narrative, semantic, or other extra-musical content. And an attempt to show that any example of "it" *does* have semantic, narrative, or representational content is, so I will argue, best understood as an attempt to show not that that particular example of absolute music *has* semantic, narrative, or representational content, but that that particular example is not an example of absolute music, so defined, at all. What has been shown, *if* it has been shown, is that that particular example has been *misclassified* as absolute music; and any "showing" of that must, if successful, also show us *why* it has been misclassified.

The extreme position, on the literary side, would be the claim that *all* "absolute music," as defined, is "absolute music" so-called; that all "absolute music" has semantic, narrative or representational content; that "absolute music," as defined, is the null class. I think this extreme position is absurd. But the opposite extreme, the claim that *no* music currently described as "absolute music," as defined, is misclassified, misdescribed as absolute music, if not absurd, is certainly a rash claim, certainly unjustified. And the best way to show *that* is to instance a case in point: a case in which we at least seem to discover that a work of what we have heretofore classified as absolute music *really is not*. And that is what I propose to do in this chapter. From this exercise we will learn what might constitute a successful demonstration that some work, previously accepted as absolute music, has been misconstrued in this regard, and how stingy we should be in how many cases we should accept as bona fide. For *most*, overwhelmingly *most*, "absolute music" so-called *is* absolute music.

The Tenth: A Preliminary Reading

The case I want to consider here is Dmitri Shostakovich's Tenth Symphony, as interpreted by Gregory Karl and Jenefer Robinson, in their essay, "Shostakovich's Tenth Symphony and the Musical Expression of Cognitively Complex Emotions." Their stated goal, in that essay, is a quite specific one: to show that absolute music is able to be expressive of "cognitively complex emotions," by showing specifically that in Shostakovich's Tenth Symphony, "there is a passage expressive of the cognitively complex emotion of hope, or hopefulness, and that if we consider the structure of the work as a whole we can attribute to the musical persona [of the symphony] the complex cognitive states characteristic of hope."[1]

In order to show that there are passages in the Tenth expressive of hope, Karl and Robinson must offer a narrative interpretation of the work in which the emotion of hope figures importantly. And it

[1] Gregory Karl and Jenefer Robinson, "Shostakovich's Tenth Symphony and the Musical Expression of Cognitively Complex Emotions," in Robinson, *Music and Meaning*, 163.

is that interpretation that interests me, not the stated goal of proving that absolute music can be expressive of complex, cognitive emotions. What I will be arguing is that the narrative interpretation they offer might perhaps be true: there is some evidence in its favor, although, as we shall see in the end, the case is far from conclusive and, in my opinion, fails.

As can be seen from the outset, Karl and Robinson, not surprisingly, given Robinson's penchant for the concept, employ the musical persona in their interpretation of the Shostakovitch work. And they begin their analysis of the Tenth Symphony with a kind of summary preview that gives the general plot outline. Remember that their specific goal is to prove that a musical passage in the work is expressive of the complex, cognitive emotion of hope. With that in mind, I quote now in full Karl's and Robinson's sketch of the Tenth's plot, as they conceive of it. They write:

The musical passage that on our view is an expression of hope is a section from the third movement of Shostakovich's Tenth Symphony. Although this is largely a pessimistic work, we argue that in our focal passage the musical persona looks forward to a future that he conceives of as more pleasant than the prevailing grim and threatening situation. He is uncertain whether this more pleasant future will occur but nevertheless strives to achieve it, despite being surrounded by memories from the past. Moreover, his contemplation of the anticipated future state provides a source of relief from these memories. In short, the musical persona, though surrounded by gloom, feels, if only briefly, hopeful for the future.[2]

Confronted, of a sudden, without preparation, by this account of what is going on in a work generally taken to be a paradigm instance of absolute music, a symphony *sans* program or title of any kind, one's first reaction is likely to be stunned incredulity. "You can't be serious," will be the response, no doubt, of even the initially sympathetic reader. "Surely this all must be a figment of your imagination. You can't be claiming that all of this is really *in* the music for all to hear."

Karl and Robinson are obviously well aware that this, or something like it, would be a natural reaction to their very specific claims. "Our

[2] Ibid., 165.

interpretation," they immediately concede, "is no doubt controversial. Certainly we do not expect a listener who encounters this piece for the first time will immediately spot the expression of hope in our focal passage." What is necessary, they say, to convince the skeptical listener of their interpretation and, in particular, the expression of hope, is that the passage which, they claim, expresses it, "is heard in the context of the symphony as a whole, which in turn needs to be heard in its historical context as an example of a particular genre."[3]

I shall have occasion to examine the argumentation that puts the symphony in its historical context later on. But for now what I want to concentrate on are some of the individual musical events that Karl and Robinson adduce to support their general outline of the symphony's plot. I will begin, as Karl and Robinson do, with the "hopeful" horn call.

"The horn call that opens the central section of the third movement," Karl and Robinson aver, "marks a turning point in the experience of the persona." As they see it, "its slow unfolding implies patience on the part of the persona; its terseness and elemental power (as a result of the horn's timbre and the leaps by perfect intervals) suggest decisiveness; and its holding on the same pitches in each of its seven soundings, despite considerable resistance, indicates steadfastness or resolve."[4]

"The horn call is answered . . . ," Karl and Robinson continue, "by a reprise of the symphony's [dark] opening theme—the persona's recollection of a grim past." This pattern is repeated a number of times. "Each subsequent sounding of the horn call is either answered by or accompanied by similar impressions of the past." In sum, then,

the horn call is the persona's resolution (vision? prayer?) for the future, its every statement answered by memories of a grim past representing that which must be overcome before the resolution can be carried through. These recollections hold the threat that the travails of the past will recur, and perhaps the persona's fear that the drama will end in the darkness with which it began.[5]

[3] Karl and Robinson, "Shostakovich's Tenth Symphony," 165–6.
[4] Ibid., 171.   [5] Ibid., 171–2.

I could go on to fill in more of the details that Karl and Robinson provide for their preliminary interpretation. But at this point I think you have an adequate idea of what they are claiming.

The Tenth: Extenuating Circumstances

Questions begin with the persona *himself*. "We say 'he' even though the character in the music is not specifically gendered."[6] How *could* one gender a "persona" by music alone?

In this music, at least, for various reasons, it is plausible to think of the musical persona as a musical persona of Shostakovich himself. The most obvious reason is that this symphony introduces a motive that Shostakovich used as a signature. It consists of D-E♭-C-B, corresponding to the German transliteration of his initials (D. Sch.). In German E♭ is represented by the syllable *es*, and H is used for B♮.[7]

Putting the letters of your name to musical notes is a tradition that goes back (at least) to Bach's *Art of the Fugue*, where the composer famously used *his* name, B♭-A-C-H (i.e. B♮), as the final subject in the closing fugue (which he did not live to complete). And making a big deal over it, when discovered, is a dangerous thing to do.[8] But in the present case, as things play out, arguing from Shostakovich's music "signature" to his being the musical persona of the work, or its being a fictional representation of him, seems to have at least some prima facie justification. So let us take that, at least temporarily, as a working hypothesis: the musical persona of the Tenth Symphony is Shostakovich, or a fictional representation of him.

But if we take it, at least provisionally, that the musical persona is the composer himself, then it is fair to ask what the historical circumstances were in which the composer/persona lived. And the answer, of course, is: Soviet Russia during Stalin's hegemony, or, to not put too fine a point on it, his, by all accounts, brutal dictatorship. So when Karl and

---

[6] Ibid., 165n.   [7] Ibid.

[8] In the case of Bach, one can see the danger played out in spades, in Hans-Heinrich Eggebrecht's bizarre book, *J. S. Bach's "The Art of Fugue": The Work and its Interpretation*, trans. Jeffrey L. Prater (Ames, Iowa: Iowa State University Press, 1993).

Robinson write that "It is as if the persona momentarily forgets the dark past and lovingly contemplates a vision of hope,"[9] it makes some sense, because the persona is Shostakovich himself, living in a time of political, intellectual, and artistic oppression, hoping for an end to the Soviet regime and a happier future.

Were the argument to stop here, I think even the formalist skeptic might be inclined to think that there is at least *some* circumstantial evidence for the interpretation of Karl's and Robinson's. But there is more evidence to come.

"Two further sources of information," Karl and Robinson tell us, "help fill in the picture":

First is what the composer supposedly said about the symphony's meaning in his autobiographical memoir, called *Testimony*, compiled and edited by Solomon Volkov:

I wrote it right after Stalin's death, and no one has yet guessed what the Symphony is about. It's about Stalin and the Stalin years. The second part, the scherzo, is a musical portrait of Stalin, roughly speaking.[10]

With this piece in place, which is to say, Shostakovich's explicit statement of intention as to what his Tenth Symphony is meant to portray, and how he intends it to be taken, we can conclude that at least a prima facie case has been made out, and at least tentatively acquiesce in Karl's and Robinson's final word on the work:

The most obvious interpretation is that the backdrop evokes the oppressive pall hanging over the Soviet Union during the Stalin era, whereas ... [the horn theme] expresses a brighter future following his death. The lively theme fails to retain its optimistic character ... The hope expressed by our focal passage proves, therefore, to be a token of a more specific type of hope than we had originally described: it proves to be false hope.[11]

Given the background information we *seem* to have, Karl and Robinson may perhaps be right in their interpretation. But what are they right *about*? It remains for us now to take stock of their conclusions,

---

[9] Karl and Robinson, "Shostakovich's Tenth Symphony," 176.

[10] Dmitri Shostakovich, *Testimony: The Memoirs of Dmitri Shostakovich*, ed. Solomon Volkov, trans. Antonina Bouis (New York: Harper & Row, 1979), 141.

[11] Karl and Robinson, "Shostakovich's Tenth Symphony," 177–8.

and state with philosophical accuracy what precisely these conclusions *really* are.

The Secret is Out

We might begin here by reminding ourselves what the specific goal of Karl and Robinson was, as they initially stated it, and what they said about it in the closing sentence of their essay. Their initially stated goal was to show, against the skeptics, that, within the "expressive structure" of a symphony, namely, Shostakovich's Tenth, "there is a passage expressive of the *cognitively complex emotion* of hope or hopefulness...", and I underscore *cognitively complex emotion*, of course, because what I call the enhanced formalist has no difficulty with the notion that a passage of music can be expressive of the cognitively *uncomplicated*, garden-variety emotions. Furthermore, in their concluding sentence, Karl and Robinson aver, on something like a note of triumph, that they have achieved even more than they proposed in their initial statement of purpose. "The hope expressed by our focal passage proves, therefore, to be a token of a *more specific* type of hope than we had originally described: it proves to be false hope."

What exactly, then, did Karl and Robinson set out to do; and what did they think they had done? Let us kind of sneak up on the question.

Karl and Robinson set out to show that a "passage of music" is expressive of a cognitively complex emotion, namely hope, and succeeded, so they thought, beyond even that goal, in showing that a "passage of music" is expressive of the yet more specific, and hence more cognitively complex emotion of "false hope." Suppose the passage in question were from an opera. Surely no formalist eyebrows would be raised by that; nor if the passage were from a symphony or tone poem with a printed program. For such musical works embody verbal texts that, it is agreed on all hands, can render music expressive of cognitively complex emotions. So, obviously, for their claim to be an interesting one—for it even to make sense—it must be that a passage of absolute music, as traditionally defined, is expressive of a specific, cognitively complex emotion. That is surely what we must, at least initially, assume them to be claiming. And the work they choose to discuss, to be sure, seems completely consistent with that assumption. For it bears, on the face of it, all the obvious marks of a work of absolute music. It has no extra-musical title or text. Its "title," if that is the right word for it, is simply: Symphony No. 10, Op. 93. If that isn't absolute music, what *is*?

The task, then, simply put, is to explain *how* a passage in Shostakovich's Tenth Symphony, Op. 93, *can* be expressive of the very specific and cognitively complex emotion of false hope. And my claim is that what Karl and Robinson have revealed, if anything, is not how a work of pure absolute music can be expressive of a specific, cognitively complex emotion, but how a work of program music, previously mistaken for a work of absolute music can, not at all surprisingly, be expressive of such an emotion. In other words, the "mechanism" that Karl and Robinson have suggested for the presence of "false hope" in the Tenth Symphony is that of program music; so in the process of revealing this "mechanism" they have, *eo ipso*, shown that the Tenth Symphony, contrary to what was previously thought, *is*, indeed, a programmatic symphony.

We have some evidence for the belief that the Tenth Symphony has a program, notwithstanding the absence of text, title, or program in the published version; the evidence comes to us in the most direct possible way: its composer has told us so, and has told us what the intended program is. (Why this evidence alone is not conclusive we will get to shortly.) Before Shostakovich revealed its secret program, we had every reason to believe that his Tenth Symphony, Op. 93, issued without text, title, or program, was an example of absolute music. After the secret is out, we have strong reason to re-classify it as a program symphony. It is as simple as that.

It is a nice question whether Karl and Robinson came up with the general outline of their interpretation before or after they gained knowledge of Shostakovich's supposed remarks anent his Tenth Symphony. They aver that "These statements [of Shostakovich's] accord well with our interpretation."[12] Well, needless to say, if the interpretation came *after* the knowledge of Shostakovich's statements. And

---

[12] Karl and Robinson, "Shostakovich's Tenth Symphony," 177.

if it came *before*, my claim would be that, in the absence of know-ledge of Shostakovich's supposed intentions, the interpretation was without rational foundation; indeed, one is tempted to say, was "off the wall."

At this point, I think, it is possible to formulate general criteria for what a *successful* argument would be for showing that a work of absolute music, so-called, is really a programmatic work.

First, the expressive pattern of the work would have to be consistent with the proposed program. A tragic program for Haydn's "Surprise" Symphony is, obviously, a non-starter.

Second, there would have to be adequate evidence, not merely conjecture, that the program was intended by the composer. The statements of Shostakovich's about the intended meaning of his Tenth Symphony, if authentic, and there is very serious doubt on this regard, as we shall see, might serve as the model for that.

Finally, and this is the so far missing piece of evidence for the interpretation of the work under discussion, there should be a con-vincing argument for *why* the program had to be discovered, and was not, from the start, an explicit part of the work. Again, the case of Shostakovich is a paradigm case. The argument is clear and convincing. The program could not be made public—had to be kept secret—because of the repressive regime under which Shostakovich labored. To express his dissatisfaction with that regime, and hope for a brighter future, explicitly, for all to perceive, would have meant the Gulag or worse. One hardly needs a better explanation than that as to why the program for the Tenth Symphony, if indeed there was one, was a secret one.

It can now be seen that, and why, the discovery of a *purported* work of absolute music *really* being a programmatic work is bound to be a very rare occurrence. It is bound to be *particularly* because the second and third criteria will be very difficult to satisfy. To start with, it is not enough to show the *possibility* of intention, which usually, in my experience, *passes* for *actuality*. That it is within the realm of possibility that a composer might have intended his work to have a program, and with a certain content, does not, even if the first criterion of success is met, and the proposed program fits the expressive structure of the work, clinch the argument by any means. Any expressive pattern will, for one thing, fit many different programs. So if it is possible, merely, that the composer intended a work to have program x, it is also possible that he intended program y, or z.

Furthermore, even if one had in hand strong evidence, in the form of written, or anecdotal documentation, that a composer intended some work with all the marks of absolute music upon it to possess a specific program, appearances to the contrary notwithstanding, I believe failure to satisfy the third criterion ought to be taken as decisive against the programmatic interpretation. This might seem counterintuitive, and so requires some elaboration.

Let me adduce, as a specific example, the slow movement of Beethoven's Quartet in F, Op. 18, No. 1. There is, as Joseph Kerman puts it, "concrete evidence" of an extra-musical significance. "According to [Karl] Amenda, Beethoven said that he composed the piece with the vault scene of *Romeo and Juliet* in mind. Sure enough, [Gustav] Nottebohm was able to read '*les derniers soupirs*' over an early sketch for the end of the movement...."[13] Once we know this, why should we not now take the movement in question to be, not as previously understood, a piece of absolute music, but a piece of program music with the referenced scene from *Romeo and Juliet* as its program?

Why don't we, then, tote up the evidence for taking the movement as absolute music, compared with the evidence for taking it as programmatic, and see what the tally sheet tells us, following Hume's admonition to "balance the opposite experiments, where they are opposite, and deduct the smaller number from the greater, in order to know the exact force of the superior evidence."[14] The evidence for the movement's being program music we have already adduced: Amenda's report that Beethoven had the vault scene of *Romeo and Juliet* in mind when he composed the movement, and Nottebohm's report that he observed, in Beethoven's own handwriting, over a sketch of the movement, the words *les derniers soupirs*. The evidence for its being absolute music is, quite simply, that that is how Beethoven presented it to the public, namely, as: String Quartet in

[13] Joseph Kerman, *The Beethoven Quartets*, 36.
[14] David Hume, *Inquiry Concerning Human Understanding*, 74 (section X, "Of Miracles").

F, Op. 18, No. 1, Second Movement, *Adagio affetuoso ed appassionato*. Full stop!

What should carry more weight with us, a reported remark of Beethoven's on the work, and "programmatic" words written by the composer on an early sketch, or the work, presented to the public, and never altered in the composer's lifetime? The answer seems all too obvious: how the work was offered to the world by the composer trumps the chance remark (if authentic), and the preliminary sketch, *in the absence of further evidence to the contrary*. But what might *further evidence* consist in, that would over-trump the composer's public presentation of his work. Obviously, what is covered by the third criterion: a satisfactory explanation for *why* Beethoven did *not* make public his true intentions, and, in effect, kept the program of the movement *secret*. It is the satisfying of the third criterion that is crucial for tipping the balance of evidence away from absolute music and towards the programmatic interpretation.

The case of Shostakovich's Tenth Symphony is not unlike that of the Beethoven Quartet movement, until the invocation of the third criterion: both issued to the public in the standard manner of absolute music, both supposedly stated by their composers after the fact to have programs, each program supposedly specified by the respective composer. Where the analogy breaks down is with regard to the third criterion. For we have an overwhelmingly convincing explanation for why Shostakovich would have had to keep his program under wraps: fear of incarceration or death. But why should Beethoven have wanted, or needed to keep from the public the fact, if indeed it was a fact, that the slow movement of Op. 18, No. 1 tells the story of the vault scene in *Romeo and Juliet*? Were the star-crossed lovers a subversive topic in Beethoven's Vienna? What possible reason could Beethoven have had for secreting such a program, if, indeed, he intended the movement to have it? In the absence of such a reason, in the absence of a convincing explanation, the public face that Beethoven gave the composition must be held to be its real face.

Beethoven, after all, knew well the difference between program music and absolute music, as did composers before him, going back at least to Johann Kuhnau's *Biblical Sonatas* (1700), and when he wanted to indulge in the former, as in the Sixth Symphony, he had no compunction about putting texts and titles to his notes, in their published form. In the absence of text or title, the slow movement of Op. 18, No. 1 stands firm as absolute music, Beethoven's reported comment about *Romeo and Juliet*, and jottings on a sketch, to the contrary notwithstanding. The third criterion stands firm.

An Interesting Implication

The general conclusion towards which the present chapter has been tending, and which has already been stated more than once before, bears repeating yet again. Absolute music, as defined, is instrumental music without text, title, program, or any other semantic, narrative, or representational content. Attempts to show that some work in the absolute music canon has semantic, narrative, or other extra-musical content either fail to do so or else, if they *seem* to do so, have really done something else: they have shown that the work in question is *not* absolute music, as defined, but some form of "program" music with a suppressed, and now revealed "program" (broadly conceived).

A rather interesting implication of the view I am developing here follows, relevant to Arthur Danto's powerful and influential theory of art. For on Danto's view, one of the criteria for something being a work of art is the so-called "aboutness" criterion. Which is to say, it is Danto's view that, necessarily, every work of art is *about* something, or the question of what it is about can at least be meaningfully raised, even if the answer is, "It is not about anything at all." As Danto puts it, with regard to works of art, necessarily, "the question of what they are about may legitimately arise."[15]

Absolute music might, then, be seen as a counterexample to Danto's theory, since, with regard to absolute music, *as defined*, the question of what a work of absolute music is about *cannot* legitimately arise since,

---

[15] Arthur Danto, *The Transfiguration of the Commonplace: A Philosophy of Art* (Cambridge, Mass.: Harvard University Press, 1981), 82.

by definition, it is not about anything. But if we see the question of aboutness in regard to absolute music from the point of view I have been developing, we do seem to have a way of working absolute music into Danto's scheme.

Imagine, as a thought experiment, a time when there was instrumental music, but no program music. At such a time the question of what a work of instrumental music means could never have occurred to anyone. It would, indeed, have been a question that could not, at the time, have been legitimately raised, even if, *per impossibile*, it had occurred to someone to ask it. Now, however, imagine, as another thought experiment, the creation of the first work of program music. At this moment of music history, it immediately would have become possible to legitimately ask of *any* work of absolute music, "What is it about?" because that question could now be understood as the more complex question, "Is it *really* absolute music, as we have always supposed, or is it program music with the program suppressed, and if the latter, 'What is it about?'"

To pursue this point a bit further, it might be useful to go back to Danto's original, ground-breaking foray into the philosophy of art, "The Artworld," first published in the *Journal of Philosophy* in 1964. In that article Danto introduced the notion of predicates entering the artworld and changing, thereby, not only the present and future state of an art, but, in an intriguing way, its past as well. Thus the idea is that before (say) there was any such thing as non-representational painting, it could never have occurred to anyone to single out a painting either as *representational*—since all paintings were and assumed necessarily to be that—or, a fortiori, *not* non-representational since it could not have occurred to anyone that a painting *could* be non-representational, and one could have no reason to apply the predicate *not* non-representational to it.

But as soon as non-representational painting enters the artworld, every painting before that time becomes *not* non-representational, and it now makes sense to say of it that it *is* representational. Every painting before this time has, so to say, gained the property of *not* being non-representational. As Danto generalizes the point: "but suppose an artist determines that H shall henceforth be artistically relevant for his paintings. Then, in fact, both H and non-H become artistically relevant for *all* paintings, and if his is the first and only painting that is *H*, every other painting in existence becomes non-*H*, and the entire community of paintings is enriched, together with a doubling of the available style opportunities."[16]

So, to return to the present case, with the advent of the first piece of program music, the predicate "absolute music" can now be applied interestingly to every example of absolute music, when before it could never have occurred to anyone to apply the predicate, as *all* instrumental music was absolute music. And, more importantly, the predicate "*not* program music" can now be applied to every piece of music that is absolute music; so, in effect, every piece of instrumental music composed prior to the composition of the first piece of program music has *gained* the predicate "*not* program music." The whole world of instrumental music has thereby been enriched, and, furthermore, it now becomes legitimate to ask of *any* work of absolute music, What does it mean?, What is it about?, which in effect is asking, is it "absolute music," properly so-called, or is it program music *a clef*?

For what it is worth, then, the argument I am making fits neatly into Danto's scheme.

Every True Englishman

Be all that as it may, it is now possible at this point, that you may suspect some funny business going on here. For it might look as if the attempt to reveal narrative, or other semantic content in absolute music is simply being assured of failure by stipulative definition, otherwise known as the "conventionalist sulk" or the "every true Englishman" argument.

"Every true Englishman does his duty," goes the last named. "But Smythers is a true Englishman, born and bred, and *he* doesn't do his duty; so the generalization is false." This calls forth the reply: "Not a bit of it. You call *him* a true Englishman? The bloke doesn't do his duty, so he is no true Englishman; for *every true Englishman does his duty*."

---

[16] Arthur Danto, "The Artworld," *Journal of Philosophy*, 61 (1964), 583.

Well we all know what has gone wrong here. The seemingly informative generalization that every true Englishman does his duty has been rendered trivially true by stipulative definition. "True Englishman" has been redefined to include doing one's duty as part of its definition; so every purported counterexample is defeated in advance.

Is that what is going on in the present case? Well, it might seem so. After all, haven't I defined "absolute music" in such a way that all purported counterexamples are defeated in advance? *By definition*, any "successful" demonstration that a work of "absolute music" has (say) narrative content will simply be ruled out of court, a priori, as being a demonstration that it is a work *not* of absolute music but a programmatic work. That looks for all the world like the "every true Englishman" argument, point for point.

But no: I think that is the wrong way to take it. Notice that in the "every true Englishman" argument, the "true Englishman" is essentially *redefined* to suit the argument's purpose. After all, in ordinary usage, doing one's duty is not part of the definition of an Englishman. We all have a pretty good idea of what a true Englishman is, and doing one's duty is not part of that idea—at least not an essential part. It is *made* an essential part *by stipulation*.

The argument being proffered here, however, about absolute music, does nothing of the kind. It starts out with a well-established definition of absolute music, not a stipulative definition. And in case you don't believe that, here it is right from the horse's mouth, the horse being the highly respected *Harvard Dictionary of Music*: "Absolute music. Music that is free from extramusical implications. The term is used most frequently in contradistinction to program music, which is inspired in part by pictorial or poetic ideas."[17] Given this definition of absolute music, which is I note again not some idiosyncratic definition tailored for an argument, but the well-established meaning of "absolute music," any "successful" demonstration that some work of "absolute music" is *not* free of "extramusical implications" (as the *Harvard Dictionary* puts it) *must* be understood as a demonstration

---

[17] Don Michael Randel (ed.), *The Harvard Dictionary of Music* (Cambridge, Mass.: Harvard University Press, 1978), 2.

that, contrary to what we thought, the work is *not* "absolute music" properly so-called. And there is nothing logically illicit in this, any more than there is in the claim that if you show a "witch" does not possess supernatural powers, you have not shown that she is a non-supernatural witch but simply that she is not a "witch" at all, as defined.

Volte-Face

One further point before I close: a point of fact, not of argument. The nasty point of fact is that *Testimony*, offered to the public by Solomon Volkov as the authentic memoirs of Dmitri Shostakovich, is, in truth, a fake pretty much from start to finish. Richard Taruskin writes, "Scholars have easily exposed *Testimony* as a fraud within only a year of its publication."[18] Or, in the words of Laurel E. Fay, *Testimony*'s most ardent and outspoken critic,

> It is clear that the authenticity of *Testimony* is very much in doubt. Volkov's questionable methodology and deficient scholarship do not inspire us to accept his version of the nature and content of the memoirs on faith. His assertion that the book itself is evidence of its own authenticity is the product of circular reasoning... If Volkov has solid proof of the authenticity of these memoirs, in the form of original notes, letters from the composer, or other documents, he must be prepared to submit them to public scrutiny. Until such tangible proof is offered, we can only speculate about where the boundary lies between Shostakovich's authentic memoirs, and Volkov's fertile imagination.[19]

But if *Testimony* overall is a fake and a fraud, not to be trusted as reliable evidence of Shostakovich's true beliefs, what of the statements contained therein concerning the "meaning" of his works? Here is what some of his former students had to say about that: "We remember how steadfastly modest and reserved Dmitri Dmitrievich was in everything concerning his compositions. One can only stare

---

[18] *A Shostakovich Casebook*, ed. Malcolm Hamrick Brown (Bloomington: Indiana University Press, 2005), 370. I am grateful to Richard Taruskin for warning me of *Testimony*'s unreliability.

[19] Ibid., 19.

openmouthed at the explications and wordy interpretations of the 'contents' of his music found in this book, ostensibly stemming from the composer himself."[20]

Nor is the Tenth Symphony exempt from this judgment. Thus Elena Basner, daughter of the composer Veniamin Basner, a close friend of Shostakovich, writes in a letter to *Izvestiia*, 8 June, 1999: "I am sorry for those who are told . . . that 'the scherzo of the Tenth Symphony was conceived as a musical portrait of Stalin!' What a primitive, protozoan level of understanding! And how vulgar."[21] And Maxim Shostakovich, the composer's son, says unequivocally of the Tenth Symphony's scherzo: "Father never said it was a portrait of Stalin."[22]

What is particularly ironic, it seems to me, about the quest for secret programs in Shostakovich's symphonies, is the fact that he was *accused* by the Socialist-Realist gang of being a musical *formalist*, the symphony being, in their eyes, the most egregious example of musical formalism. And one would think it far more likely that, in light of this, the composer would have "disguised" his formalism by giving out that his untitled symphonies really did have programs when, in fact, they had none.

In any case, nothing in *Testimony* that purports to be a statement by Shostakovich about the meaning of his works can be taken seriously, if the experts and his friends are to be credited. And if not they, *who?* So what I take to be absolutely essential to Karl's and Robinson's interpretation of the Tenth Symphony, namely, the composer's supposedly stated program for it, turns out to be completely fraudulent. Without it, their interpretation of the work seems utterly beyond belief, its detail too much to accept without the backing of the composer's imprimatur. And to quote the composer himself concerning such interpretations as Karl and Robinson put on his Tenth Symphony: "When a music critic writes that in such-and-such a symphony the Soviet office-workers are depicted by the oboe and clarinet, and the Red Army soldiers by the brass section, you want to shout, 'Not true!' "[23]

---

[20] Ibid., 81.   [21] Ibid., 139.   [22] Ibid., 315.
[23] Quoted in ibid., 336.

What can we learn from this? One lesson, at least, is that firm evidence for secret musical programs is very hard to come by, another, that we should exercise a healthy skepticism towards such purported evidence when it is proffered, and a third, that the *desire* to put narrative interpretations on works now included in the absolute music canon, on the part of those practicing what is known as the "new musicology," is so strong that they are likely to accept evidence for their interpretation that cooler heads will find less than convincing. But what we should not, and cannot conclude from the Shostakovich debacle is that it is impossible to discover cases in which there *is* a secret, heretofore unknown program for a work of "absolute music," so-called, which, upon the discovery, leads us to reclassify it as a work of program music. And the requirements for such a discovery are, of course, what this chapter is about. The structure of the argument stands even though the claim for Shostakovich's Tenth Symphony collapses in a cloud of recalcitrant facts.

Conclusion

To sum up then, my argument is that the logically proper way to see the spate of recent attempts to put narrative interpretations on the works of absolute music, accepted as such in the canon, is to see them as attempts to demonstrate that these works are not works of absolute music at all but, in reality, programmatic works mistakenly taken to be works of absolute music. For to do otherwise—in particular, to describe these interpretations as imparting narrative content to absolute music, as defined—is a logical howler.

Now taken simply as an abstract conclusion about how correctly to describe the quest for narrative content in the absolute music canon, my conclusion may appear perfectly benign. For all practical purposes, it would seem, it leaves the practice of narrative interpretation undisturbed—merely re-described. However, I have also argued that the bar for successful narrative interpretation of the absolute music canon—which is to say, the successful demonstration that an alleged work of absolute music is in reality program music *a clef*—must be raised. It is not enough to produce a narrative interpretation that fits the expressive pattern of the work; not enough to demonstrate that the composer *could have* intended such a narrative in his work; not enough, even, to demonstrate, as in the case of the slow movement of Op. 18, No. 1, that at some point in the creation of the work the composer *did* have such an intention. What must also be shown is why, in the event, the work was given to the public as absolute music, with no program attached. And that final criterion is seldom met—indeed, seldom even addressed.

I am under no illusion that what I have said will change musical practice in the slightest degree. The conclusions of philosophers seldom make much impression on anyone except themselves. And I imagine that the quest for narrative content in the absolute music canon will continue on its merry way, which is just another example, in my experience, to support the conviction I have had for many years that, in the last analysis, a philosophical cause, even a philosophical cause *celebre*, more often than not turns out to be a cause without an effect.

At this point there is nothing more to be said. So I move on to other matters. Part I of this book laid out the early foundations for musical formalism, and the incipient quarrel it generated between literature and music. In Part II, I have tried to counter some of the recent attempts to discredit musical formalism by producing narrative interpretations of works in the absolute music canon. It remains now, in the third and final part, to give a positive defense of musical formalism. For it is not without its problems. And any responsible defense must try to meet them.

PART III:
The Fate of Formalism

8

The Failure of Formalism and the Failure of its Foes

Introduction

The argument of this book—the philosophical story, if you will, that it has told so far—has been that since the rise of absolute music, in the second half of the eighteenth century, there has existed a "quarrel" between those roughly describable as "formalists," who wish to characterize absolute music solely in terms of its musical structure, and "phenomenological surface," and those, whom I shall now simply call "narrativists," who believe that we cannot do full justice to the significance and nature of this music without discussing what they take to be its narrative content: what it says, or, more usually, what "story" it "tells."

Why did this quarrel arise when it did? The all too obvious answer is that it arose when it did because what it was *about*, namely, absolute music, arose then. How could the quarrel arise before there was a *subject* of the quarrel? The answer is, of course, correct; but it is only part of the *full* answer. Or, to put it another way, the appearance of a subject for the quarrel was a necessary condition for the quarrel; however, surely not sufficient. There are, after all, many things abroad that we could quarrel about because they are there, and do not.

Furthermore, absolute music did not first spring fully armed from the head of Zeus in the second half of the eighteenth century. For if one means, roughly, by absolute music, music for instruments alone, without title, text, or program, then it is perfectly clear that there was absolute music long before the second half of the eighteenth century: at least, in fact, as far back as the Renaissance, and very likely before.[1] So we must mean something more specific by the assertion that the late eighteenth century witnessed the "rise" of absolute music than that it first made its appearance then, since it didn't.

Just what happened to absolute music in the second half of the eighteenth century is, of course, a question for music historians, not philosophers. But can we not safely say, *at least*, that while prior to this time, by and large, vocal music of one kind or another was the center of the composer's professional attention, by the end of the eighteenth century absolute music could, and sometimes did, become a composer's major concern, the way he defined himself and the foundation of his reputation?

Given this newly attained status, would it not seem reasonable, then, that the nature and human appeal of absolute music should become pressing questions? But questions for *whom*? Well, for, among others, *philosophers*. And why philosophers? That is a question which now must be pursued. For the whole of this book has been converging upon the *philosophical* question of what the nature and human interest of absolute music is, with formalism and narrativism as the contending parties. The purported failure of formalism, and the ultimate fate of formalism, in providing an answer to the question of absolute music's nature and interest, or value if you like, is the logical subject for the final chapters. But before we get to that, it would be useful to know *how* this question became a *philosophical* question, and what the current state of play with regard to that question is. That is the subject of the present chapter. To the former topic I turn in the next section.

Music as Art

The philosophical concern with what *we* call the fine arts began, everyone would agree, with Plato and, in particular, his dialogues,

---

[1] The Bamberg Codex, a rich source of thirteenth-century polyphony, contains a piece, *In seculum viellatorus* ("The Fidler's *In seculum*"), the title of which, we are told, "indicates that it is an instrumental composition, probably to accompany a dance." David R. Rothenberg, "The Marian Symbolism of Spring, ca. 1200–1500: Two Case Studies," *Journal of the American Musicological Society*, 59 (2006), 338. Of course the piece has a title, and was meant to dance to, not listened to with rapt attention, as a Beethoven symphony in Carnegie Hall. And to call it "absolute music" would be anachronistic in the extreme.

Ion, and *Phaedrus*, and Books III and X of the *Republic*, where epic and dramatic poetry, painting, sculpture, and "music" (whatever Plato really meant by that) were given close scrutiny. But, as is well known, Plato did not think of all of these human practices as *of a kind*, which is to say, "the fine arts," as we do. For painting, sculpture, and music were "crafts" (*techne*), while poetry was an "inspirational" practice and product, along with prophecy and, arguably, at least in the *Meno*, the acquisition of virtue.

The distinction between a craft and an inspirational practice cashes out in terms of the following. A craft, be it carpentry, shoemaking, or painting, possesses a rational, explicit method for its successful employment. And because of this I can be taught, I can learn how to make good tables, or good shoes, or good paintings. There is a rational procedure for producing these things. But for producing good poetry, Plato claimed, in the *Ion* and *Phaedrus*, no such procedure existed. There was no "method" for making good poems. No good poet could tell you how he made good poems. Nor could you be taught to make good poems, because there was no explicit procedure, no method to be imparted by instruction. Poetry, in other words, was not a craft, not *techne*. Rather, the good poet was merely a conduit for the muse or the god, who spoke through the poet, or "inspired" him to produce his poems. He, essentially, "took dictation."

Now whether or not Plato really believed that muses or gods literally dictated to the poets, or merely meant this as an elaborate metaphor for the fact, cause unknown, that the poets created good poetry without a method, they knew not how, is a question I cannot answer. Suffice it to say, for present purposes, that Plato perceived a truth about poetry: that there is no explicit method, no set of rules for making good poems. And he used this truth to distinguish poetry from the rest of what we would call the fine arts, which, clearly, has the implication that Plato had no conception of the fine arts, as we understand them, since poetry was different in kind from the others, in this important respect.

The standard, widely accepted story of how we go from Plato, to here and now to our own conception of the fine arts, is told by Paul Oskar Kristeller, as has been mentioned before, in his seminal two-part article, "The Modern System of the Arts."[2] In it, Kristeller identifies the approximate point in time at which the various arts coalesced, came to be seen as of a kind, and to constitute the "Modern System" of his title. "Only the early eighteenth century, particularly in England and France, produced elaborate treatises written by and for amateurs in which the various fine arts were grouped together, compared with each other and combined in a systematic scheme based on common principles." And, furthermore, as a result of the formerly disparate arts coalescing into a system, the modern discipline of philosophical aesthetics came into being. "The second half of the century, especially in Germany, took the additional step of incorporating the comparative theoretical treatment of the fine arts as a separate discipline into the system of philosophy."[3] With this second development the still ongoing project of defining the fine arts, in other words, giving a philosophical account of why they are of a kind, came into being.

It is these developments in eighteenth-century thought that provide the explanation for why, in the second half of the century, the issue of absolute music arose, and, in particular, what its value and interest for human beings might be. First, it was *there*. Second, it was, as never before, *prominently* there. Third, it had become, not without a struggle and still but tenuously, a member of the newly formed "modern system of the arts." Fourth, the modern discipline of philosophical aesthetics was now on the scene, to press the issue with a rigor characteristic of a *philosophical* discipline that would not accept easy answers, common wisdom, or received opinion. Fifth, the debate over whether, and why absolute music might be numbered among the fine arts inevitably included consideration of what value absolute music has for us and what we enjoy in experiencing it. It is these latter two considerations that, I believe, have driven the anti-formalists, the foes of formalism, to conclude that formalism, even of the "enhanced" variety, is a failure: a failure in that it cannot account for why absolute music is of value to us, and for why experiencing it should pleasure or satisfy us as deeply as it does. It is those worries of the anti-formalists,

---

[2] Paul Oskar Kristeller, "The Modern System of the Arts," in Kivy, *Essays in the History of Aesthetics*.

[3] Ibid., 62.

or "narrativists," as I will sometimes call them, and their attempts to deal with those worries, that will occupy us here.

Music as Representation

The three major philosophical players in the struggle for absolute music's elevation to the pantheon of fine art were Kant, Hegel, and Schopenhauer. For Kant and Hegel the stumbling block was absence of a text. Neither had a problem with texted music, which they readily granted fine-art status, because the text provided the semantic, conceptual component that both thought, in their different ways, a necessary ingredient in the fine art mix. But both wavered in regard to music without text, not unequivocally deciding for or against the fine-art status of absolute music.

These struggles of Kant and Hegel, with absolute music, I have discussed elsewhere;[4] and my latest views on Kant, relevant to present concerns, are laid out in Chapter 2. But it is Schopenhauer I want to turn to now, as providing the entrance to the specific issues we are concerned with in this place, namely, the importance and interest to human beings of the "strange" phenomenon of absolute music. And make no mistake: it is a "strange" phenomenon, occupying but a small segment of place and time in the world's musical life.

By the time Schopenhauer came on the scene in 1819, with the first volume of *The World as Will and Idea*, we can see, in retrospect, that there were three options on offer then for bringing absolute music into the system of fine arts. Kant had already, as I suggested in Chapter 2, pushed the fine arts in the direction of formalism; but he was by no means a total formalist himself, and absolute music's lack of semantic or conceptual content remained for him an impediment to its entrance into the system.

Also on offer, I would venture to say, was some form or other of an "expression" theory, that could be gleaned from the various musical writers on "music and the emotions," who flourished in

---

[4] See, Peter Kivy, "Kant and the *Affektenlehre*: What he said and what I wish he had said," in Kivy, *The Fine Art of Repetition: Essays in the Philosophy of Music*; and "Music, Will, and Representation," in Kivy, *New Essays in Musical Understanding*.

the late eighteenth and early nineteenth centuries. This is certainly the route Hegel was contemplating, when he wrote of music in the *Lectures on the Fine Arts*, first published in 1835, that "what alone is fitted for expression in [absolute] music is the object-free inner life, abstract subjectivity as such." Which is to say, then, that "the chief task of [absolute] music consists in making resound . . . the manner in which the inmost self is moved to the depths of its personality and conscious soul."[5]

The third possibility, beside formalism and expression, was some form of representation theory. Vocal music, as we have seen, was easily conceived of as a representation of the passionate speaking voice, and had been since the end of the sixteenth century. But elaborate forms of absolute music proved recalcitrant to representation theories, for obvious reasons. (What could a symphony or a string quartet "represent"? Surely not the speaking voice, passionate or no!) And by the time Schopenhauer came to consider the question of what about absolute music might make it a fine art, "representation" would surely have seemed a remote possibility: an "outmoded" alternative. But it was just this alternative that Schopenhauer chose, not by revamping the concept of representation; rather, by finding something "new" for music to represent that would lend the notion of music as representation more plausibility, in the age of Haydn, Mozart, and Beethoven.

This is not the place to give an elaborate exposition of Schopenhauer's complex (and bizarre) metaphysics—a metaphysics unlikely to appeal to the contemporary reader as a plausible picture of the world. For it is neither *how* Schopenhauer thought absolute music represents, or *what* he thought it represents, but *why* he thought it represents that is of interest to us here, and that might suggest to us an early instance, perhaps the earliest, of the motivating force that drives recent anti-formalist, narrative interpretations of the absolute music

---

[5] G. W. F. Hegel, *Lectures on Fine Art*, trans. T. M. Knox (Oxford: Clarendon Press, 1975), vol. II, 891. A proto-expression theory of art was already in evidence in Thomas Reid, in the late eighteenth century. On this see, Peter Kivy, "Reid's Philosophy of Art," in Terence Cuneo and René van Woudenberg (eds.), *The Cambridge Companion to Thomas Reid* (Cambridge: Cambridge University Press, 2004).

canon. Suffice it to say (very briefly) that Schopenhauer conceived of the world in a three-tiered ontology, beginning with the phenomenal world, presented to us as "idea" (in the first English translation) or "representation" (in the more recent one); the world of Platonic ideas lying behind the phenomenal world of individuals; and finally, the ultimate reality itself, the Kantian "thing in itself," characterized by Schopenhauer as a striving will whose "expressions" are the Platonic ideas and the phenomena.

It is Schopenhauer's contention that, contrary to received opinion, the fine arts do not represent the phenomenal world, the world delivered to us by the external senses, but, rather (with the exception of absolute music) the Platonic ideas, and absolute music the striving will itself. As Schopenhauer says of music, the most Romantic of the fine arts: "Therefore music is by no means like the other arts, namely a copy of the Ideas, but a *copy of the will itself*, the objectivity of which are the Ideas."[6] In this respect, he insists, the art of music "stands quite apart from all the others."[7]

The crucial point for our purposes, as I have said, is not what absolute music represents, or how it represents it, but *that it represents* at all, and, in particular, *why* Schopenhauer thinks absolute music *must* be thought representational. Here is the argument (such as it is): "That in some sense music must be related to the world as depiction to thing depicted, as the copy to the original, we can infer from the analogy with the remaining arts, to all of which this character is peculiar; from their effect on us, it can be inferred that that of music is on the whole of the same nature, only stronger, more rapid, more necessary and infallible."[8]

It is difficult to make out just what the structure of the argument is here. But the older, Haldane and Kemp translation, is of some help. It reads as follows: "That in some sense music must be related to the world, as representation to the thing represented, as the copy to the original, we may conclude from the analogy with the other arts, all of

---

[6] Arthur Schopenhauer, *The World as Will and Representation*, trans. E. F. J. Payne (Indian Hills, Colorado: The Falcon's Wing Press, 1958), vol. I, 257.
[7] Ibid., vol. I, 256.   [8] Ibid.

which possess this character, and affect us on the whole in the same way as it does, only that the effect of music is stronger, quicker, more necessary and infallible."[9]

If Haldane and Kemp have it right, the argument must go something like this. Absolute music seems to have the same qualitative effect, produce the same subjective "feel" as the other fine arts. The other fine arts are representational arts, and achieve their effect through representation. Therefore, it is reasonable to conclude that music is representational as well.

As an argument, it leaves something to be desired. One might even be tempted to say that it is full of holes.

For one thing, it is not at all clear what exactly "the same way" *is* in which *all* of the fine arts, including absolute music, "affect us." For, clearly, in many respects we are affected quite differently by the various fine arts which, after all, are very different from one another. For another, even if there *were* one single, principal effect on us of all of the fine arts, including absolute music, and given that all of the fine arts, with the exception of music, are representational, as, indeed, they were in Schopenhauer's day, the conclusion that music must *therefore* be representational is a non sequitur. For it must further be shown that the effect we are talking about could *only* be brought about through representation, to get the desired conclusion. (A bullet in the head and arsenic in the stomach both have the same lethal effect; but that hardly implies that bullets are poison.)

But again, my interest here is not in the details of Schopenhauer's argument, or even for the time being, in its plausibility; rather, I am concerned with what exactly lies behind it. And *that* is, I suggest, the felt need to explain what absolute music could possibly mean to us, why it should interest and pleasure us, given its apparent (at least) character of pure contentless form. Furthermore, Schopenhauer's explanations for the appeal and importance of absolute music set the agenda for the anti-formalist critique. Although Schopenhauer never explicitly stated the formalist position, for the sake of refuting it—it was after all, not given full expression, as we have seen,

⁹ Arthur Schopenhauer, *The World as Will and Idea*, trans. R. B. Haldane and J. Kemp (4th edn.; London: Kegan Paul, Trench, Trübner, 1896), vol. I, 331.

until Hanslick did so, some thirty years later—any reader of Kant's third *Critique* could not be unaware of the formalist possibility for absolute music; and that Schopenhauer was a reader of the *Critique of Judgment* is beyond question. Thus there is some reason to construe Schopenhauer's view of absolute music as a representational art not merely to be a view stated *in vacuo*, as it were, but a *response* to the perceived inability of a formalist view to explain what the value and appeal of absolute music could possibly be, even though Schopenhauer did not explicitly formulate what he was doing in just that way.

But why begin with Schopenhauer? Why place such emphasis on him as the *fons et origo* of the anti-formalist critique? The reason is this. What this book is about is the formalism/anti-formalism debate in music theory construed as a *philosophical* debate in that branch of philosophy which we know today as aesthetics. Schopenhauer is the first philosopher of the first rank to place absolute music firmly and unequivocally in the domain of fine art. Furthermore, he is the *only* philosopher not only to take absolute music *very seriously*, but actually to place it above all of the other arts in significance and importance. Reason enough, I think, in all of this, for seeing Schopenhauer's musical representationalism as the opening shot in the campaign against musical formalism, even though the latter doctrine had not yet, in Schopenhauer's day, received a fully systematic exposition.

What I am suggesting, then, is that we understand Schopenhauer's theory of absolute music as a representational fine art—indeed, if it were *not* representational it could not be, on Schopenhauer's view, a fine art—as first of all, an implicit recognition of the *failure of formalism* to adequately explain what it is that *so* deeply interests and pleasures us in absolute music; and second, an attempt to provide a non-formalist explanation: this in answer to the question that, he believes, the formalist cannot answer, namely, what it is in absolute music that so deeply interests and pleasures us. And his answer is: the same theory that *obviously* makes all of the other fine arts agreeable and interesting: *representational content*.

But if Schopenhauer's theory of absolute music prefigures present-day perceptions that formalism is a failure, and representational or narrative content the answer to that failure, then, I suggest, it also suffers from the failure of present-day representational and narrative analysis of the absolute music canon to provide an answer to the question that formalism is supposed to have failed to give. And so it will be instructive to see just *how* Schopenhauer's theory has failed in answering the question of absolute music's value for us.

Schopenhauer's Failure

One might, I suppose, begin by pointing out that *representation* as an *explanation* of why absolute music pleasures us seems to rely, if it is to be convincing, on our understanding of why representation itself pleasures us. And it is not at all obvious that we *do* have such an understanding. Why representation pleasures us may well be as mysterious as why absolute music does; so we are simply being offered a second mystery to explain the first.

Aristotle, as is well known, made allusion to an "instinct" for representation in human beings, and provided at least the outline for an explanation of what it is in representations that pleases us. What he said merits full quotation. Aristotle wrote in *Poetics* IV:

Speaking generally, poetry seems to owe its origin to two particular causes, both natural. From childhood men have an instinct for representation and in this respect man differs from the other animals in that he is far more imitative and learns his first lessons by representing things. And then there is the enjoyment people always get from representations. What happens in actual experience proves this for we enjoy looking at accurate likenesses of things which are themselves painful to see, obscene beasts, for instance, and corpses. The reason is this. Learning things gives great pleasure not only to philosophers, but also in the same way to all other men, though they share this pleasure only to a small degree. The reason why we enjoy seeing likenesses is that, as we look, we learn and infer what each is, for instance, 'that is so and so.' If we have never happened to see the original, our pleasure is not due to the representation as such, but to the technique or the colour or some other such cause.[10]

The instinct for representation, then, is twofold, according to Aristotle. It is a propensity for enjoying the act of representing things, which is to say, "imitating" them. And it is a propensity for enjoying

---

[10] Aristotle, *Poetics*, trans. W. Hamilton Fyfe, 13–15.

representations; which is to say, we enjoy perceiving representations of things. It is the latter that is relevant to present concerns.

It sounds right that we "instinctively" enjoy perceiving representations, if by that is meant nothing more than that we all, without being taught, seem naturally, from earliest childhood, to look at pictures with pleasure, and play with dolls and other "representational" toys with obvious relish. The question is *why* we enjoy experiencing the representations of things. That we do is obvious. Why we do seems rather mysterious.

Aristotle's well-known and, after all, predictable answer is that we naturally enjoy learning, and representation is a learning instrument: "as we look, we learn and infer what each is, for instance, 'that is a so and so.'" But if you read the passage carefully, you will see that Aristotle does not seem to be saying that we learn from representations anything about the things represented, in lieu of having present the things represented, the way we can learn anatomy from medical illustrations or about Russian society by reading Tolstoy's novels. Rather, it is recognizing that, which is to say, finding out that, "learning" that the painting is a representation of Mont Sainte-Victoire. It is the pleasure of recognition: recognizing Mont Sainte-Victoire in the painting; learning "that is a so and so," that is a likeness of Mont Sainte-Victoire. That, at least, is what I take Aristotle to be saying.

Perhaps, it might be suggested here, it is not so much the recognition that X represents Y that pleasures us in representation, according to Aristotle, but, rather, the "excellence" of the representation. He does, after all, emphasize, in the passage quoted above, that "we enjoy looking at *accurate likenesses* of things which are themselves painful to see . . . ," which is to say, representations well brought off. But I rather think it is not the excellence of the representation that is being enjoyed, in itself; rather, the enhanced recognitional experience that the more accurate representation affords. That, at least, is what I take Aristotle to be saying.

Furthermore, what follows from this account of the kind of learning that takes place in our experience of representations, and that pleasures us, is that if we are not acquainted with the object of representation, then we cannot recognize that it is what the representation represents, and hence cannot gain the pleasure of recognitional learning from experiencing the representation. This does not mean that, for example, I must have seen Mont Sainte-Victoire to be pleased by the painting of it in the way being considered. For although I cannot recognize that it is Mont Sainte-Victoire, in the absence of direct acquaintance with that famous mountain, I can recognize that it is a painting of a *mountain*, and gain the pleasure of recognitional learning by recognizing *that*. But if I have never seen a mountain, any mountain at all, if I come from Flatland, then the painting of Mont Sainte-Victoire can afford me no pleasure of recognitional learning at all, as of a representation of a mountain. And Aristotle does not fail to make that inference. As he concludes: "If we have never happened to see the original, our pleasure is not due to the representation as such, but to the technique or the colour or some other such cause."

It appears to me that, with some important qualifications and amplifications to come later on, Aristotle has basically the right idea about at least one of the very important ways in which representations afford us pleasure. And under that working assumption, we can see straightaway that Schopenhauer's theory of musical representation fails as an explanation, along Aristotelian lines, for how music can please through representation and, indeed, collapses into the very formalism it is meant to supplant.

Recall what the object of musical representation is, according to Schopenhauer, namely, the metaphysical will that underlies all of reality as we know it. But it is, of course, the notorious "thing-in-itself," in Schopenhauer's version, of which Kant insisted we can know nothing, and which Schopenhauer thought is inaccessible to direct acquaintance. And if it is, as Schopenhauer thought, inaccessible to direct acquaintance, then its musical representation cannot provide the experience of recognitional learning or, by consequence, the pleasure of that experience. For if I do not know that the thing-in-itself looks like, sounds like, or whatever, then I cannot hear it in the music and say "that is so-and-so," *that* is the metaphysical will. Which means, in Aristotle's words, that "our pleasure is not due to the representation as such, but to the technique or the colour or some other such cause," that is to say, the aesthetic parameters of formalism. So if, *per impossibile*, absolute music *were* as Schopenhauer thought, a direct copy of the metaphysical will, it would not be able to provide the pleasures of representation through recognitional learning, because recognition would be impossible, since we could not recognize it in the music, lacking, as we must, prior acquaintance with it. You can't *re*-cognize what you have never *cognized* in the first place.

Schopenhauer's attempt to move absolute music into the class of representational arts, as, at least, an implicit (if unstated) response to the failure of the protean musical formalism of his time to provide the grounds for our pleasure and interest in it, is a philosophical move repeated ever and again in present-day attempts to find the grounds that formalism fails to find. Only the representational model now favored is, as we have seen in preceding chapters, dramatic and narrative fiction. But that aside, the present-day move is similarly motivated, and comes a cropper something like the way Schopenhauer's does. Making that claim good will be my task in the rest of the present chapter.

Aristotle Amplified

In the previous section I expressed the view that Aristotle basically had it right about how at least one aspect of representation pleasures us in our experience of it. But in order to make use of this Aristotelian insight we certainly must enlarge upon what is, after all, a small fragment of a work itself a fragment. I turn to that task now.

It will be recalled that in the passage quoted above, Aristotle ascribed the pleasure taken in perceiving representations as the pleasure of a particular kind of learning, recognitional learning, which is to say, recognizing that a particular representation is a representation of a so-and-so: recognizing that the picture is the picture of a mountain (for example). But as we read on in the *Poetics*, we discover that this is not the only kind of learning experience that representation affords, at least the representation known as "tragedy," which is what, of course, the portion of the *Poetics* that survives is principally about. For in section IX Aristotle famously said that "The difference between a historian and a [tragic] poet . . . is that one tells what happened and the other what might happen. For this reason [tragic] poetry is something more scientific and serious than history, because [tragic] poetry tends to give general truths while history gives particular facts," where by a general truth is meant "the sort of thing that a certain type of man will do or say either probably or necessarily."[11] And since, as Aristotle had already said, in the passage from section IV quoted above, that "Learning things gives great pleasure . . . ," it would obviously follow that this form of learning, learning about "general truths," affords pleasure in spectators, just as recognitional learning does.

At this point the question will perhaps arise as to whether this second kind of learning might be the learning that absolute music provides about Schopenhauer's metaphysical will. But we can reject this suggestion straightaway for the obvious reason that recognitional learning is a pre-condition for the second kind of learning, which I shall call from now on, "informational learning." I cannot learn from a representation, "general truths" about men, for example, without first recognizing that there are men, and various other things, depicted in the representation. And similarly, I cannot derive information about Schopenhauer's metaphysical will without first recognizing it represented in the music; but because there is no prior direct acquaintance with the will, that prerequisite recognitional learning cannot, in the nature of the case, take place. Thus there is no aid and comfort for Schopenhauer's theory of musical representation in Aristotle's second kind of representational learning.[12]

Nevertheless, the first and second kinds of learning from representations that Aristotle addresses, recognitional learning and informational learning, are certainly, I want to argue, principal players in our experience of representational art (broadly conceived) and our pleasure in it. So I want to pursue the matter further.

Surely we have all experienced Aristotelian recognitional learning, and taken pleasure in it, both in pictorial and literary representations.

---

[11] Aristotle, *Poetics*, trans. W. Hamilton Fyfe, 13–15.

[12] I have been arguing that Schopenhauer's theory of musical *representation* is of no help in understanding how absolute music pleasures us. But this is not to be taken as a complete repudiation of Schopenhauer in this regard. As I have argued elsewhere, Schopenhauer's idea of the power of music to "liberate" us from certain of life's vicissitudes is indeed a valuable idea when itself "liberated" from his rather cumbersome and, to the modern mind, implausible metaphysics. On this see, Peter Kivy, *Philosophies of Arts: An Essay in Differences* (Cambridge: Cambridge University Press, 1977), chapter 7, "The Liberation of Music."

We say things like, "How perfectly Rembrandt has captured in a few broad strokes the leathery skin of the elephant; that's just the way it is"; or, "How perfectly Jane Austen has portrayed the pride and prejudice of her two main characters, and the misunderstanding and reconciliation that result therefrom; why that's *so true* to my experience"; and so on. Who can deny that such recognitional learning events occur frequently in our encounters with visual artworks and literary fiction? And who can deny that they afford us one of the principal pleasures of the representational arts? Aristotle is right on the money, here, as he so frequently is in characterizing everyday behavior in moral and aesthetic contexts.

Informational learning is a far more contentious matter in philosophy of literature. For information is customarily conveyed by the expression of propositions. And there are those who deny as well as those who affirm what might be called the propositional theory of literature, which is to say, the theory that *some* literary works have as *one* of their artistic functions, the expression, usually by implication or suggestion, of general propositions with a philosophical, moral, political, psychological, or other conceptual content, that the reader is meant to be persuaded of, or at least to seriously consider. Obviously Aristotle embraced such a theory in the *Poetics*, with regard to tragic poetry, in stating that tragic poetry provides what I have been calling informational learning. And I myself am a supporter of it, arguing in its favor on a number of occasions.[13]

It is not my intention to re-argue here the plausibility of informational learning as one source of pleasure we take in artistic representations and, especially, the artistic representations of narrative fiction. Rather, for the sake of argument here, I am going to assume its truth, as I am the truth of recognitional learning as another source.

To sum up the argument of the chapter so far, it is that the failure of musical formalism to explain why and how absolute music interests and pleasures us motivated Schopenhauer to suggest that it does both,

---

[13] See Kivy, *Philosophies of Arts*, chapter 5; "On the Banality of Literary Truths," *Philosophic Exchange*, No. 28 (1998); and *The Performance of Reading: An Essay in the Philosophy of Literature* (Oxford: Blackwell, 2006), sections 24–6, and 28.

as do the other fine arts, through representation: in the special case of music, representation of the thing-in-itself, which is to say, for Schopenhauer, the metaphysical will-in-itself. Furthermore, the argument has been that given Aristotle's two proposed sources for the pleasure and interest we take in artistic representation, recognitional learning and informational learning, Schopenhauer's theory of music representation fails to provide either source, that is, either recognitional or informational learning, because of the peculiar object of representation that he proposes. Hence, Schopenhauer's representational theory of absolute music fails to remedy the failure of formalism, fails to provide a plausible answer to the question of why and how absolute music interests and pleasures us.

Does this mean that *no* representational account of absolute music can answer these questions? Certainly not. For obviously, the failure of Schopenhauer's attempt devolves on the peculiar or, more strongly, the bizarre object of representation that Schopenhauer proposes as the *only* object of musical representation. The theory itself, then, is peculiar, even bizarre, because it not only proposes a peculiar or bizarre object of musical representation but proposes that music can have only one object of representation, whereas the other fine arts can represent, at least it seems obvious to most of us, any and all of the objects of human experience; and even on Schopenhauer's view, with the exception of music, the fine arts, although they are confined to the representation of one *kind* of object, the Platonic ideas, there are many such ideas that, presumably, they can represent. Surely representationalism can do better than *this* for absolute music, the defender of musical representation will argue.

Indeed, the defender of musical representationalism will, doubtless, claim that the accounts of absolute music as fictional or dramatic narrative, that I have canvassed and criticized in Chapters 5 and 6 *do* do better. So in the present chapter I want now to re-open the case for absolute music as narrative or dramatic representation. In particular, I want now to view the theories examined in the aforementioned chapters as implicitly affirming the failure of formalism to explain our pleasure and interest in absolute music, and providing an implicit answer of their own—an answer, I shall argue, as unsuccessful as Schopenhauer's.

Fictional Narrative and Recognitional Learning

Let us begin with the musical persona, the subject of Chapter 5.

It will be recalled that Jenefer Robinson imputes to an instrumental work by Brahms, the Intermezzo in B-flat minor, Op. 117, No. 2, a protagonist, a musical persona, who, in the short compass of the work, experiences "yearning" at the outset and at the end "has accepted that yearning is to be his fate, has recognized that he will not achieve his desire, and sorrowfully, reluctantly, has resolved himself to the realization."

In Chapter 6 we are confronted with two somewhat different "fictional narratives" (broadly conceived).

Fred Maus presents us with, essentially, a drama of actions without characters in the first movement of Beethoven's Op. 95 string quartet. Thus the movement begins with "an abrupt initial outburst, and a second outburst that responds to many peculiar factors of the opening but also ignores some of its salient aspects . . . ," and so on. However *whose* actions these are is left undetermined, for "in musical thought, agents and actions sometimes collapse into one another," because "musical texture does not provide any recognizable objects, apart from the sounds, that can be agents," and so musical actions "reflect a pervasive *indeterminacy* on the identification of musical agents."

Although he seems more willing to put some detail and some agency into his interpretations, in the present instance, Anthony Newcomb's interpretation of the second movement of Mahler's Ninth Symphony holds, as does Maus, to what might be called the "musical agency uncertainty principle." The interpretation, to remind the reader, is that "There is a struggle in Mahler's movement, but it is not at all a heroic struggle. Foregrounded are issues of weakness of will, of lapses of attention, of addiction to external glitter, entertainment, and the racy life, of banalization and brutalization of the initial clumsy image, and of the realization only intermittently, and too late of the need to resist." But when we come to ask "Who or what did this?"—who are what the story is about—"In music, the answer to this question *must* . . . remain indeterminate."

I have examined all three of these authors' interpretations, and their problems, in detail in previous chapters. And it is not my intention to repeat all of that yet again. What I do intend is to now view them in the specific role of answers to the perceived failure of formalism to provide an explanation for why and how absolute music interests and pleasures us.

Well, to begin with the good news is that all three of these interpretations avoid at least the first objection to Schopenhauer's approach, to wit, that it cannot accommodate recognitional learning because the object of representation is such that it cannot be experienced, and hence music's successful representation of it, if it *is* successful, cannot be recognized. For all three interpretations propose for the object of musical representations perfectly ordinary things, actions, agents, events, states of mind, that all of us experience throughout our lives.

But, alas, the bad news is that, in this regard, it is a hollow victory only, for the narrativist approach. For the requirement for recognitional learning in artistic representation is twofold, or, rather, there are *two* requirements. The object of representation must have been experienced by the perceiver for recognition to take place. *That* requirement the narrativists have fulfilled.

But there is a second requirement for recognitional learning in artistic representation. That requirement is that the object of representation must be *recognizable* in the representation and that absolute music fulfills *that* requirement is a point of some contention.

When Aristotle wrote, in the *Poetics*, about what I have been calling recognitional learning, he of course had in mind, as do I, the experience we all have, unaided by expert commentary, of recognizing the objects of representation in the representational arts, be it the Prince of Denmark ranting in a graveyard, or the picture of a man's face with a bandaged ear. And it is in reacting to *those* kinds of representations that we experience recognitional learning; it is these kinds of representations that elicit in us the expletive, "Why *that's* exactly how it is!"

But that kind of recognitional learning, that kind of "Why *that's* exactly the way it is" experience, we never get from absolute music. True, some of us, witness Robinson, Maus, and Newcomb, do, by what I would call laborious digging and tortuous interpretation, come up with representational stories for works in the absolute music repertoire. But many of us who read these stories fail to hear them in the music. Whatever is going on here, it is not what I meant (or I think Aristotle meant) by recognitional learning.

Furthermore, recognitional learning is supposed to be a way of partially making good the failure of formalism to account for our interest and pleasure in absolute music. But can it, in the form in which it is given us in the stories of Robinson, Maus, Newcomb, et al.?

Let us make the reasonable assumption that the pleasure we take in recognitional learning has its source in the interest we take in recognitional learning: which is to say, our pleasure is directly coupled with how interesting we find the recognitional learning—the more interest, the more pleasure. But under this assumption it becomes clear that the recognitional learning provided by such stories as those told by Robinson, Maus, and Newcomb, if they provide any at all, is monstrously *uninteresting*, hence the pleasure it can provide vanishingly small.

Let us remind ourselves what interests us in the artistic representations that *do* provide substantial recognitional learning. What interests us in *Hamlet*? What interests us in *Pride and Prejudice*? That is, what interests us in the representational aspects of these works that provides recognitional learning and the pleasure thereof?

Clearly it is these works' representational fullness: the depth and the detail of these fictional representations capture our interest and, by consequence, produce the pleasure and the satisfaction we take in such art works. And it is just this depth and detail that are absent from the minimal, abstract scenarios of Robinson, Maus, Newcomb, and their ilk. Whatever paltry interest or pleasure these minimal scenarios, with their "indeterminate" personae, and agent-less actions can provide for those who manage to hear them in the music, such vanishingly small rewards cannot answer for what it is about absolute music that so deeply interests and pleasures us. Viewed as a response to formalism, the fictional interpretations of these foes of formalism are failures as well.

But, furthermore, the problem of absolute music that formalism has failed satisfactorily to address would remain even if the stories and characters the foes of formalism heard were as deep as *Hamlet* and as intriguing as *Pride and Prejudice*. For the unpleasant fact would remain that large numbers of devoted, sophisticated listeners to the absolute music canon listen in a formalist manner *without* hearing anything but *the music*; no personae, no stories, no psychodramas, no nothing. I know this for a fact because *I* am one of their number.

Fictional Narrative and Informational Learning

If recognitional learning and the pleasures thereof fail to accrue to absolute music at all, or at most in a degree incapable of explaining our interest and pleasure in absolute music, surely informational learning must, in light of this, seem an even less likely or promising option. For informational learning is conveyed, mostly, through the expression of propositions; and absolute music's potential for expressing propositions seems even more remote from its nature than its potential for representing stories.

We are, remember, exploring the possibility of absolute music, as a representational art, providing a source of recognitional learning or informational learning. But if the analogy to the arts of fictional representation is to be taken seriously, then there are two ways that absolute music, if it *were* an art of fictional representation, could express propositions, as a means to informational learning, corresponding to the ways that fictional works do: through sentences directly expressing propositions, and through works as wholes, or aspects of works, expressing propositions indirectly by implication or suggestion.

As for the possibility of absolute music containing sentences that express propositions, it is a possibility that seems hardly worth considering. For even if one could, *per impossibile*, come up with a plausible account of how absolute music might contain sentences directly expressing propositions, it is very hard to believe the propositions would be such as to merit our interest or produce any informational learning worthy of the name.

But, in fact, much of what such fictional arts as drama, movies, and the novel express as informational knowledge is expressed by the *works*, not by individual sentences within them, in the form of implied or suggested propositions (although sentences of course play a major role in this). And what implies or suggests these propositions are the stories and characters that constitute the fictional works. Furthermore, what makes it possible for serious fictional works to imply or suggest interesting, thought-provoking propositions are their deep, detailed, and complex plots, inhabited by deep, detailed, and complex characters. That being the case, we are up against the same stumbling block to informational learning in absolute music that we were with regard to recognitional learning, to wit, the paltry, completely uninteresting "plots and characters," if they deserve the names, bereft of depth, detail, and complexity: bereft of all of the things that make it possible for a fictional work of art to suggest or imply interesting, thought-provoking propositions that result in pleasure-provoking informational learning.

The conclusion, then, seems compelling, that absolute music is incapable of providing significant, if any, recognitional learning, or significant, if any, informational learning; and both, it would seem, for the same reason: its incapability of embodying stories and characters of significant depth, detail, or, therefore, interest, if indeed it can embody them at all. It seems to follow, furthermore, that if the production of either the pleasure of recognitional learning, or that of informational learning, is offered as an answer to the failure of formalism to explain our pleasure and interest in absolute music, or even partially answer it, that must itself be a failed project. So where do we go from here?

Facing Failure

In the present chapter, I have investigated the possibility of the kinds of narrative interpretation put on absolute music by Robinson, Maus, and Newcomb being offered as attempts to provide an explanation for the interest and pleasure that we take in absolute music. And I have argued that if they are so offered, they fail of their purpose.

But one thing those failed answers to the failure of formalism have right, if indeed they were so intended: formalism's defenders *have* failed to give an adequate explanation for the deep interest and pleasure that absolute music, in the Western canon, provides to its devotees: interest and pleasure to such a degree that it emboldens them to put the masterpieces of the canon alongside those masterpieces of the great poets, novelists, painters, and sculptors, from antiquity to the present. Why should the busts of Beethoven and Bach be worthy to occupy their niches in the same venue as Shakespeare or Michaelangelo? Formalists have failed to tell us. And the narrativists are right to call them out on it, and offer an answer of their own. At least they have tried and failed, which is better than not trying at all. So in what follows I will give it a try myself.

9

Attention, Ritual, and the Additive Strategy

Introduction

For more years than I care to remember, I have defended against all comers, what I have called in this book, and elsewhere, enhanced formalism: the view that absolute music, music without text, title, or program, pure instrumental music, in other words, is to be understood and appreciated as a structure of sound, sometimes an *expressive* structure of sound, without either representational, narrative, or semantic content. I call it enhanced formalism because, as I have said before, I believe absolute music possesses expressive character, is expressive of the garden-variety emotions, whereas traditional formalists, beginning with Hanslick, have denied this. And I call it formalism, though with reluctance, because I believe it is not merely musical form that matters for understanding and appreciation but other characteristics of musical sound as well. Nevertheless, I continue to call it formalism because it seems too late to change the name without causing undue confusion. Most people know that musical formalists, so-called, do not think musical form the only property of absolute music relevant for proper appreciation and understanding.

In any event, I have defended enhanced formalism over the years with a confidence sometimes approaching a kind of evangelical zeal. The present book is a continuation of that defense, perhaps my last effort in the cause. And in the next three chapters, I want to try to give some indication of how I think the defender of musical formalism must proceed, in answering the very real problems that the view presents. But in the end, after all this time, and after all of my attempts to answer the foes of formalism and defend its integrity, here and elsewhere, the phenomenon of absolute music *still* seems to me, when all is said and done, a divine mystery.

Paying Attention

I want to begin with what might be called the "attitude of rapt attention" to works of absolute music, the "aesthetic attitude," if you like; and with a story.

A friend of mine, a world-class astrophysicist, teaches in his university on occasion, an undergraduate course known there, and at other places, as "physics for poets." I had the pleasure of attending his lectures, one semester, and was present when he introduced to the class Christian Huygens' discovery of the mathematics of the pendulum. He described the mathematics as "deeply moving." And there was no doubt that this was not mere hyperbole, to impress a class of unscientific humanities majors, but a sincere expression of feeling "from the heart."

I wish I too could have been deeply moved by Huygens' mathematics; I envy my friend that; I just don't have the right circuits for it. I do, though, have some of the right circuits for absolute music. And when I raptly attend to the right stuff I too am deeply moved, moved sometimes to tears.

Now I can't imagine any better example of "rapt attention" than that attention given to mathematics, except perhaps for the rapt attention that I, and others like me, give to absolute music in the concert hall. And my point is that this attitude of rapt attention to the formal structure of absolute music gets a bum rap; that we are indulging in a conceptually "pure" activity, emotionally sterile, completely devoid of emotional involvement, *much in the manner of a cold, calculating mathematician*, contemplating a complicated proof or equation, completely devoid of that enemy of rational thought—*emotional involvement*. Of course, as you can see, this bum rap is doubly bum. It tars emotionless, "intellectual," rapt aesthetic attention to absolute music with the same brush it tars emotionless, rapt intellectual attention to mathematical theorems and proofs. But *neither* deserves the tarring; neither is "emotionless"; and as we all ought to know by now, *pace* Star Trek, emotion and intellect are not at cross purposes.

Lost Rituals

The attitude of rapt attention to absolute music, in the modern setting of the concert hall, is frequently contrasted unfavorably, with music in its ritual settings, before the advent of modern musical institutions.

I should like to begin with a reminder to anyone who longs, uncritically, for music's lost interactive settings, and the rituals that went with them. A great many of these settings were venues for rituals, rewarding and pleasant though they may have been, that consisted in various ways of making noise and ignoring the music. If that is what you are longing for you are not longing for any *musical* ritual but a ritual at which music was an all but silent presence.

No doubt the musical ritual that comes most readily to mind as both richly rewarding *and* truly musical is the religious ritual in which music plays an important part: to instance two cases in point, the Protestant service for which Bach wrote the cantatas, and the Catholic one for which we have polyphonic settings of the liturgy dating back to the late Middle Ages. Any one of the faithful in either of these religious settings, who also possesses the requisite musical sensibility, will lay claim with some justification, no doubt, to an experience richer and deeper and more rewarding than the secularist's purely art-dominated experience, even when in the liturgical setting, with its ritualistic choreography as an added artistic object: for it *will* be for the secularist, merely an artistic object, not a religious one.

Music as religious ritual is lost to the secularist; similarly, the core ritualistic significance of Handel's Coronation Anthems is lost to the republican. What remains for them both, and for those who have lost the other ritual settings in which music was experienced before the advent of the concert hall and the public concert, is concert-going itself. Is *that* a ritual worth the trouble? Or should we all retire to our "home entertainment" centers and flick a switch in splendid isolation?

Now concert-going takes many forms. But there is one kind of concert-going, the "subscription" concert, that is known in every city in the Western world large enough to support a symphony orchestra, or a program of visiting ensembles. And what I would like to do in the rest of this section is to examine its claim to be a musical ritual in more than name alone. I begin with an analogy.

It has been said in jest that a Unitarian is someone who believes there is, *at most*, one God. It is a religion, if that is the right word for it, that has stripped just about all of what we think of as religious ritual from its practice except for the gathering together, on Sunday, and the presentation, by the "leader," of what might be termed a sermon, but is more in the character of a moral or philosophical lecture.[1]

I once asked a member of a Unitarian congregation why he participated. (He was, as a matter of fact, a non-practicing Jew.) His reply was that he wanted to feel, at least once during the week, that he was in contact with something bigger than himself, and his ordinary daily life, and that he wanted an opportunity to sit for a while, in the presence of others, to think about something "important." The same function is served by the Ethical Culture Society, with no commitment at all to a "higher being," even "at most."

I believe that, for many of those who subscribe to symphony concerts, the same motivations are in place as for Unitarians and Ethical Culturists. My two maiden aunts attended regularly, I was going to say "religiously," the Sunday afternoon subscription series of the New York Philharmonic. Like the Unitarian I mentioned, they too were non-practicing Jews; and I firmly believe that they too, like him, were where they were every Sunday afternoon to feel themselves in communion with other people, in the presence of something bigger than themselves and their ordinary work-a-day world. I am not denying that they were in Carnegie Hall to hear beautiful music; it was, however, beautiful music that they felt in their blood and bones to be something of importance—not ephemeral but deep and enduring. There were *at least* four gods: Haydn, Mozart, Beethoven, and Brahms; and Arturo Toscanini was the high priest. This was not entertainment: it was holy communion.

No doubt the subscription concert's days are numbered, as are those of the symphony orchestra, except perhaps in the largest world capitals.

---

[1] There is also music, usually secular music; but I will leave that out of consideration here.

But while they last, before we descend entirely into the solipsism of the electronic audio cave, it can provide for us—those of us secularists who want or need it—some vestige of that healing and benediction that Bach's audience may have experienced in *Thomaskirche*, on a Sunday morning in Leipzig.

But let's admit it. We still have not faced up to the question of why and how it is that absolute music can move and enthrall those of us susceptible to its power as deeply and totally as it does. If it did not have this power to move and enthrall, we would scarcely treat our encounters with it in its acknowledged temple, the concert hall, as ritual communion rather than bread and circus. I think that power remains a mystery we should place high on the aesthetic philosopher's "most wanted" list. Malcolm Budd, whose philosophical skills and insights I very much admire, has argued that there is no mystery, at least no philosophical mystery, here at all. And I want now to consider his argument.

The Mystery of Music

I can find no better way to state the problem, the mystery as I see it, of absolute music, than to begin with these words of Budd's: "The difficulty is to provide an account of the nature of [absolute] music which both recognizes the abstractness integral to it and does justice to its artistic achievements by rendering intelligible music's capacity to generate products of exceptional intrinsic value. What appears puzzling is that human beings find it profoundly rewarding to absorb themselves in abstract processes that seem to be about as far removed from everything they value in their extramusical lives as anything could be."[2]

Now it must be pointed out at the start that Budd is interested in the general question of music's value as an art whereas I have been concerned, more specifically, with its power to move and enthrall us as an art. But I do not think that these questions can be prised apart, because of the way I construe the experience of being emotionally

---

[2] Malcolm Budd, *Values of Art: Pictures, Poetry and Music* (London: Penguin Books, 1995), 125–6.

moved by music. According to the oldest and, I imagine, most widely held belief, at least among non-philosophers, about how music moves us, sad music moves us to sadness, happy music to happiness, and so on. On this view, musical value and music's power to move are more or less independent of one another, since there can be music almost devoid of musical value yet identifiably happy, sad, and so on, as well as music of the highest value essentially devoid of expressive properties. On my view, however, music moves in virtue of its perceived beauty, or, in other words, of its perceived good-making qualities qua music.[3] So, on my view, what makes music valuable, *qua* art, moves us emotionally, qua art. Thus it seems reasonable on my view to treat Budd's explanation for musical value, and his denial that there is a "mystery" about it as, *eo ipso*, an explanation for what it is in absolute music that moves and enthralls us, and a denial that there is a "mystery" about *that*.

Budd begins his demystification, if I may so call it, of absolute music, by distinguishing between "psychological" and "constitutive" questions concerning its value.

Constitutive questions about music's artistic potential concern the identification of features of music in virtue of which it has whatever artistic capacities it does possess: they concern *what* it is about the art of music that endows it with its artistic potential. Psychological questions call for causal explanations of the effects the valuable features of music have on the responsive listener: they concern *why* the listener finds these features so rewarding, and hence why he values them.[4]

Psychological questions, or the psychological question, Budd sets aside as unanswerable, given the present state of the discipline. "If the puzzlement [about absolute music] is psychological," he writes, "it cannot be resolved at present, since the science of psychology is still in a primitive stage of development."[5]

I am not nearly as certain as Budd seems to be just where philosophy ends and psychology begins (or vice versa); and that goes for the philosophy of art and the psychology of art as well. But that possible

---

[3] For more on this see, Peter Kivy, *Music Alone: Philosophical Reflections on the Purely Musical Experience*.

[4] Budd, *Values of Art*, 158.   [5] Ibid.

disagreement does not stand in the way of my taking seriously Budd's attempt to answer the constitutive question (or questions). That attempt I now intend to examine.

Basically, I would characterize Budd's method of demystification as the "additive" method. What he does is to enumerate as many of the characteristics as he can of music that we value, that make it interesting as an art, and then say, in effect: Well, what *more* do you want for an explanation of absolute music's power over us. If it has this, and this, and this; if it has *all* of these things, *of course* it will be valuable to us; *of course* it will enthrall us; *of course* it will move us deeply. There is a good deal of very good sense in this method. So let us spend a moment on some of the characteristics of absolute music Budd addresses, and how they add up.

"In the first place, the feeling that music's power as an abstract art is problematic is vulnerable to the consideration that abstractness does not preclude an abstract work of art from possessing aesthetically valuable qualities of many different kinds, qualities that are not peculiar to music."[6]

"Secondly, the range of aesthetically appealing abstract forms is in fact widespread...." And music has the advantage that whereas it takes considerable effort to perceive the abstract forms in nature, and in representational art, "music presents nothing but such forms," so relieving us of "a task that is often possible only to a very limited extent...."[7]

Finally: "In virtue of the resources available to abstract music..., it is possible to compose musical processes that possess to the highest degree the quality of dramatic action, as was realized supremely in Beethoven's music...."[8]

So, given the above, "Is it any wonder that the embodiment of abstract forms in music and the remarkable enhancement of their appeal when composed *with art* should result in a colossal magnification of their power?"[9]

As I have said, I think that what I have called Budd's "additive" method has a lot of good sense to it. And, as a matter of fact, I tried

---

[6] Ibid., 164.   [7] Ibid., 165.   [8] Ibid., 167.
[9] Ibid., 169.

out a similar strategy myself once upon a time.[10] However, neither my own earlier reflections, nor Budd's, have succeeded in dispelling my sense of mystery concerning the power over us of absolute music. Here is why I think Budd has failed me in this regard.

Budd's first suggestion is that we might be mystified by absolute music's power over us because of the mistaken belief that its "abstractness" precludes its possessing aesthetically valuable qualities. He rightly points out that this is certainly not the case and, furthermore, that many of the aesthetically valuable qualities absolute music does possess "are not peculiar to music," suggesting, of course, that if there is no mystery attached to the power over us of the other objects that possess these aesthetically valuable qualities, that should help dispel the sense of mystery surrounding the power of music.

I have difficulties with this first demystification strategy. To begin with, I do not think the sense of mystery has anything to do with the mistaken belief that the abstractness of absolute music precludes its possessing valuable aesthetic qualities. I do not think that many people have this belief. On the contrary, I think most people who concern themselves with these matters at all believe that absolute music possesses all of those valuable formal and "sensual" aesthetic properties that other abstract aesthetic structures possess. The mystery is why absolute music seems to wield an involving and emotive power over its devotees that many of these other structures do not, even though they possess some of the same aesthetically valuable aesthetic qualities.

Furthermore, those abstract structures that, I imagine, do exercise over their devotees emotive power equal to the power absolute music exercises over enthusiasts like me, pure mathematics and theoretical physics, for example, present, one would think, the very same mystery they have been wheeled in to dispel. It is no consolation to me to consider that the pure abstract structure of mathematical proof may possess many of the same aesthetically valuable qualities possessed by Beethoven's late quartets. If the former has the same emotive power over the susceptible, I find it equally mysterious. We now have two mysteries instead of one.

[10] See, Peter Kivy, "The Fine Art of Repetition," in Kivy, *The Fine Art of Repetition*, 327–59.

The second point is that the abstract forms in music are out front, on immediate display, whereas those of nature and the representational arts are embedded, and need effort to dig out. So, one supposes, the abstract forms of absolute music are able to exert more power over its audience than nature and the representational arts over theirs. The point is well taken. But one wonders just how much mileage can be got from it.

Clearly, the way both Budd and I construe absolute music, *all* it *is* is "abstract forms" (some of which are "expressive" forms). And I suppose it to be just plain common sense that there will be far more in the way of abstract form in an art devoted solely to that end than in the art of representational painting or drama, where there is, to use the old cliché, both form *and* content. We should, then, not underestimate the power of absolute music, because of its lack of "content," but remind ourselves that what it lacks in "content," it more than makes up for by far exceeding the arts of "content" in its formal aesthetic qualities.

It is a valid point—up to a point. But the problem is, the "mystery" is: how can it be that absolute music *more than makes up for* its lack of content by its profusion of formal properties? How can it be that the profusion of form has the power it does over us? That is what mystifies me.

I am somewhat disturbed by Budd's description of how we exper- ience abstract form in nature and in the representational arts (if I am understanding him correctly in this regard). He makes it sound as if we experience it by stripping away the content; abstracting from the object perceived, is how he puts it.[11] Certainly we do do this sort of thing when we want to "take apart" an artwork for study or didactic purposes. But it is not, or should not be the way we experience an artwork "aesthetically," or as an artwork, the way it was meant to be experienced. For then we are meant to experience "form" and "content" as welded together in a seamless whole. And it is just this seamless whole, this double whammy of form-enhanced content, content-enhanced form that we feel comfortable in believing explains the enormous emotive power such artworks as *King Lear* or the Sistine

---

[11] Budd, *Values of Art*, 165.

Ceiling, have over us as well as, by the way, opera, music drama, and other forms of texted music.[12]

Thus there is no advantage accruing to absolute music over the representational arts by its giving us the abstract aesthetic qualities without the labor of stripping them away from a content in which, in the representational arts, they are embedded. We were never meant to experience abstract qualities of the representational arts by stripping them away, "abstracting" them from content, in the first place. It is their double effect, and its absence in absolute music, that makes us see the power of the latter as a deeper mystery. It takes two to tango; and absolute music is a solitary dancer. Yet against all intuitions, she tangos anyway. *That's* the mystery.

Finally, music and drama. It is an oft-repeated claim that absolute music, from the time so-called sonata form comes to dominance, can best be described in dramatic terms: as a kind of "wordless drama," or, at least, as possessing a distinctly "dramatic" character. This we saw amply demonstrated in Chapter I. And as Budd quite rightly observes, this dramatic character of absolute music seems to have been "realized supremely in Beethoven's music." But the problem is that the drama analogy, when you scrutinize it, turns out to be a very infelicitous one, for all of its popularity in the literature. It provides little explanation, if any at all for absolute music's power.

Let us say that there are two possible claims concerning absolute music and drama: the strong claim that absolute music is wordless drama, and the weak claim that absolute music has certain dramatic qualities. Of the strong claim I will say, to start with, that it immediately comes a cropper in many instances in the face of the fact that in music, unlike drama, it is fairly common, as I have argued previously, for whole sections to be repeated "verbatim," as it were. So if you think, say, of the first movement of Beethoven's *Eroica* Symphony as a wordless drama in four acts, you will find that the first scene of the first act, which is to say, the exposition of a sonata movement, is performed twice before the second scene is played. Thus, the repeat, one of the commonest features of absolute music, and taken quite for

---

[12] On this see, Peter Kivy, *Osmin's Rage: Philosophical Reflections on Opera, Drama and Text.*

granted as we have seen before, would be altogether bizarre in spoken drama.[13] The analogy, to say the least, is an "imperfect" one. All this, of course, is old news to us: it is the same objection brought against the persona theory in Chapter 5.

But let us put this problem aside and ask ourselves how it would help solve the "mystery" of absolute music if we thought of symphonies, sonatas, string quartets, and the rest, as wordless dramas. What is it in spoken drama, we should ask ourselves first, that so thoroughly enthralls and deeply moves us? I answer, not surprisingly, the characters, what they say, what they do, what happens to them. What else? And there is the problem. In absolute music there are no characters, or their sayings, or their doings; nothing happens to anyone. So what is the cash value of this "wordless drama"? As an answer to the mystery of absolute music, the account is empty. For the things any real drama, properly so-called, that enthrall and move us "wordless" musical drama does not possess. (We have been over all of this before.)

What of the weak thesis then: that sonatas, symphonies, string quartets, and the rest, are "dramatic"? My problem with it has always been that I am not quite sure what exactly is being claimed. Sometimes we refer to sudden changes of one kind or another as "dramatic"; or we may say that some course of events proceeds to its conclusion with "dramatic inexorability." Sonata movements certainly impress us sometimes, with just such "dramatic" features: sudden musical changes and a strong sense of goal direction. As well, we frequently hear in this kind of music "dramatic conflict." Thus, as Budd describes the first movement of the *Eroica*, "...Beethoven builds a gigantic musical structure in which a series of dramatic conflicts engendering tremendous tensions and climaxes is worked out, the music ending with a final resolution of the elements of the conflict."[14]

I think, by the way, that we tend to fixate on the so-called "dramatic" qualities of sonata form, rather than the other metaphorical literary qualities of absolute music, such as the "conversational" quality of the string quartet, for example, or the quality of rational

---

[13] On this see, Kivy, "The Fine Art of Repetition."
[14] Budd, *Values of Art*, 168.

"discourse" that many, both in the Baroque and Classical periods, heard in instrumental music. But as we have seen, they hold out no more promise than the dramatic model, and for the very same reason: they are defeated by the repeat. But one war at a time, so back to the dramatic, in the weaker sense.

What benefits can we reap from the fact that we sometimes like to describe a sudden modulation as a "dramatic" change, two contrasting themes as "struggling dramatically" with one another, a musical composition as progressing inexorably to its "dramatic" conclusion with the fatal necessity of a Greek tragedy; things like that? What we *can't* get is the privilege of assuming these ways of speaking imply the satisfactions they token are the satisfactions of real, spoken drama, for the same reason that thinking of absolute music as wordless drama cannot yield us the satisfaction of real, spoken drama. When we are astounded, and moved by a dramatic change, in real, spoken drama, it is a change of *someone's* fortunes or situation or relationships that astounds and moves us. When we are astounded and moved by struggle in a drama, it is the struggle of characters, with personalities and beliefs, that astound and move us. When we are astounded and moved by the inexorable course of a spoken drama, to its ultimate tragic or triumphant denouement, it is the tragedy or triumph of characters whom we have come to love or hate or understand. That we can call absolute music "dramatic" does not give us those things, anymore than calling it "wordless drama" does.

Of course this is not to say that these "dramatic" elements of absolute music are not worthwhile, and enthralling, and moving. They *are*; and that is just the mystery. How *can* they be when they lack all of the content that accounts for their fascination and emotive power in spoken drama?

At this point I do not know what more can be said about the mystery that surrounds the incredible power with which the abstract art of absolute music grips and moves us. It is like no other I have ever experienced—which, of course, may be nothing more than testimony to my impoverished experience. And what has been said by other philosophers, myself included, has not lessened my sense of bafflement.

But one thing we should know by this time, from the preceding chapters, is that the literary model, in any of its forms, is not going to help. We are up against, yet again, the ancient quarrel. If we are to have an explanation for the power of absolute music, it will not come from the literary camp.

Perhaps I am unknowingly longing for the *psychological* explanation that Budd points out psychology is far from ready to give. I don't know; and I have never been sure, in the first place, as I have said before, just where the boundaries of philosophy lie. In any case, I still look to philosophy for an answer. Right now, for the mystery of absolute music, which still seems to *me* to *be* a mystery, philosophy still seems to me to be the only game in town, and literature is not one of the players. Could morality be?

In the next chapter I am going to explore this possibility with the utmost skepticism. And yet in the end, surprisingly enough, and surprising most of all to myself, I am going to reach a somewhat positive conclusion, which will then be amplified in the final chapter.

10

Musical Morality

Introduction

It may appear as if the subject of music and morality is totally irrelevant to present concerns. But a moment's reflection will suggest that that is not by any means the case.

Our theme is the ancient quarrel between literature and music. And it is one of the most frequently cited functions of fictional literature to express morel beliefs and have an effect on our moral lives. As well, if we construe the term "literature" broadly to include philosophical "literature," which is to say, philosophical texts then, of course, the ethical writings of the major philosophers of the Western tradition can also be considered relevant to the "ancient quarrel." Thus, in a word, the paradigmatic way in which we convey moral knowledge, and attempt to influence moral behavior, is through "literature," broadly conceived to include both narrative fiction and non-fictional texts in the area of moral philosophy.

If absolute music, then, is a possible conveyor of moral beliefs, and purveyor of moral influence, it must measure up to the capabilities of literary texts, broadly conceived. The moral claims of absolute music, if such there be, become, then, a special case of the ancient quarrel between literature and music, alongside of the narrative claims made for it, which we have been considering above. We are, once again, embroiled in the conflict of the antithetical arts. So with the charge of "irrelevancy" answered, let us examine now the moral claims of absolute music.

The Bad and the Beautiful

In an altogether chilling scene in the movie version of *Schindler's List*, German soldiers have discovered an apartment where Jews are hidden: some in closets, some in attics, some even in spaces between walls, and between ceilings and floors. While these soldiers are in the process of shooting the terrified people hiding there, one of their number spies a piano and sits down to play. "Bach?" asks a comrade. "No, Mozart" another soldier replies. (It sounds to me like Bach.)[1]

The point of the scene is all too clear. The knowledge, love, and appreciation of the most sublime musical works of Western civilization can apparently exist alongside of, indeed as an accompaniment to the cruelest, most barbaric acts imaginable. Love of Bach does not engender love of humanity, or of the good. Or, put another way, the music of Bach is not a moral force in the world. A lover of Bach is no more likely to be a morally upright human being than a lover of chess or baseball. As a recent writer has eloquently put the point: "The question of music's ambivalence is always a disturbing one; the question of Beethoven in Auschwitz is terrifying"; and again: "musical language is either amoral or it expresses a notion of morality that includes tyrants—which is the same thing."[2] To instance a specific case in point, "SS leader Reinhard Heydrich," otherwise known as Hangman Heydrich, "who was instrumental in organizing the Final Solution . . . played the violin and could be deeply stirred by a Schubert sonata."[3]

Interestingly enough, another Holocaust narrative also, by the way, like *Schindler's List*, a historical narrative, not a fictional one, might be seen to make exactly the opposite point.[4] It is the remarkable memoir, *The Pianist*, by Wladyslaw Szpilman, brought to the screen

---

[1] The movie is based on Thomas Keneally's book, originally published as *Schindler's Ark* (London: Hodder & Stoughton, 1982).

[2] Esteban Buch, *Beethoven's Ninth: A Political History*, trans. Richard Miller (Chicago: University of Chicago Press, 2004), 219 and 266.

[3] Joachim Fest, *Inside Hitler's Bunker: The Last Days of the Third Reich*, trans. Margot Bettauer Dembo (New York: Ferrar, Straus and Giroux, 2004), 35.

[4] There has, by the way, been some question raised about the historical accuracy of *Schindler's List*, both the book and, by consequence, the movie. But that is beside the point.

by Roman Polanski. In the climactic scene, both of the book and of the movie, Szpilman, a Jewish pianist and composer, is discovered by a German officer close to the end of the war, after having hidden in Warsaw through the entire German occupation. For reasons that will become apparent in a moment, I am not going to reveal to you what transpires by describing the scene in Polanski's version, or quoting from Szpilman's book. Rather, I will quote from the advertising blurb on the back cover. Here is what it says:

On September 23, 1939, Wladyslaw Szpilman played Chopin's Nocturne in C-sharp minor live on the radio as shells exploded outside—so loudly that he couldn't hear his piano. It was the last live music broadcast from Warsaw: that day, a German bomb hit the station, and Polish Radio went off the air.

    Though he lost his entire family, Szpilman survived in hiding. In the end his life was saved by a German officer who heard him play the same Chopin nocturne on a piano found among the rubble.[5]

Now I assume we are supposed to infer from the way the scene is described that there is a causal connection between the German officer's hearing the Chopin nocturne and his saving the pianist's life. We are supposed to argue *post hoc propter hoc* to the morally healing powers of great music. But the fact is that the advertising blurb is a total misrepresentation of what transpired, if, that is, it is intended to imply that Chopin's Nocturne in C-sharp minor had the moral effect of deflecting a vicious Nazi killer of Jews from his intended purpose. For the German officer in question, Captain Wilm Hosenfeld, we know from the diaries he kept, was already suspicious of the National Socialists as early as 1939, and by the time Wladyslaw Szpilman crossed his path, in 1945, was a committed anti-Nazi. It did not require Chopin's Nocturne in C-sharp minor to prevent him from killing the pianist. He had no such intention in the first place.

    I think I know why the writer of the blurb misrepresented the book in this way. Advertising blurbs, after all, are intended to make prospective buyers into *buyers*; and the way to do that is to make them think that the book in hand will tell them what they *want* to be told.

---

[5] Wladyslaw Szpilman, *The Pianist*, trans. Anthea Bell (New York: Picador, 1999), back cover of the paperback.

We *do* want to be told—*want* to believe—that great music such as that of Bach, Mozart, and Chopin has power for the good. We do, at least some of us, have a strong intuition that you can't love Bach, Mozart, and Chopin, and love genocide too. Yet there *is* that scene in *Schindler's List*—and, alas, it rings true too. So which vision, then, is the true one? Is it the benign vision of music's morally uplifting powers, or the cynical one of music and sadistic cruelty in perfect moral harmony?

Preliminary Distinctions

So far I think the question being raised has remained too vague to be dealt with in a convincing way. A reasonable next step must be, then, to try to make it clear enough for meaningful analysis and discussion.

The question, as previously posed, is whether the music of such great composers as Bach, Mozart, and Chopin is a "moral force" in the world: a moral force, that is to say, for the good. And I will begin by reminding the reader that the music about which this question is raised is pure instrumental music: music without a text or dramatic setting; in other words, absolute music; music alone.

The reason I want to confine myself to such music in this discussion is that once words and dramatic representation come into the picture, the question ceases to be one of *music*'s moral force but of the moral force of artworks about which there is much less doubt. There is no question that if you think, for example, dramatic works can exert moral force, then you are surely going to think that music drama or opera can. That, I presume, is why the Viennese aristocracy was so wary of Mozart's and Da Ponte's plan to make an opera of Beaumarchais' *Marriage of Figaro*, with all of its revolutionary overtones. They had no such problem with Mozart's piano concertos or symphonies, even though *they* were written in the same musical "language" as the operas.

But once we understand that it is absolute music, music alone, whose moral force we are questioning, we still are in need of some clarification with regard to the concept of "moral force" itself. What *is* that? What *is* it we are asking whether or not music has?

I would like to distinguish three ways in which we can construe the concept of moral force, although I make no claim that these three ways exhaust the possibilities. And I shall raise the question, with regard to each of them, as to whether absolute music possesses moral force.

One way in which something can possess moral force is to possess the power to convey or impart moral insights and theoretical knowledge. Prime examples are philosophical texts like the *Nicomachean Ethics* or Kant's *Grundlegung*. I shall call this *epistemic* moral force.

A second way in which something might possess moral force is to possess the power to make people act in a moral way: to do the right thing. Good parenting can do this. Moral indoctrination can. Even behavior-altering drugs. Nor need one necessarily be aware that one is being so influenced. I shall call this *behavioral* moral force.

Finally, we may construe moral force as the power to build moral character; to make someone, as it were, a better human being, either in the more obvious moral dimensions, or in any other way that might be broadly conceived as part of the moral. I shall call this *character-building* moral force. Any one of the things mentioned above that possesses moral force, either in the epistemic sense or in the behavioral sense can also possess it in the character-building sense.

I need now only point out, before getting on with the question of music's possible moral force, that the three concepts of moral force that I have just distinguished are, obviously, closely intertwined with one another.

Thus, the epistemic force of the *Nicomachean Ethics*, or Kant's *Grundlegung*, might well be thought of as imparting to those texts behavioral and character-building moral force as well: which is to say, if I read and am convinced of the moral theories put forth in one of these texts, these moral convictions may result in my behaving in a more morally upright manner than heretofore, or result in the moral improvement of my character. As well, the building up of my moral character, no matter how it is achieved will, presumably, have a beneficial effect on my moral behavior, and, furthermore, the improvement of my moral behavior, no matter how *it* is achieved, may, if it becomes a permanent aspect of my person, constitute, *eo ipso*, an improvement in my moral character.

These complications, however, we may safely put aside. For our purposes the three concepts of moral force can be treated as completely separate. Our question is, simply, does music, that is to say music alone, absolute music, possess moral force in any of these three senses? And to that question I now turn, beginning with epistemic moral force.

Music and Moral Knowledge

There is a very general argument that would, at a stroke, scotch the idea of music's possessing epistemic moral force.

Consider the examples that immediately come to mind when one thinks of moral force in the epistemic sense: philosophical treatises, principally, as well as religious and moral tracts, ancient moral codes and, of course, the foundational documents of the world's religions: the Bible, the Koran, and so on. These are the kinds of works whose purpose is the imparting of moral knowledge, whether in the form of theory and analysis, or moral teaching and exhortations of a more practical cast.

Now there is a view, widely held in the philosophy of art, that works of art are unable to, and, by consequence, are not in the business of conveying moral insights. Nor is it a recent view, having been embraced by numerous philosophers and critical theorists of the nineteenth and twentieth centuries, epitomized by Oscar Wilde's well known remark that "There is no such thing as a moral or an immoral book. Books are well written, or badly written. That is all."

Literary fiction is no doubt the best candidate for an art form, one of whose purposes is, at least sometimes, the conveying of moral knowledge. But, so the skeptical argument goes, even serious novels and plays, by the great literary artists of the Western tradition, fail the test. For even if one can extract from them moral theses and precepts, these alone do not make for knowledge of any real consequence. What makes such works as the *Nicomachean Ethics*, or the *Grundlegung* important sources of moral knowledge is not merely the moral precepts and theses that they put forth; it is the arguments provided in their support, and the systematic theoretical framework of which they form a part. None of this, however, so the skeptics claim, is in evidence in literary works of art. They may, indeed, at times express moral precepts and theses. However that cannot alone make them sources of moral knowledge in any important way, lacking, as they do, the necessary analysis and argumentation. Whatever the business of literary artworks, then, the skeptic insists, it cannot be the exerting of epistemic moral force. And what goes for literature goes, a fortiori, for the other arts.

The argument, then, against the possibility of music possessing moral force in the epistemic sense is short and sweet:

(1) No artworks possess epistemic moral force.
(2) Works of absolute music are artworks.
(3) Therefore, no works of absolute music possess epistemic moral force. Q.E.D.

Well it seems like a nice enough argument. But I do not think it will wash for the simple reason that I do not share the moral skeptic's claim that literary works of art are not sources of important knowledge: do not possess epistemic moral force. I am a defender, along with a few others in the philosophy of art, of the view that *some* works of literary fiction *are* capable of conveying important moral knowledge: do indeed possess epistemic moral force as part of their *raison d'etre* qua artworks.[6] Thus the general argument cuts no ice with me because I believe the major premise is false. Nevertheless, I do believe that the conclusion is true. Showing that, however, requires a different argument, but it is not far to seek.

Recall again our prime examples of works with epistemic moral force: the *Nicomachean Ethics*, Kant's *Grundlegung*, the great documents of the world religions. Clearly these texts are complicated systems of sentences expressing, among others, moral propositions, and supporting arguments for them in a more or less systematic fashion, depending on the text in question. Literary works, like novels and plays, are also texts comprised of large numbers of sentences. The difference is, with regard to moral content, that literary works express moral propositions, if they express them at all, *indirectly*. As Peter Lamarque and Stein Olsen describe the view I am espousing, although it is a view

---

[6] See, for example, Peter Kivy, *Philosophies of Arts: An Essay in Differences* (Cambridge: Cambridge University Press, 1997), chapter 5.

they vigorously oppose, "literature at the 'literary level' is for the most part fictive, i.e. . . . . characteristically its content is fictional and its mode of presentation is not that of fact-stating. But . . . at a different level literary works do, perhaps must, imply or suggest general propositions about human life which have to be assumed as true or false"[7]—moral propositions, of course, being one of the principal kinds.

Now the point is that the crucial feature held in common by philosophical texts, religious texts and, if you accept the view, literary texts, which enables them to possess epistemic moral force, is that they all are capable of expressing complex propositions extensively, and in a systematic way. Therein lies their epistemic moral force. And if that is true, it bodes ill for the epistemic moral force of absolute music, for the obvious reason that absolute music is either totally impotent to express propositions of any kind; or, if it can express propositions at all, can do so only at the most primitive, banal level. You would get more propositional content out of a third-grade reader than out of the first eight of Beethoven's symphonies. (I omit the ninth for obvious reasons.)

It seems to me a no-brainer that absolute music *cannot* express propositions, even indirectly, as some claim literary fiction can. It seems to me absurd to even try to provide an argument for this contention. For if an argument is meant to go from the more certain to the less, it is difficult for me to find anything I am more certain about than that absolute music does not, because it cannot, express propositions. The best I can do is to present for your consideration, two of the propositions that, after considerable exegetical labor, have been extracted from great works of the absolute music canon, and ask you to consider with an open mind whether anything amounting to moral knowledge worthy of the name can be claimed for them.

Jerrold Levinson, who is certainly one of the leading philosophers of art of our times, and a prolific writer on musical subjects has, with great difficulty, in an essay called "Truth in Music," extracted a proposition from Mozart's G-minor Symphony (K. 550) to the effect that in the experience of a single individual happiness *could* naturally

---

[7] Peter Lamarque and Stein Olsen, *Truth, Fiction, and Literature: A Philosophical Perspective* (Oxford: Clarendon Press, 1994), 321.

follow unhappiness. This is a special case of what Levinson takes to be a general rule of musical exegesis that if a musical work is expressive of two different emotions in successive passages, it is saying that in the experience of a single individual the second emotion could naturally succeed the first.[8]

In an even more elaborate job of work, this time of the music-historical kind, the musicologist David P. Schroeder has extracted the following message from Haydn's 83rd Symphony: "opposition is inevitable and the highest form of unity is not the one that eliminates conflict": it is the message of "tolerance over dogmatism"; and Schroeder goes on to assert: "It is precisely this message that can be heard in many of Haydn's late symphonies."[9] That this is the sum total of moral knowledge conveyed by a large group of the greatest works in the absolute music canon, if true would be, it hardly needs pointing out, a pretty conclusive argument against the notion that absolute music has as one of its major tasks the moral enlightenment of humanity.

My own view is that neither author has succeeded in showing absolute music capable of expressing propositions. But even if we give them their propositions, what have we got? Hardly the stuff to make moral theories with; hardly the stuff to impart epistemic moral force of any significant kind to works of absolute music. Even when they are not banalities, they are isolated moral precepts with neither rational argument nor critical analysis behind them. How could there be? How could absolute music *do* that. And without such backing, their epistemic moral force is nil.[10]

Let's face it. That absolute music is capable of expressing arguments, making moral generalizations, and constructing moral theories, is simply too bizarre a view to be entertained even for a fleeting

---

[8] Jerrold Levinson, "Truth in Music," in Levinson, *Music, Art and Metaphysics: Essays in Philosophical Aesthetics*, 298.

[9] David P. Schroeder, *Haydn and the Enlightenment: The Late Symphonies and their Audience* (Oxford: Clarendon Press, 1990), 88.

[10] This is a conclusion, by the way, that I suspect Levinson would endorse, in spite of his belief in the ability of absolute music to express propositions. For the judgment he himself passes on the propositions he thinks absolute music can express is essentially a negative one, to the effect that they don't much matter, one way or the other, to the artistic value of the works that express them.

moment. But not to worry, the defender of music's moral force is bound to reply. Who was ever silly enough to attribute *epistemic* moral force to absolute music anyway? That's just a red herring. It is the *other* two kinds of moral force, the *behavioral* and the *character-building* that are the viable candidates for musical morality.

Fair enough. So let's have a look at the remaining candidates.

Music and Moral Behavior

The history of musical thought, from antiquity, is littered with claims regarding music's power to influence human behavior, as well as abundant attempts to explain how it's done. If I had the time, it would be a waste of time to canvass them. I would have to start with Orpheus.

In any event, I do *not* have the time. So I will confine myself to two accounts of how absolute music might influence human *moral* behavior: what I shall call the *emotive* account and the *recognition* account.

The oldest philosophical question about music that still survives in the literature, as we have seen, is that of its supposed intimate relation to the human emotions. As any reader of the *Republic* knows, Plato thought that "music," as the translators render the Greek word, could arouse emotional states in the listener: what I have been calling in this book the "garden-variety" emotions, like love, fear, happiness, sadness, and a few others. He was, as you will recall, very concerned about this because the arousal of such emotions might, he feared, prove harmful to the citizenry.

As a matter of fact we know little, if anything really, about what the "music" Plato talked about was like; how it sounded. But we certainly know enough to conclude that he was very likely talking about sung music with a text, not anything even remotely like absolute music in the modern Western tradition. In any event, Plato's (and Aristotle's) belief in the power of music to arouse the garden-variety emotions re-emerged, with a vengeance, at the end of the sixteenth century, has remained a presence ever since, and was extended, not without difficulty, to absolute music as well, by the end of the Enlightenment.

But why should this be relevant to the topic at hand? Well, clearly, because the garden-variety emotions are prime motivators of actions.

So if absolute music can arouse the garden-variety emotions, it can, thereby, initiate behavior; and if it can arouse emotions to initiate *moral* behavior, it has, thereby, behavioral moral force.

Has anyone ever really espoused this emotive account of music's behavioral moral force? Only rarely, at least in my reading experience; but there are instances. Thus, for example, the British theorist and composer, Charles Avison, wrote: "...I think we may venture to assert that it is the peculiar quality of music to raise the *sociable* and *happy* passions...,"[11] the implication, I think, being that the *sociable* passions are ones that motivate social, cooperative behavior—surely a moral plus in Avison's mind.

As well, I have before me now a curious book that I picked up in a rather scuzzy second-hand book store, by the Reverend H. R. Howeis, M. A., called *Music and Morals*. It must have been extremely popular in Victorian England, for my copy is of the fifteenth edition, published in 1888. In it the good Reverend, with more enthusiasm than argument, avers that "if, as we have maintained, music has the power of actually creating these mental atmospheres [i.e. the emotions], what vast capacities for good or evil must music possess."[12] And, it becomes clear, these "vast capacities for good or evil" are to be cashed out, on his view, in terms of *behavior*. For he adds: "Everything, it may be said, music included, which excites an emotion not destined to culminate in action, has a weakening, enervating effect upon character."[13]

Without pursuing the matter any further, I think we can make quick work of the emotive account. It has two fatal flaws; and if the first one won't do it in the second will.

To start with, my own view, stated before, is that absolute music *cannot* arouse the garden-variety emotions. According to one very popular theory of the emotions, already anticipated, as we have seen, by Hanslick, and sometimes called the *cognitive* theory, the garden-variety emotions are *typically* aroused by the forming of beliefs appropriate to the emotions, which take intentional objects, and then

---

[11] Charles Avison, *An Essay on Musical Expression* (3rd edn.; London, 1775), 4.
[12] H. R. Haweis, *Music and Morals* (15th edn.; London: W. H. Allen, 1888), 48.
[13] Ibid., 49.

eventuate in some appropriate mode of behavior. Thus, I become afraid by coming to the belief that I am in danger of life and limb, as when I spy a full grown lion advancing towards me. My fear takes an intentional object, namely the lion, and initiates the appropriate action: standing my ground, aiming my rifle, and shooting the beast, if I am Earnest Hemingway; running like hell if I am a terrified philosopher.

The all too obvious point of the story is that absolute music simply does not have the resources to do this sort of thing, as Hanslick pointed out. How could it? What beliefs could music elicit in us to make us afraid, or angry, or sad? What would the intentional objects of these emotions be? And what would be the appropriate actions?

The theory of the emotions that I have evoked above is not, needless to say, the only one abroad. And it would be beyond the scope of this chapter to try to canvass them all. But there is one other, at the cutting edge right now, called by Jenefer Robinson the *affective appraisal* theory, which she has, as a matter of fact, employed to the end of showing how absolute music might arouse the garden-variety emotions. A brief look at Robinson's attempt would perhaps help to further elaborate my point.

According to Robinson[14] a passage of music might arouse a garden-variety emotion in the following way:

(1) The passage, as I hear it, occasions in me a state of excitement or arousal.

(2) I subsequently become puzzled about what garden-variety emotion was experienced when I heard the passage, even though *I wasn't experiencing any.*

(3) Consequent upon the puzzlement the personal associations I bring along with me cause me to label the state of arousal or excitement felt when listening to the passage of music with the name of a garden-variety emotion, say, "fear."

(4) The labeling of the arousal or excitement experienced when I heard the passage *causes* me *now*—finally, one is tempted to say—to become *afraid.*

[14] See Jenefer Robinson, *Deeper than Reason: Emotion and its Role in Literature, Music, and Art*, 400–12.

Whatever the real possibility of this process producing a garden-variety emotion in the listener—and step (4) is problematic, to say the least—it hardly seems a case of the *music's* producing the emotion. What *it* does, *if* it does it, is to stimulate the *listener* to produce a garden-variety emotion in her self, some time after the event. Surely, though, the claim we are investigating, that music possesses moral force through emotive arousal, is the claim that musical masterpieces possess the power of themselves, in their own character as art works, to directly arouse garden-variety emotions and, thereby, alter moral behavior (for the better). On Robinson's account, however, music simply provides emotive excitement or arousal (which I do indeed agree that it does, since I think absolute music can be deeply moving).[15] The rest is hostage to fortune. So there does not seem to me to be any basis here on which to build a theory of *music's* moral force through arousal of the garden-variety emotions. And that is the point at issue.

My general conclusion, then, about this line of thought, is that absolute music simply does not possess the materials necessary to arouse the garden-variety emotions in listeners, in any artistically relevant way. Some very good philosophers do not agree with me on this, and have postulated some very ingenious ways to explain how music might, the above objections to the contrary notwithstanding, arouse the garden-variety emotions. Two of the best are my good friends, Jerrold Levinson and Stephen Davies. But—and here is the second fatal objection to the emotive account of moral force in music—*both* of them are forced to concede that the emotions aroused by music *do not have any motivational force whatever.* Thus Davies admits that when music arouses the garden-variety emotions, "Not only does the [emotive] response lack many beliefs which, standardly, would lead to action, it also lacks the beliefs that give intensity to those feelings."[16] And, in a similar vein, Levinson is forced to admit that "weakening of the cognitive component in emotional response to music generally results in inhibition of most characteristic behaviors and in the significant lessening of behavioral tendencies."[17]

---

[15] On this see, Peter Kivy, *Music Alone: Philosophical Reflections on the Purely Musical Experience*, chapter 8.

[16] Stephen Davies, *Musical Meaning and Expression*, 307.

[17] Jerrold Levinson, "Music and Negative Emotions," in *Music, Art and Metaphysics*, 313.

It is scarcely surprising that Davies and Levinson are forced to concede the motivational impotence of the garden-variety emotions they believe music can arouse. For not only is there lacking in the musical experience just those things that render emotions motivational: appropriate beliefs, and intentional objects for the emotions to take. It is, as well, *a plain fact* that musical listeners do not do the things they ordinarily would if they were made *motivationally* sad, fearful, angry, and the like, by music. They do not fight, or flee, or vent their anger by thrashing the conductor.

Well, it might be replied, of course people don't "act out" their emotions in the concert hall: they are educated to repress them. But even repressed emotions have their signs or symptoms, or the repressing of them does. And that is no more in evidence in the concert hall than the expression of the emotions themselves.

Thus, of the two current views on offer, that music is impotent to arouse the garden-variety emotions, and that it can arouse the garden-variety emotions, but in a benign form in which they cannot motivate action, *both* are fatal to what I have been calling the *emotive* account of absolute music's moral force, in the behavioral sense. That, then, leaves us with what I called the *recognition* account; and to that I now turn.

Suppose there were some feature of absolute music that we *recognized* in it when we listened attentively, and with understanding; and that recognizing this feature resulted in our moral behavior improving. This would constitute a moral force in the music of a behavior-enhancing kind: just what we are looking for.

Now we must be careful here not to choose features that absolute music cannot possess, like propositions and arguments—the features we recognize in moral treatises and some narrative fiction, and which might well have a positive effect on our moral behavior. It must be a feature we could all agree absolute music can possess. What could such a feature be? Certainly "harmoniousness" is a reasonable candidate. And the claim would then be that the recognition of this aesthetic feature, in the music that possesses it, will motivate the listener to seek harmony in her interactions with other people, which is to say, try to get along with them, be tolerant of their points of view, and so on: in other words, to, in those respects, behave in a more morally commendable manner than heretofore.

Well, it is a very nice idea. The problem is: *there is absolutely no evidence that listening to music possessing harmoniousness makes people behave in the way stated, or improve their behavior in any other way.* Indeed, if there *is* any evidence, one way or the other, it is against the proposal rather than in its favor, which is exactly the point of the scene in *Schindler's List* that I discussed earlier.

Here it might be objected that we must not make too much of the *Schindler's List* phenomenon. After all, one might well imagine, instead of the German soldier spying a piano, his spying, rather, a copy of Kant's *Grundlegung*, and, being of a scholarly disposition, sitting down to read it while his comrades proceed with their gruesome work. But surely, the objection goes, this is not evidence against the contention that the *Grundlegung* possesses moral force! If *it* doesn't, what *does*?

But we must be careful not to confuse the two kinds of moral force at issue here. The *Schindler's List* scene as altered above is, to be sure, evidence against the moral force of the *Grundlegung* in the *behavioral* sense, not, however, in the *epistemic* sense. And it is the latter, not the former, that the objector must have in mind. For it is no news that moral knowledge frequently fails to motivate, or at least to *fully* motivate. ("The better path I gaze at and approve; the worse I follow.") To not put too fine a point on it, moral philosophers, as a group, show no evidence of being more morally upright than philosophers of science or philosophers of art.

But absolute music is another matter entirely; for we have already given up the idea that it can possess epistemic moral force at all. We are now working on the idea that it *may* possess behavioral moral force on what I have been calling the *recognition* account. There is no evidence that it does; and thought experiments like the scene in *Schindler's List*, as well as plain old empirical evidence like the music-loving Austrians' participation in the Holocaust, suggests that it does not. So we are right back where we started.

This leaves us, within the parameters I have set for myself, one remaining option: what I called the *character-building* sense of moral force.

Music and Character

In a strange little volume called *Beethoven: His Spiritual Development*, the British scientist, science popularizer, and amateur musician, J. W. N. Sullivan wrote in 1927: "The function of the kind of music we have been discussing is to communicate valuable spiritual states testifying to the depth of the artist's nature and to the quality of his experience of life."[18] And in our encounter with such music, of which Beethoven's is, for the author, the highest achievement, Sullivan avers that "We do feel, in our most valued musical experiences, that we are making contact with a great spirit, and not simply with a prodigious musical faculty."[19]

Now if something like this is true, then one might argue that, at least in some sense or other, great music uplifts us; makes us, for the period of the listening experience, feel a kind of exaltation. Whether the feeling is the result of the composer's really being, as Sullivan puts it, "a great spirit" and not just someone with a "prodigious musical faculty," doesn't really matter. It is the feeling *that* we are in such a presence that does the work, whether or not we are. And surely, even though this experience has no lasting beneficial effect on our characters (and there is no evidence that it does) it would not be wrong to say that *during* the experience, at least, we are better people; our characters are, during that experience, themselves made better. Furthermore, the sense in which, during the experience of great absolute music, we are better people, with improved characters, might fairly be construed as, at least broadly speaking, a "moral" sense of "better" and "improved." In the ancient sense of morals being about living well, and being self-fulfilled, during our all too brief encounters with great music perhaps we music lovers are, indeed, experiencing a heightened state of moral consciousness.

The claim is just vague enough to possibly be true. That might sound like damning with faint praise, but it was not so intended. The claim is vague because the experience it attempts to depict is one that,

---

[18] J. W. N. Sullivan, *Beethoven: His Spiritual Development* (New York: Vintage Books, 1960), 36.
[19] Ibid., 21.

although many people have had it, is complex enough, and subtle enough to defy our ordinary linguistic powers. I suppose that is what poets are for. And Sullivan was close to the mark when he wrote that "The musical critic who wishes to describe these experiences is faced with precisely the same task as the literary critic who wishes to describe the significance of a poem and, like the literary critic, he is likely to achieve but a stammering success."[20]

But if we can achieve only, in Sullivan's words, "a stammering success" in describing the feeling of mind-expanding exaltation that great music can impart to the listener prepared for it, can we achieve more than "a stammering success," it might well be asked, in saying what it is *about* absolute music that imparts this experience? The simple answer is that we can: it is the beauty, the magnificence of the music. The not-so-simple answer is to point out the elements in musical masterpieces that have this cumulative effect on us. That, however, is a job not merely for the philosopher but for the music theorist, the musicologist, and all others engaged in the analysis and the criticism of the absolute music canon. I have contributed to that project elsewhere myself, and will say no more about it here.[21] That absolute music in its highest manifestations, has this uplifting, character-building power, as described above, seems obvious enough, difficult though it may be to spell out in what that power resides. And I will leave it at that.

So here, at least, and at last, is a sense in which I am prepared to acquiesce in the moral force of absolute music, skeptic though I am. In the circumscribed way described above, absolute music can have moral force—moral force of the character-building variety. The late Robert Solomon described it as a force that, in the right kind of music, "sweeps us away"; it is an "experience of spirituality in music": an experience of what he called "naturalized spirituality," which is to say, spirituality with no religious or other supernatural overtones.[22]

That having been said, there are I think, two good reasons for not making too much of this conclusion, and one good reason not to make too little. Let's hear the bad news first.

---

[20] Ibid., 32. [21] See Kivy, *Music Alone, passim.*

[22] Robert C. Solomon, *Spirituality for the Skeptic: The Thoughtful Love of Life* (Oxford: Oxford University Press, 2002), xv.

First off, if you were looking for a way in which absolute music might have some *lasting* moral influence for the good—and I place emphasis on "lasting"—in the way either of imparting moral insight, facilitating moral behavior or improving moral character, you will have come away empty. Absolute music, I have argued, is impotent in all three respects.

Second, if you were looking to be told that absolute music has some *unique* thing to contribute to the moral life, you will come away empty. For the uplifting, character-enhancing effect of absolute music, of which I have been speaking, and which Sullivan describes as an experience in which "We do feel . . . that we are making contact with a great spirit . . . ," is by no means an experience exclusive to absolute music. All great works of art provide such uplifting, character-enhancing experiences to those susceptible. And so too, we have ample testimony, does the contemplation of elegant mathematical proofs, elegant scientific theories, elegant scientific experiments, for those capable of understanding them.

Thus absolute music shares with many other human activities the propensity to produce, in human beings, a kind of ecstasy that might seem appropriate to describe as character-enhancing, consciousness-raising and, therefore, in some vague, perhaps attenuated sense, morally improving, *while it lasts*. But being just one of many such activities, absolute music seems to lose that special, magical connection to morality that goes back, one suspects, to its Pythagorean and Orphic roots. If that bothers you, then you have just received my second piece of bad news about the relation of absolute music to the moral life, in the character-building sense.

So what's the good news? Simply that absolute music *does* have the effect that it does, of character-uplifting, consciousness-expanding described above; and to that extent, it can, as well, be described as morally uplifting. There is no evidence that this ecstatic, character-uplifting experience has any lasting effect at all on moral behavior or moral character in the long haul. Nor is it some mysterious, Orphic or Pythagorean quality that music alone possesses. (It is not the harmony of the spheres.) But never mind all of that. Music *does* possess it. And *while* you are experiencing its effect, *you* are the better for it, and so is the world. So we should forget about what absolute music can't be and cannot do, and thank God, or evolution for what it *can*.

The question, however remains: What more can we say about what I have characterized as the morally uplifting effect of absolute music, in its highest manifestations? And will it help us solve what I have been calling the "mystery" of absolute music? To these questions I turn in the next (and final) chapter.

11

Empty Pleasure to the Ear

Introduction

When the Council of Trent read the riot act to the composers of liturgical music and laid it upon them that "The whole plan of singing in musical modes should be constructed not to give *empty pleasure to the ear*, but in such a way that the words may be clearly understood by all . . . ," their admonition had, I believe, a double barb. Obviously, it was meant, first and foremost, to remind the composers that the experience of music in the Christian service was to be a *religious experience* for which the musical setting of the text was to be a means, not a *musical experience* as an end in itself. For, as the admonition continues, the end result of "singing in modes" is to be that "the hearts of the listeners be drawn to the desire of heavenly harmonies, in the contemplation of the joys of the blessed . . . ."[1]

But I said there was a double barb; and here is the second, not just a dig at music in the church that does not serve its purpose; rather, a dig, *wherever it is to be found*, at *music itself.*

What would one be hearing, as the Council of Trent saw it, if one were listening to pre-Tridentine polyphony in church: polyphony in which "the words may [*not*] be clearly understood by all . . ."? One would, for all intents and purposes, be hearing music alone: in other words, *absolute music.* And *that* kind of music, the Council avers, is an *empty* pleasure. Would it be fair to say a useless pleasure; a frivolous pleasure; a trivial pleasure; a mere diversion; a guilty pleasure, even; not worthy of a human being. In other words, implicit in the Council of Trent's admonition against music in the liturgical service that fails

---

[1] See supra, Chapter I, fn10.

to perform its proper function is a put down of music itself, even where it has no further function than just being *music*, because music is merely, in *just* being *music*, "an *empty* pleasure to the ear." And an empty pleasure is at best valueless, and more often harmful or even morally repugnant.

I am reminded here of the lines from Pope's *Essay on Criticism*, which, no doubt, the Council of Trent would have greeted with approbation:

> But most by Numbers judge a Poet's song;
> And smooth or rough, with them is right or wrong:
> In the bright Muse though thousand charms conspire,
> Her voice is all these tuneful fools admire;
> Who haunt Parnassus but to please the ear,
> Not mend their minds; as some to Church repair,
> Not for the doctrine, but the music there.[2]

To hear and to judge a poem merely by its "Numbers" is to hear it as sound without sense: as music, one might say, "to please the ear" but not to "mend" the mind, as "some to Church repair,/Not for the doctrine but the music there." So music is senseless "poetry": there are only the "numbers" to hear. It is what "tuneful fools admire": which is to say, "empty pleasure to the ear."

Are we mistaken in seeing here, in these two judgments, so widely separated in time and context, the same put down of pleasure for its own sake, and music without "sense," for providing only that? Well why should this surprise us? There is, after all, an ancient quarrel between philosophy and *pleasure*, as well as a long-standing fascination with it. And what seems to be developing here is the defense of absolute music, as defined, as a defense of "empty pleasure to the ear," and an explanation of *why* "empty pleasure to the ear" may be of as great importance for us as those pleasures and satisfactions that the philosophers compare it to so unfavorably. The conclusion of the previous chapter, remember, was that the experience of absolute music in its higher manifestations is the experience of a character-uplifting, consciousness-expanding kind that might, broadly speaking

---

[2] Alexander Pope, *An Essay on Criticism, Selected Works*, ed. Louis Kronenberger (New York: Random House, The Modern Library, 1951), 41.

at least, even be called a "moral" experience. If *that* experience is the experience of a species of "empty pleasure," perhaps there is more to be said for it than the Council of Trent understood. So let us now praise "empty pleasure to the ear."

Pleasure

What *is* "empty pleasure to the ear," as the Council of Trent applied it to music? To answer this question it would seem obvious that we would need to know what *pleasure* is, what an *empty* pleasure is, and what it would mean to be a pleasure *to the ear*. And the answer to the last is not as obvious as one might initially suppose.

To try to "define" the word "pleasure," in the philosophical sense of giving some sort of necessary and sufficient conditions, or a "conceptual analysis," would be, at this point in time, a mug's game. And, in any case, I certainly have nothing new to add to any such project. The concept of pleasure has been a subject of philosophical discussion from Plato to the present. And here is no place to embark on such troubled waters.

But there are a few obvious things to say. To begin with, we are not to think of "pleasure" as the name of some unique, identifiable feeling, or *qualia*, that is common to all the experiences we describe as pleasurable, the way, we might say, the sensation of "sweetness" is common to all our experiences of sweet things: a clearly identifiable sensation common to all instances.

That "pleasure" is not, like "sweetness," some unique, identifiable qualia is easily shown by simply enumerating some of the great variety of things and experiences that we say "give us pleasure," "pleasure us," or, more colloquially, that we say we "enjoy." I enjoy a cup of tea, a performance of *Hamlet*, my afternoon swim at Nobska beach, the solving of a problem, patting my neighbor's dog, a good meal, orgasm, the cessation of pain (as Plato so acutely observed in the *Phaedo*), the sounding of concert "A" by the oboe when tuning the orchestra, the overwhelming monumentality of the *Eroica* Symphony, and so on. To say that there is some single, identifiable sensation called "pleasure," common to all of these things and experiences, seems to me monstrously implausible.

As is well known to philosophers in general, ethicists in particular, Jeremy Bentham attempted to reduce all such pleasures or enjoyments as were listed above to a single quantifiable unit, so that the differences among them were simply to be cashed out in *quantity*, which, in the case of a presently experienced enjoyment or pleasure, was to be measured in terms solely of its *intensity* and its *duration*.[3] Thus, on Bentham's "hedonic calculus," the overwhelming ecstasy of my listening to the *Eroica* Symphony, and the pleasant sensation of my drinking a sweetened cup of Earl Grey tea differ only in the intensity and duration of some common hedonic unit. And such considerations led Bentham to coin the epigram, which either outrages or amuses depending upon your philosophical predilections, that, in principle, poetry is no better than push-pin (which one gathers was a popular but trivial game enjoyed in Bentham's time).[4]

Again, as is well known in philosophical circles, John Stuart Mill, recasting Bentham's hedonistic utilitarianism, insisted that the dimension of *quality* be added to the calculus of *duration* and *intensity*. "It would be absurd," he wrote, "that, while in estimating all other things quality is considered as well as quantity, the estimation of pleasure should be supposed to depend on quantity alone."[5] Which is to say that Mill thought "some kinds of pleasure are more desirable and more valuable than others."[6] And if the equation of push-pin with poetry is a paradox, or a *reductio ad absurdum* of Bentham's hedonic calculus, Mill's bringing of *quality* into the calculus was meant to save the day. For if a game of push-pin should produce the same intensity and duration of pleasure in one person as reading a fine poem does in another, there is always the higher quality of poetry-pleasure over push-pin-pleasure to achieve the sought-for conclusion that, *pace* Bentham, poetry *is* better than push-pin.

Mill's attempt to secure the dimension of quality for the hedonic calculus, and to secure the conclusion that the pleasures he favored *were*, on some objective standard, of higher quality than those he

---

[3] Jeremy Bentham, *The Principles of Morals and Legislation* (London, 1789), chapter IV, section ii.

[4] Traditionally attributed to Bentham, but I have know idea of the source.

[5] John Stuart Mill, *Utilitarianism*, ed. Oskar Piest (New York: Liberal Arts Press, 1957), 12.

[6] Ibid.

despised, is notorious for its logical difficulties and, in the end, general unconvincingness. But, fortunately, there is no need for us to cut through this logical thicket, or to find some way other than Mill's to establish his conclusion. For the fact is, I don't care much about his conclusion for present purposes (although I will return to it briefly later on).

My purpose here is not to provide an argument against the Benthamite's "skeptical" claim that playing push-pin is as good as listening to Beethoven's *Eroica* if it provides the same duration and intensity of pleasure to the push-pin player as the experience of the *Eroica* does for the musical enthusiast. And it is precisely to answer such a skeptic that Mill appeals to the higher *quality* of pleasure in the latter as opposed to the former. If push-pin produces the level of ecstasy in its enthusiasts that absolute music in the Western canon does for its, then so be it. My only aim is to defend this experience of moral ecstasy against the charge of its being "empty pleasure to the ear," in some pejorative sense, on the part of those who think sense must be added to sound to avoid the charge, not by denying that absolute music is an empty pleasure to the ear, but by pleading guilty to the charge, and defending empty pleasure to the ear against its detractors.

The purpose, then, of this brief encounter with the concept of pleasure—of which more anon—is to prevent us from reifying pleasure, and turning it into some kind of negotiable quantity of a hedonistic calculus. "Pleasure" is what we are experiencing in all of those instances enumerated above. And that is all we need to know, at present, about what pleasure *is*.

Empty Pleasure

What *is* an *empty* pleasure? Perhaps we could begin answering that question by asking what a *non-empty* pleasure might be.

It is clear that what the Council of Trent was opposing to empty pleasure to the ear was a pleasure that possessed religious content. And it is at least plausible to suggest that what Pope was contrasting with what when he contrasted those "Who haunt Parnassus but to please the ear" with those who haunt it to "mend their minds" was empty pleasure to the ear with a pleasure that possessed some *useful* conceptual content meant to have some beneficial effect—some "mending" effect—on the intellect of the reader of poems, or at least impart knowledge, even if of "What oft was thought but ne'er so well express'd...."[7]

But if what makes a pleasure *non-empty* is some kind of useful effect contained in the pleasurable experience, or resulting from it, a rather paradoxical conclusion follows for those who think that narrative content might, *of itself*, save absolute music from the charge of *merely* empty pleasure to the ear, and so of little account. For there is deep in the human psyche a desire for being told a story, either by listening or looking or reading, that has nothing to do with utility, whether intellectual or moral, that might accrue to the experience, but is indulged in for the pure pleasure of the story-telling. As Peter Lamarque and Stein Olsen put the point I am trying to make: "Those with knowledge of literature and a feel for the literary seek a special kind of pleasure from the works they read...; and *a pleasure that is not instrumental or utilitarian but a pleasure in the literary for its own sake.*"[8]

I am certainly not denying that some story-tellings are intended to have effects beyond the pleasure that story-telling affords. Some great works of literature express deep philosophical and moral theses that their audience is supposed to understand and think about—are meant to "mend the mind."[9] But others, some no less great, are "merely"—*merely?*—ripping good stories. And for reasons not fully understood, or perhaps even partially understood, the pleasure that human beings take in stories is very deep and abiding. But it affords nothing beyond itself; it is an "empty pleasure."

There is the irony. In trying to save absolute music from the charge of being an empty pleasure to the ear the narrativist has tried to make absolute music a story-telling, which turns out to be *another* empty pleasure. Furthermore, the way that story-telling can become

---

[7] Pope, *Essay on Criticism*, 40.

[8] Peter Lamarque and Stein Haugom Olsen, "The Philosophy of Literature: Pleasure Restored," *The Blackwell Guide to Aesthetics*, ed. Peter Kivy (Oxford: Blackwell, 2004), 211; italics mine.

[9] On this see, Peter Kivy, *The Performance of Reading: An Essay in the Philosophy of Literature*, sections 23–8.

a non-empty pleasure is by being a vehicle for the expression of deep moral and philosophical theses. And if understanding absolute music as a story-telling is a hard sell, which has been the argument of this book, understanding it as a story-telling capable of expressing deep moral and philosophical theses is going to be mission impossible.

Listening to stories then, and listening to absolute music, are turning out *both* to be empty pleasures. And if you think the empty pleasure of stories is a pretty damned important pleasure, why should you think it not so of the empty pleasure of listening to absolute music, at least when it is at the level that those deeply devoted to and deeply moved by the masterpieces of the absolute music canon can attest to?

But remember: the charge is that absolute music is an empty pleasure *to the ear*. What is the pleasure delivered by story-telling an empty pleasure *to*? Perhaps here we may find what makes the latter an *important* empty pleasure and the former not, if it really *is* no more than an *empty* pleasure.

Pleasure to . . .

To get right to the point, it might seem perfectly obvious that while absolute music is an empty pleasure to the ear, the experience of stories is an empty pleasure to the *mind*. And, *of course*, the philosophers will tell you, a mental pleasure is far superior to a pleasure to the ear, which is a "mere" pleasure of sense.

That experiencing stories is a pleasure to the mind I don't suppose requires a huge defense. A story has to be comprehended, understood, the sequence of events remembered, to be enjoyed. And it hardly needs saying that understanding, or comprehension, and memory are mental activities. Even when a story is told in the form of a play or a movie, as opposed to a silently read fictional work, where sights and sounds are part of the experience, the story, *qua* story, must be a pleasure to the mind; for whatever pleasures may accrue to the senses of sight and hearing in the experience, the story must be cognized to be experienced; and so the pleasure of the story-experience, the story-telling, is a mental pleasure.

But absolute music possesses no narrative content to be cognized by the mind. It is, as E. M. Forster described Beethoven's Fifth Symphony in *Howards End*, a "beautiful noise," thus a sense pleasure *merely*.[10] And, of course, Jimmy Legs has been down on "mere" pleasures of sense, as opposed to mental pleasures, in Western culture since time immemorial. He has been down on *empty* pleasure as well.

We shall get to the case against—and *for*—empty pleasures of all kinds later on. But we must first take a close look at the claim that absolute music is an empty pleasure to the sense and not the mind. For as I see things, it is plainly false.

Sounds, of course, pure and simple, may well be pleasures solely to the sense of hearing, as a sweet thing is to the palate. Thus the sound of the concert "A" of the oboe, tuning the orchestra, would be a pure pleasure to the auditory sense. There is nothing to *think* about; it is a simple sensation.

However, *music*, as opposed to individual sounds, is quite another matter. As I have argued at length in a previous book, *Music Alone*, music—at least the music of the classical Western canon, which is to say, the music under discussion here—is not merely a thing of the sense, but a thing of the mind as well. It required an entire book to argue this point; and I obviously cannot re-argue it again here. I will, though, take the liberty of quoting myself in an effort to give the reader the gist of what I was, and am maintaining. In *Music Alone*, "I . . . tried to show that our enjoyment of music alone [that is, absolute music] is of cognitively perceived musical sound. This is a conscious activity, and the music is not an uncognized stimulus to pleasure, like a drug or a tickle, but a cognitive object for us."[11]

Beethoven's Fifth Symphony is not just a "beautiful noise," like the chirping of a bird, the jangling of wind chimes, or the oboe's concert "A." It is a complex sound structure that is heard as a series of connected musical events. Listeners, of course, vary in their musical knowledge and musical experience, and so differ in the "intentional objects" of their music perception and appreciation. A musically educated listener will have as her intentional object when listening to the first movement of the mighty Fifth a tightly knit, monothematic movement

---

[10] Of course I am not attributing that view to the author. It is "said" by the narrative voice of the novel. And, anyway, it is something of a literary hyperbole.

[11] Peter Kivy, *Music Alone: Philosophical Reflections on the Purely Musical Experience*, 91.

in sonata form, and she will recognize the transformations of the opening motive as they occur throughout the movement. She will perceive that the Trio section of the Scherzo is a fugato, and hear it appropriately as such. And so on. Whereas a serious but musically uneducated music lover will perceive and appreciate an intentional object certainly like his musically educated companion's in many respects, and yet unlike it in that he will not, clearly, be able to perceive and appreciate it under descriptions such as "monothematic sonata form" or "fugato." Nevertheless, it will not be a "mindless" experience for him any more than it is for his more musically educated companion.

Perhaps there are—I have no doubt that there are—purely "mindless" listeners to the absolute music canon who hear it only as beautiful noise. But the point is that the serious music lover, trained or untrained or in between, as the case may be, listens to music, not noise, and listens to cognized musical events under whatever descriptions his or her musical concepts and vocabulary facilitate. And, therefore, absolute music, in the Western canon, no less than narrative fiction, is a *pleasure to the mind*.

Of course absolute music *is a pleasure to the ear*—a pleasure in hearing—and it would surely make no sense denying it in affirming that absolute music is a *pleasure to the mind*. Should we, then, construe the pleasure of absolute music as a combination of two different musical pleasures, one to the mind and one to the sense of hearing? I do not think that is the right way to go. It seems to bifurcate the pleasure in a way contrary to our actual experience of music. But nor am I really sure how we should construe the matter, and I do not want to spend time on it here. It will have to suffice for present purposes to say that the pleasure of absolute music is an *aural pleasure of the mind* and leave it at that.

The important point is that pleasure in absolute music, like pleasure in stories appreciated for their own sake, as stories, *is* a pleasure to the mind. So although both are *empty* pleasures, as defined above, fictional narrative does not have a value beyond that of absolute music because it produces empty pleasure to the mind, absolute music empty pleasure to sense. So if you think experiencing stories is an important part of human life, empty pleasure though it may be, there is no reason to think the experience of absolute music is *not* an important part of life too, empty pleasure though *it* may be, because it does not, like stories, constitute a pleasure to the mind. For it *does* provide pleasure to the mind, as I have argued above.

But now two objections loom. First of all, even if absolute music is an empty pleasure, in part, to the mind, it is, nevertheless, an *empty* pleasure. What then is it but "mere" sonic wallpaper; a "mere" decorative art.

And, second, that the pleasure taken in stories for their own sake is empty pleasure, in many people's minds in the past and present, is redeemed by its being empty pleasure taken in *stories*, in literary fiction, rather than in some other, less "worthy" activity, such as push-pin or, in Pope's eyes, reading poetry only for the numbers. If it has no intellectual payoff, if it doesn't, as Pope put it, mend the mind, then it is an idle pursuit, not worthy of an educated audience. This is not a "made up" objection. There is a long-standing indictment of pleasure taken in fiction—in "mere story-telling," that dates back at least to Plato. It is all one whether *empty* pleasure is derived from the mind or the senses. Jimmy Legs is down on empty pleasure *tout court*.

First, then, to the charge that if absolute music gives empty pleasure, even if to the mind as well as the sense, it then must be a "mere" decorative art, and so, of course, something of no account.

"Mere" Decoration

I have been arguing for many years that philosophers of art fail to realize, fail to accept how *different* absolute music is from the other fine arts. Since the end of the eighteenth century, when pure instrumental music came to be seen as one of the fine arts, it was, naturally, a philosophical imperative to find the common thread that connects it with the rest of the fine arts. The project was to figure out how they were *all the same*. So convinced did I become, at one point, of the gap between absolute music and the rest of the fine arts that I suggested it makes more sense to consider it not as a fine art at all but, rather, one of the decorative arts.[12]

---

[12] Peter Kivy, "Is Music an Art?," reprinted in Peter Kivy, *The Fine Art of Repetition* (Cambridge and New York: Cambridge University Press, 1993), 360–73.

Of course there are problems here. For one, Michelangelo "decorated" the ceiling of a chapel; but we would hardly call that "decorative art." Second, decorative art decorates *something*; some *thing*, but absolute music, as was once pointed out to me, does not decorate anything: it just is an entity in itself.

I am not very much troubled by either of these objections. As for the first, it is obviously possible for something to be both decorative and fine art at the same time, the Sistine Ceiling being a case in point. As is well known, fine art prior to the "modern system of the arts," was not produced, usually, to exist autonomously as self-contained objects whose sole purpose was to be contemplated in the "aesthetic attitude," but as objects in places, in environments, if you like; and the "decorations" of the Sistine Ceiling constitute just such an "object": a work of fine art and a work of decorative art in the same package. There is no problem in that.

As for the second objection, it is based on a false premise. A work of decorative art is decidedly not always a "decoration of . . . ." The cut crystal object resting on my desk is what is known as a "decorative object." Of course it can be thought of as decorating whatever it rests on: right now my desk, later my coffee table, if I choose to put it there. Thus I find no problem in thinking that a symphony decorates my aural space, wherever I happen to be hearing it. It too is a "decorative object." And just like the cut crystal object on my desk, it can be contemplated for itself, whatever it is "decorating."

I do not want to make, and argue for the claim that absolute music *is* a decorative art. I have no theory of my own about what fine art *is*. And so I do not have the philosophical means to distinguish *it* from decorative art in the first place. What I *do* intend is to rely on our intuitive notion of what decorative, as opposed to fine art is, and to explore the hypothesis that absolute music belongs to the former category.

The villain of the piece is Kant, whom the denigrators of musical formalism frequently allude to as both being a musical formalist, and expressing his formalism in terms of the view that absolute music is "sonic wallpaper," which, of course, is meant by the anti-formalists as the most obvious and devastating *reductio ad absurdum*. Kant was saying that the symphonies of Haydn and Mozart (none of which he was likely ever to have heard) were "mere" sonic wallpaper. (How silly can you get?) But you will recall from Chapter 2 that Kant's description, or rather, *analogy*, was "designs à la Grecque." And if you think of the kinds of decorations that adorn the walls of Rococo residences, palaces, and churches, which obviously is what Kant had in mind, "mere" seems hardly the appropriate way of describing them. When Kant spoke of the arts of decoration he spoke of them in no way disparagingly, nor should *we*.[13] But, of course, *in the West*, Jimmy Legs is down on the decorative arts as well as on empty pleasure.

But it is otherwise in the *East*. And I suggest to anyone who thinks of the decorative arts as "merely" decorative arts that they take a trip to Spain to look at the decoration that adorns the Moorish architecture. You might start in Granada, with the Alhambra. You will, however, have to get a ticket at least a month in advance. It seems to be a tourist attraction exceeding in popularity, for example, the Sistine Chapel, which requires for entrance merely a brief wait.

What is the viewer's reaction to the decorative arts displayed on the Alhambra's walls and ceilings and floors? My own reaction was one of awe, not unlike what I feel in the presence of a great work of absolute music, and one could feel as well as hear testimony to that same reaction among one's fellow visitors. It only trivializes absolute music by calling it a decorative art if you have in mind the wrong comparison class, which Westerners normally do. One might just as well denigrate "mere" representational art because you have in mind those paintings of girls with big eyes instead of the *Polish Rider*.

Hanslick, in comparing the progression of sounds in a musical composition to "the play of colour and shape in a kaleidoscope," writes: "The main difference between such a musical, audible kaleidoscope and the familiar visible one is that the former presents itself as the direct emanation of an artistically creative spirit, while the latter is no more than a mechanically ingenious plaything."[14] Of course, the contrast is between the chance arrangement of colored glass shards, one after the other, made into symmetrical patterns by the optics of the thing, and the rational, planned sequence of sounds by a thinking, creative

[13] See, Immanuel Kant, *Critique of Aesthetic Judgement*, trans. Meredith, 188 (§51).
[14] Hanslick, *On the Musically Beautiful*, trans. Payzant, 29.

human agent. But the contrast might be taken a step further to be between rationally constructed visual patterns, but by talentless hacks, "mere wallpaper," like the kind that decorates cheap motels, and the stirring patterns adorning the Alhambra, or the Alcazar, or a Rococo church, that make us gasp with wonderment, that "take our breath away," and seem to "emanate" not merely from an "artistically creative spirit" but an artistically creative spirit of *genius*. Why can there not be genius for abstract decoration, as there is for representational painting?

Stephen Davies describes some masterful games of chess that, in his words, "illustrate to a jaw-dropping degree the inexhaustible fecundity, flexability, insight, vitality, subtlety, complexity, and analytical far-reachingness of which the mind is capable."[15] But that is a perfect description, as well, of the experience of the Alhambra and Alcazar decorations. And for Davies it *also* describes his experience of the *Eroica* Symphony. For, as he observes, "in creating the very greatest music, composers display to an extraordinary degree many of the general cognitive capacities seen also in outstanding chess; namely, originality, far-sightedness, imagination, fertility, plasticity, refinement, intuitive mastery of complex detail, and so on."[16] And again, one can say the same, *mutatis mutandis*, of the Alhambra and Alcazar decorations, as well as other great examples of the decorative art.

When one experiences the *Eroica* Symphony, *or* the *Polish Rider*, *or* the Alhambra and Alcazar, one has, in one respect anyway, the *same* experience: the experience of being in the presence of creative *genius*. And about *that*, if I may take the liberty of quoting myself: "When we experience great works of art, we find ourselves unable to conceive how (by what means) such works could have been brought into being, and this engenders in us a sense of wonder, a sense of miracle that is a necessary part of our aesthetic experience."[17] That is the experience of genius. And the decorations of the Alhambra and Alcazar, no less than the *Eroica* Symphony, the *Polish Rider*, or *Hamlet*,

---

[15] Stephen Davies, "Profundity in Instrumental Music," *British Journal of Aesthetics*, 42 (2002), 351.

[16] Ibid., 351–2.

[17] Peter Kivy, *The Possessor and the Possessed: Handel, Mozart, Beethoven, and the Idea of Musical Genius*, 249.

produce in those susceptible that very experience. So it expresses no disrespect—it is not a put down—if we decide that the symphony is in the category of the first-named rather than of the other two. "Merely" is not in the equation.

I have been arguing in this section, that if one chooses the right comparison class of decorative art, namely that art in its highest manifestations, there is no reason to believe that it does not have the same ability to produce the kind of mind-uplifting ecstasy in the susceptible viewer that absolute music, in its highest manifestations, does in its appreciative audiences. Of course it does not follow from this that absolute music *is* a decorative art—merely that the experience of it is, in the way described, consistent with the hypothesis. Both are capable of producing a kind of experience that, in the preceding chapters, I have said might be rightly called, in a broad sense of the term, a "morally" uplifting experience. In the next section, then, I want to delve deeper into the experience so described.

The Religious Analogy

In a thought-provoking essay called "Art and the Aesthetic: The Religious Dimension," Nicholas Wolterstorff calls our attention to an aspect of Clive Bell's book, *Art*, that contemporary philosophers of art pretty much ignore. Concentrating almost entirely on Bell's well-known and much criticized "definition" of art, these philosophers, at least the ones in the Anglo-American tradition, pay short shrift to how diffused Bell's language is with *religious* overtones and allusions. "The language Bell uses here to develop his 'aesthetic' hypothesis," Wolterstorff points out, "carries unmistakable echoes of religious language; indeed it *is* religious language."[18]

I confess that I am as guilty as the rest in never having paid the attention due the religious (and metaphysical) aspects of Bell's reflections on art. But it is never too late to learn. And having been stimulated by Wolterstorff's remarks to return to Bell's *Art*, after years of neglect, I too have been struck by how similar Bell's descriptions are,

---

[18] Nicholas Wolterstorff, "Art and the Aesthetic: the Religious Dimension," *The Blackwell Guide to Aesthetics*, ed. Kivy, 326.

of what he calls the "aesthetic emotion," to traditional descriptions of religious and mystical experience. (Nor does Bell himself leave the connection unmade.) Furthermore, what strikes me about Bell's descriptions of his "aesthetic emotion" are how closely they resemble the kind of ecstatic experience of absolute music I have been trying to describe in the last and present chapter.

I am going to examine some of these descriptions in a moment. But before I do I must make a necessary stipulation.

I want my reader to assume with me, contrary to fact, for the sake of the argument, that the remarks of Bell that I am about to quote refer *solely* to absolute music, as defined in this book. They refer, as a matter of fact, to *all* of the arts, in Bell's text. And my own views with regard to art *tout court* are very different from Bell's in many respects. But as descriptions of the musical experience, where absolute music is concerned, they are, I believe, spot on. And so I am going to treat them here as exclusively descriptions of the absolute music experience.

Religion and art, Bell says (and for "art" read "absolute music") "have the power of transporting men to superhuman ecstasies...."[19] Or again: "The contemplation of pure [artistic] form leads to a state of extraordinary exaltation and complete detachment from the concerns of life...."[20] That art "is a means to a state of exaltation is unanimously agreed," Bell says; "and that it comes from the spiritual depths of man's nature is hardly contested."[21] "The appreciation of art is certainly a means to ecstasy...."[22] And so on.

What could be the cause of this exalting kind of experience that absolute music, in its highest manifestations, has the power to impart to its devotees? Bell seems to provide two explanations for it—and remember, he is talking about art *tout court*, and I merely about absolute music—and does not, so far as I can see, try to reconcile them. In any case, I will simply present them as separate theses, neither of which is original with him, having long histories in the literature. I will then go on to suggest that they *are* two parts of a unitary explanation which I will reject, or, at least, suggest is in want of any real evidence in its favor.

---

[19] Clive Bell, *Art*, 63.   [20] Ibid., 54.   [21] Ibid., 59.
[22] Ibid.

"Why do certain arrangements and combinations of form move us so strangely?" That is Bell's question. And he answers: "It seems to me possible, though by no means certain, that created form moves us so profoundly because it expresses the emotion of its creator."[23]

Many will recognize this as the good old—or perhaps bad old—"expression theory of art." In any case, it appears obvious that it alone does not, even if true, answer the question that Bell offers it as a response to. Why should the fact that the *Eroica* Symphony (say) expresses Beethoven's emotion cause it to produce in us the experience of ecstasy that Bell speaks of?

Well, if by "expression" is meant something like "produce in another," which self-expression theorists normally *do* mean, then Beethoven, presumably (according to Bell's explanation) experienced ecstasy in his creation and simultaneous contemplation of his symphony, and listening to the symphony reproduces that ecstasy—i.e. a token of the type—in us. But that simply pushes the question one step back without answering it. For we now want to ask: "What is it about the creation and contemplation of his *Eroica* Symphony that produced the ecstasy *in Beethoven?*"

What Bell next argues is that the ecstatic aesthetic experience, of which he has been speaking, is in the character of what is usually called a "religious experience," or, more generally, a "mystical experience," in which the subject comes to believe that some transcendent or ultimate "reality" is being directly revealed to him. As Bertrand Russell described it: "Belief in a reality quite different from what appears to the senses arises with irresistible force . . . ."[24] And in his classic study of the so-called "religious experience," William James wrote: "It is as if there were in the human consciousness a *sense of reality, a feeling of objective presence, a perception* of what we may call 'something there,' more deep and more general than any of the special 'senses' by which the current psychology supposes existent realities to be originally revealed."[25]

---

[23] Clive Bell, *Art*, 43.

[24] Bertrand Russell, "Mysticism and Logic," *Mysticism and Logic and Other Essays* (London: George Allen and Unwin, 1951), 19.

[25] William James, *The Varieties of Religious Experience: A Study in Human Nature* (New York: The Modern Library, 1929), 58.

It is just such a "religious" or, if you will, "mystical" experience of some ultimate, transcendental reality in terms of which Bell describes the experience of "aesthetic emotion," where he writes, for example: "There would be good reason for supposing that the emotions which artists feel in their moments of inspiration, that others feel in the rare moments when they see objects artistically, and that many of us feel when we contemplate works of art, are the same in kind. All would be emotions felt for reality revealing itself through pure form."[26] Or again, "we become aware of its essential reality, of the God in everything... Call it by whatever name you will, the thing I am talking about is that which lies behind the appearance of all things—that which gives all things their individual significance, the thing in itself, the ultimate reality."[27]

Bell is following here, as Wolterstorff points out, a tradition, "whether wittingly or not, I do not know," that goes as far back as the *Enneads* of Plotinus and Plato's *Symposium*.[28] Nor does the idea that music, in particular, provides a "window to the absolute" lack a tradition. It was well entrenched in Schopenhauer, as we have seen, and was the stock-in-trade of the German Romantics, with Beethoven's Fifth Symphony especially singled out as the metaphysical conduit.[29] But the question must surely arise as to *why* glimpsing the absolute, or thing in itself, or ultimate reality (whatever that may be) *should* produce the ecstatic state that the music lover can, in her finer moments, experience.

What Wolterstorff calls the "Christian story" of course has a reassuring answer to that question. For the Christian name of the ultimate reality is "God." And what, then, is revealed to us in the ecstatic, mystical experience is God and/or the heavenly kingdom. And if the Christian story is true, a glimpse of *that* is beyond price and should be capable of engendering ecstasy and then some.

But what if the Christian story is false, as I and many others believe? There remains at least the metaphysical story, which is to say, the story to the effect that what is revealed by the ecstatic musical experience

---

[26] Bell, *Art*, 46. [27] Ibid., 54.

[28] Wolterstorff, "Art and the Aesthetic: The Religious Dimension," 328.

[29] On this see Bonds, *Music as Thought*.

is ultimate metaphysical reality: the thing in itself behind the mere experiences of the phenomenal world. Well, let it be remembered that ultimate reality, the thing in itself, bears the appearance of the Lisbon earthquake and the Holocaust. So why a glimpse of *it* should cause anything but horror and revulsion is beyond my comprehension. That the reality behind those ghastly events should cause *ecstasy* in the music lover (unless a hardened sadist) seems hard to credit.

So if the secularist is going to reject the Christian story, as I do, and if the analytic philosopher, or just plain common sense, is going to reject the metaphysical story, as I do, what is left? Of course what is left is what we started with: a kind of aesthetic ecstasy which takes as its intentional object absolute music at its highest manifestations, and the common sense conviction that the perception of the music is the source of the ecstatic experience, whether or not there comes with it a "feeling" of communication with a "reality" beyond, for a "feeling" is all there is to it.

But we are *also* left with the same old question: *Why* and *how* does absolute music do this? We seem to be back where we started.

Well not *exactly* back where we started. We do, after all, have a better idea than we did at the end of Chapter 10 about what *kind* of pleasurable experience we are talking about when we talk about the "pleasure" afforded by absolute music, and a better idea to what the "pleasure" appeals, which is to say, not merely an empty pleasure to the ear but to the mind as well, and a pleasure of such significant intensity that it has been compared with the experience of the mystic and the religious ecstatic.

However, we are still no closer to really understanding how absolute music can have this effect on those of us who are susceptible. Malcolm Budd saw no mystery in it and thought that whatever explanation those who *do* find it a mystery, as do I, are really yearning for is a psychological explanation that is yet, if ever, to come. I think there *is* more to it than psychology. But the bad news is that I do not know *what* more. In other words, I am going to leave you (and me) *with* the mystery.

What I can do, and will try to do, in the final sections of this chapter (and of this book) is to argue that a lot of the animosity directed against the formalist position on absolute music is motivated and nurtured by the age-old prejudice in the West *against* "empty pleasure" as a worthwhile pursuit: as a pursuit worthy of the enlightened human life. And, furthermore, I will put up what defense I can *for* "empty pleasure to the ear" (and mind). There is a kind of "utilitarian Puritanism," if I may so put it, at work here, which needs to be exposed and extirpated.

Pleasure Again

The doctrine of Epicurus, in the *Letter to Menoeceus*, is familiar to everyone with even a tincture of philosophy. It reads: "we recognize pleasure as the first good innate in us, and from pleasure we begin every act of choice and avoidance, and to pleasure we return again, using the feeling as the standard by which we judge every good."[30] The doctrine, of course, is ethical (and psychological) hedonism, and in one form or another it has played a prominent role in the history of ethical theory. If it were true, pleasure, even empty pleasure to the ear (and mind) would hardly need a defense. It would be the only game in town. "The art of music," says Mill, "is good for the reason, among others, that it produces pleasure; but what proof is it possible to give that pleasure is good?"[31] Pleasure is pleasure, no matter what its source; and that absolute music, in its higher manifestations, gives the depth and intensity of pleasure that it does, to its devotees, is all the defense it needs against any *other* pleasure, whether of the mind or of sense or of both. Push-pin *is* as good as poetry, if it delivers the goods (which I doubt)—and so too would be absolute music.

I am no ethical or psychological hedonist. I believe neither that pleasure is the only good nor the only human motivational force. I surely believe, with Aristotle, "that pleasure is not the Good...";[32] and I believe with him, as well, "that happiness must contain an element of pleasure...."[33]

---

[30] Epicurus, *Epicurus to Menoeceus*, *Ethical Theories: A Book of Readings*, ed. A. I. Melden (New York: Prentice Hall, 1950), 115.

[31] Mill, *Utilitarianism*, 7.

[32] Aristotle, *Nicomachean Ethics*, trans. H. Rackham (Cambridge, Mass.: Harvard University Press; and London: William Heineman, 1962), 591 (X.iii.3).

[33] Ibid., 613 (X.vii.3).

Whether Aristotle would have thought the pleasure of absolute music a superior pleasure because of its source is a nice question. Was there anything comparable to the tradition of Western absolute music in Aristotle's culture? In one place in the *Nicomachean Ethics* he does indeed refer to "the pleasure afforded by the music of the flute . . . ," but gives no indication there whether he considered it one of the higher pleasures.[34] And the pleasurable activity he praises to the skies, at the end of the *Ethics*, not altogether consistent, some think, with what has gone before, is "philosophy or the pursuit of wisdom [which] contains pleasures of marvelous purity and permanence . . . ."[35]

Shall we defend the pleasure of absolute music as being pleasure of a higher *quality* than the pleasure of push-pin? That is a dangerous path to tread, as we know from Mill's much-criticized attempt to provide a standard by which the qualities of pleasures might be adjudged "higher" or "lower."

Aristotle, in the above-quoted passage, praises the pleasures consequent upon the pursuit of wisdom as being pure and permanent, and a little later on in terms of "self-sufficiency," since its pursuit "requires [only] the necessaries of life . . . ."[36] Of course times have changed; and the pursuit of *scientific* wisdom, anyway, requires far more than the "necessaries of life," as anyone knows who has observed a scientist in the throes of writing up a grant proposal or trying to get lab space from her university. And as for purity, I am not very clear about what Aristotle means by it or why it should be praiseworthy. (Does he mean there is, in "pure" pleasure, no admixture of pain?)

Permanence may well be a praiseworthy quality for a pleasurable activity to possess. It would be comforting to know that at least the "wholesome" activities that now pleasure me will continue to do so in the years to come. But physical and mental decline aside, there seems little reason to think that if you enjoy push-pin more than Pushkin in your maturity, that will not be the case in your old age as well.

[34] Aristotle, *Nicomachean Ethics*, 601 (X.v.314). Actually Aristotle uses the example of flute music to illustrate how something can distract someone from study. But he gives no indication that he thinks the pleasure of flute music is a low or unworthy pleasure, although we can be sure he thought the pleasure in study superior.

[35] Ibid., 613 (X.vii.3).   [36] Ibid., 615 (X.vii.4).

Aristotle, at least at the end of the *Nicomachean Ethics*, was firmly defending the intellectual pleasures, although throughout the earlier parts of the book the active pleasures were highly touted. Would Aristotle have considered the pleasures of absolute music, in its highest manifestations, "intellectual pleasures," if he were alive today to enjoy them? Well, not to the extent that they are empty pleasures *to the ear*. But they are not, so I have argued here and elsewhere, *mindless pleasures*. Yet whether the kind of intellectual activity involved in following a complex fugue or a tightly constructed symphonic movement would have satisfied Aristotle's requirements for a thing intellectual is a matter, obviously, of sheer conjecture.

All in all then, I would not like to try to argue for the higher quality of pleasure in absolute music over push-pin or its equivalent along Aristotelian lines. But what about Mill's, shall we say, more "democratic" standard for hedonic quality?

Mill proposed, as is well known, the following standard for judging the quality of pleasures:

> If I am asked what I mean by difference of quality in pleasures, or what makes one pleasure more valuable than another, merely as pleasure, except its being greater in amount, there is but one possible answer. Of two pleasures, if there be one to which all or almost all who have experience of both give a decided preference, irrespective of any feeling of moral obligation to prefer it, that is the more desirable pleasure.[37]

Taking the word "desirable," over which a great fuss has been made by interpreters of Mill, to mean something like "worthy of desire," I read Mill as saying that if all or most people who have experienced the pleasures of push-pin and the pleasures of absolute music in its highest manifestations prefer the pleasures of absolute music to the pleasures of push-pin, the former pleasures are more worthy of desire, or, in other words, are of higher quality.

But can this really be the standard of quality? Surely not, without begging the question in favor of the outcome one wants. A "vote," even if the voters have experienced both the pleasures of push-pin and the pleasures of absolute music, cannot decide the question of which

---

[37] Mill, *Utilitarianism*, 12.

pleasures are more desirable, unless "desirable" is taken (mistakenly) to mean "able to be desired," "susceptible of desire," which Mill has frequently been accused of doing. If "desirable" is taken in the evaluative sense of "worthy of desire," as I think it must, then a vote cannot decide the issue of which pleasures are the more "desirable." Only an argument can do that, if anything can. Mill has apparently taken the "able" of "desirable" as equivalent to the "ible" of such words as "visible" and "audible," which of course bear no value implications at all. Obviously if most people see something, it is visible, if most people hear something it is audible; but if most people desire it, nothing follows about its desirability.

In any case, I have no wish to defend the pleasures of absolute music on grounds of their supposed higher quality. Whatever my intuitions on the matter, I shall simply assume that pleasure is pleasure; and *it* is its own defense, when the impediments to its rightful place in our lives are removed.

Pleasure's Prerogative

I referred previously to what I called a kind of puritanical utilitarianism with regard to empty pleasure to the ear (and to everything else). Let me begin to explain what I mean with an example.

Not too long ago a "finding" was reported in the *New York Times* to the effect that listening to the music of Mozart, prior to taking an examination (that had something to do with geometry), improved the scores of the listeners over non-listeners. Why Mozart? Why classical music? Would the choice of music have made a difference? How about Bach, for instance? Such questions were never broached. But what was crystal clear from the reportage was the message that now at last we had a plausible reason to think listening to Mozart's music a good thing, to be encouraged among the youth (at least at examination time). We *finally* found a *use* for the stuff: it makes us smarter (or at least better at taking certain kinds of examinations). All this fuss about Mozart was *finally* vindicated. We found the utilitarian payoff.

Obviously this is just another instance of the well-established truth that there is nothing, no matter how silly, that someone will not eventually attribute to absolute music in its cause. (Who needs enemies with friends like these?) But it is also an example of the *kind* of thing that well-meaning and in many cases highly intelligent thinkers attribute to the absolute music experience, which is to say, use, or some other non-musical payoff. There is a kind of Gradgrindian mentality at work here that must find a utility or a lesson in every innocent pleasure, pleasure itself not being enough, perhaps a waste of time, worse still harmful in some way or, at least the product of mere "amusement," which Aristotle described as "a form of rest," necessary "because we are not able to go on working without a break, and therefore . . . not an end, since we take it as a means to further activity."[38]

How deep, pervasive, and current this desperate need to "save" pleasure from the charge of emptiness or uselessness really is was brought home to me yet again, recently, in reading a charming and insightful article in which the author analyzes and extols what she calls "the aesthetic in ordinary experience," arguing that "our everyday lives have an aesthetic character that is thoroughgoing and available at every moment, should we choose to attend to it."[39]

Here are some of what might well be described as "innocent aesthetic pleasures," that the author has in mind:

I drink tea out of a large mug that is roughly egg-shaped, and clasp it with both hands to warm my palms. When I am petting my cat, I crouch over his body so that I can smell his fur, which at different places smells like trapped sunshine or roasted nuts, a bit like almonds but not quite. I scratch my head with a mechanical pencil that allows me to part my hair and reach exactly the right spot on my scalp. I move my wedding ring back and forth over the knuckle that offers it slight resistance, and jiggle it around in my right palm to enjoy its weight before sliding it back on.[40]

"Empty" pleasure, if ever there was such a thing, one would think; and surely "innocent" pleasure into the bargain.

Yet even stroking your cat somehow needs justification; some payoff beyond the pleasure it affords, "innocent" though that pleasure

---

[38] Aristotle, *Nicomachean Ethics*, 611 (X.vi.6).
[39] Sherri Irvin, "The Pervasiveness of the Aesthetic in Ordinary Experience," *British Journal of Aesthetics*, 48 (2008), 30.
[40] Ibid., 31.

may seem, because in fact, if it *is* "empty" pleasure, how then can it be "innocent" pleasure? And, not surprising, the defense offered is a moral one. "The aesthetic aspects of everyday life take on obvious moral relevance insofar as they affect my tendency to do or pursue what is morally good."[41] More specifically: "If we can learn to discover and appreciate the aesthetic character of [ordinary] experiences that are already available to us, perhaps we will be less inclined to think that we must acquire new goods that make different experiences available. Perhaps we can discover that we already have enough, or even more than we need, to be satisfied; and this might make room for giving something—time, energy, or money away."[42] And so on.

The possible connection between moral improvement and such ordinary aesthetic pleasures (if aesthetic they are) as stroking your cat or feeling the warmth of a tea mug, seems, to say the least, tenuous and strained; all the more reason to wonder why it is posed at all. The answer is that no matter how innocent and trivial a pleasure may be, if it is an "empty" pleasure, it cannot be abided. There must be a payoff. Had the Council of Trent considered the stroking of cats, I have no doubt there would have been an interdict forthcoming if the pleasure were not productive of religious or moral sentiment.

But I wonder if a music lover, untainted by philosophy, would not intuitively feel that someone who was looking for a use or a lesson or other practical payoff in Mozart's instrumental music was somehow "missing the point." One has first to have an ax to grind before such an obvious source of the deepest human satisfaction requires for it some further utilitarian justification.

Epicurus thought pleasure the *only* unqualified human good. Aristotle quite rightly denied this. But he nevertheless thought quite rightly that it was *a* human good, and a pretty important one at that, since a requirement for happiness. Has there ever been a philosopher who has denied that pleasure is at least *a* human good? Does the claim require a defense (except perhaps for some kind of religious ascetic or mortifier of the flesh)?

Of course the word "pleasure" is a word of such general signification, particularly in the mouths of philosophical hedonists, that it has

---

[41] Irvin, "Pervasiveness of the Aesthetic," 41.   [42] Ibid., 42.

become a rather "pallid" appellation, which is to say "pleasant." It was a real *pleasure* to take a warm bath after a *pleasant* walk in the park on a chilly afternoon. Ho Hum! Is *that* how I want to describe my experience of Bach's monumental organ prelude and fugue in E flat, known as the "Saint Ann"? A pleasant prelude followed by a pleasurable fugue?

The problem is, I would suppose, that philosophical hedonism has appropriated the pleasure word to cover every satisfaction or positive experience, from the sublime to the trivial. It has lost its pre-theoretical meaning and become a term of art. As a term of art, it then becomes applicable both to the experience of a warm bath *and* to the experience of a monumental prelude and fugue by a transcendent genius.

What we need to do is to rescue the experience of absolute music from the clutches of that damning word "pleasure." In the ordinary sense of the word, the experience of absolute music, in its highest manifestations, is *not* a "pleasure." It is, as I have described it in this chapter, and in the previous two, a transporting experience. It is of the depth and intensity frequently characterized as comparable to the kind of ecstasy described by mystics and those who believe they have had what is called a "religious experience." In short, it is orders of magnitude beyond what the pallid word pleasure conjures up, in its ordinary, pre-systematic use.

Furthermore, if one wants to call the above described musical ecstasy a "pleasure," then one might well argue that its very intensity and depth entitle it to be called a pleasure of higher *quality* than the pleasure of push-pin. For it is common usage and common sense to describe things that exceed the norm to a high enough degree as having achieved a higher "quality" in a pre-systematic meaning of *that* word. To instance a case in point, artistic creativity comes in varying degrees; but *beyond* a certain point we call it "genius."[43] I mention this as an aside, as I do not wish to re-introduce the flap over the quality of pleasure. It has caused enough trouble, and there is no need for it in my defense of *musical* pleasure. *Degree* will suffice.

My defense is simplicity itself. The feeling of ecstasy, exaltation, passionate enthusiasm, or however you want to characterize it, that

---

[43] On this see, Peter Kivy, *The Possessor and the Possessed*, 251–4.

absolute music in its highest manifestations calls forth in its devotees, is of an intrinsic worth beyond price, and during the time one is experiencing it one is, on that account, a better person. It may not have a lasting effect, or motivate one to noble acts. In fact, as I have argued in Chapter 10, I do not think that the musical emotion, of which I speak, does motivate, or have a lasting effect on human character. That, however, is beside the point; for as Robert Solomon observes: "It is tempting for philosophers (with an ax to grind) to say that what makes love and other feelings admirable is their consequences, the fact that they tend to result in morally good actions . . . [B]ut the worth of our feelings does not just depend on the desirability of any resultant actions or their consequences."[44]

The experience of absolute music, as above described, needs no defense or is its own defense, if one puts aside what I have called the pervasive mentality of the puritanical utilitarian who requires some kind of practical payoff for every human experience or activity. There is nothing *wrong* with empty pleasure to the ear (and mind) that absolute music affords in such depth and abundance. There is nothing *wrong* with absolute music affording that and nothing more. There is everything *right* with it. And what the musical Gradgrinds offer us as the supposed extra-musical payoff of absolute music is too poor a stuff to make *anything* worthwhile that isn't worthwhile to begin with. If absolute music is not worthwhile *without it*, it is not worthwhile *with it*. But it *is* worthwhile without it because it affords a deep, satisfying, even exalting experience; and such experience is not and need not to be a means to something else; it is an end in itself, as all pleasure is, in the broad (philosopher's) sense of the word. Nor, for the matter of that, does the pleasure of push-pin need a defense. And the only defense one can put up for absolute music over push-pin is the depth and intensity of the experience that its devotees undergo. Their credibility is enhanced, of course, if they have had the push-pin experience as well, with which to compare it; and that perhaps is what reasonably remains of Mill's insistence that the arbiter of quality in pleasure is the one who has been on both sides of the tracks.

---

[44] Solomon, *Spirituality for the Skeptic*, 34.

But what of the push-pin player who experiences the absolute music canon and *still* opts for push-pin? What can we say further to him? We can, of course, continue to talk with him, and continue to press upon him the virtues of the musical experience. If, however, you are looking for a knock-down argument, à la Mill, to *prove*—whatever that might mean in the present case—the superiority of the musical experience to the push-pin one, I don't think there is such an argument; and I think we should just learn to live with that. If you can't live contentedly with human diversity, at least of the harmless (and slightly amusing) variety, even if you are convinced as I would be that it is human *perversity*, you are not going to be a happy camper. One need not *defend* absolute music against push-pin, or the narrative and representational arts, for that matter. For those who have experienced its ecstatic effects, *that* is all the defense it needs, or can ever have, push-pin notwithstanding.

There is, however, a debt outstanding, a promissory note to be paid. Where is the *explanation* for the power absolute music, in its highest manifestations, has over its devotees? Alas, in the event, I have none to offer. I know what the explanation is *not*. It is not its narrative content, or its dramatic content, or any other literary content that it has been said from time to time to possess. For me, its power over us remains a divine mystery. Or, in other words, I haven't the foggiest.

What I *do* know, by direct acquaintance, is the deep, powerful, ecstatic effect absolute music has on me, and, by description, on others who have experienced and described it. It may not be, I am sure it is not, an enduring moral force in the world, or a revelation of a deeper reality. But it sure is great while it lasts. And if it makes us better in the moment, by affecting us in the way that it does, well, that is more than can be said for most human experience, and more than enough to justify the esteem in which it is held.

Absolute music may not be the savior of the world. But what is?

Bibliography

Ambros, Wilhelm August, *Die Grenzen der Musik und Poesie: Eine Studie zur Aesthetic der Tonkunst* (Leipzig: H. Matthes, 1855).

____ *The Boundaries of Music and Poetry: A Study in Musical Aesthetics*, trans. J. H. Cornell (New York: G. Schirmer, 1893).

Aristotle, *Nicomachean Ethics*, trans. H. Rackham (Cambridge, Mass.: Harvard University Press; and London: William Heineman, 1962).

____ *On Poetry and Music*, trans. S. H. Butcher (Indianapolis and New York: Bobbs-Merrill, 1956).

____ *The Poetics*, trans. W. Hamilton Fyfe (Cambridge, Mass.: Harvard University Press; London: William Heinemann, 1953).

Arnheim, Rudolph, *Film as Art* (Berkeley: University of California Press, 1957).

Avison, Charles, *An Essay on Musical Expression*. 3rd edn. (London, 1775).

Bell, Clive, *Art* (New York: Capricorn Books, 1958).

Bentham, Jeremy, *The Principles of Morals and Legislation* (London, 1789).

Bernstein, Lawrence F., " 'Singende Seele' or unsingbar? Forkel, Ambros, and the Forces Behind the Ockeghem Reception during the Late 18th and early 19th Centuries," *The Journal of Musicology*, 23 (2006).

Bonds, Mark Evan, *Music as Thought: Listening to the Symphony in the Age of Beethoven* (Princeton: Princeton University Press, 2006).

Bouwsma, O. K., *Philosophical Essays* (Lincoln: University of Nebraska Press, 1969).

Braunbehrens, Volkmar, *Maligned Master: The Real Story of Antonio Salieri*, trans. Eveline L. Kanes (New York: Fromm International Publishing Company, 1992).

Brown, Malcolm Hamrick (ed.), *A Shostakovich Casebook* (Bloomington, Indiana: Indiana University Press, 2005).

Buch, Esteban, *Beethoven's Ninth: A Political History*, trans. Richard Miller (Chicago: University of Chicago Press, 2004).

Budd, Malcolm, *Values of Art: Pictures, Poetry and Music* (London: Penguin Books, 1998).

Carroll, Noel, *A Philosophy of Mass Art* (Oxford: Clarendon Press, 1998).

____ "Art and Mood: Preliminary Notes and Conjectures," *The Monist*, 86 (2003).

Carroll, Noel, *Theorizing the Moving Image* (Cambridge: Cambridge University Press, 1996).

Carter, Tim, "Two Monteverdi Problems, and Why They Matter," *The Journal of Musicology*, 19 (2002).

Cone, Edward T., *The Composer's Voice* (Berkeley, Los Angeles, London: University Of California Press, 1974).

Cuneo, Terence, and Renė van Woudenberg (eds.), *The Cambridge Companion to Thomas Reid* (Cambridge: Cambridge University Press, 2004).

Danto, Arthur C., *Analytical Philosophy of Action* (Cambridge: Cambridge University Press, 1973).

—— "The Artworld," *Journal of Philosophy*, 61 (1964).

—— *The Transfiguration of the Commonplace: A Philosophy of Art* (Cambridge, Mass.: Harvard University Press, 1981).

Davies, Stephen, *Musical Meaning and Expression* (Ithaca, New York: Cornell University Press, 1994).

—— "Profundity in Music," *British Journal of Aesthetics*, 42 (2002).

Eggebrecht, Hans-Heinrich, *J. S. Bach's "Art of Fugue": The Work and its Interpretation*, trans. Jeffrey L. Prater (Ames, Iowa: Iowa State University Press, 1993).

Einstein, Alfred, *Gluck* (London: Dent, 1954).

Empson, William, *Seven Types of Ambiguity*. 2nd edn. (London: Windus, 1947).

Fest, Joachim, *Inside Hitler's Bunker: The Last Days of the Third Reich*, trans. Margot Bettauer Dembo (New York: Peter Strauss and Giroux, 2004).

Gluck, Christoph Willibald, *The Collected Correspondence of Christoph Willibald Gluck*, trans. Stewart Thomson, eds. Hedwig and E. H. Mueller von Asow (New York: St. Martin's Press, 1962).

Hanslick, Eduard, *On the Musically Beautiful: A Contribution towards the Revision of Of the Aesthetics of Music*, trans. Geoffrey Payzant (Indianapolis: Hackett, 1986).

—— *The Beautiful in Music*, trans. Gustav Cohen, ed. Morris Weitz (New York: The Liberal Arts Press, 1957).

—— *Vom Musikalisch Schönen: Ein Beitrag zur Revision der Aesthetik der Tonkunst*, 20th edn. (Wiesbaden: Breitkopf & Härtel, 1980).

Haweis, H. R., *Music and Morals*, 15th edn. (London: W. H. Allen, 1888).

Hegel, G. W. F., *Lectures on the Fine Arts*, trans. T. M. Knox, 2 vols. (Oxford: Clarendon Press, 1975).

Hodges, Sheila, *Lorenzo Da Ponte: The Life and Times of Mozart's Librettist* (Madison, Wisconsin: University of Wisconsin Press, 2002).

Hume, David, *Inquiry Concerning Human Understanding*, ed. Eric Steinberg. 2nd edn. (Indianapolis and Cambridge: Hackett, 1993).

Irvin, Sherri, "The Pervasiveness of the Aesthetic in Ordinary Life," *The British Journal of Aesthetics*, 48 (2008).

James, William, *The Varieties of Religious Experience: A Study in Human Nature* (New York: Random House, The Modern Library, 1929).

Kant, Immanuel, *Anthropology from a Pragmatic Point of View*, trans. Mary J. Gregory (The Hague: Martinus Nijhoff, 1974).

_____ *Critique of Aesthetic Judgement*, trans. James Creed Mereditih (Oxford: Clarendon Press, 1911).

_____ *Critique of Judgment*, trans. J. H. Bernard (New York: Hafner, 1951).

_____ *Critique of Judgment*, trans. Werner S. Pluhar (Indianapolis: Hackett, 1987).

_____ *Critique of the Power of Judgment*, trans. Paul Guyer and Eric Matthews (Cambridge: Cambridge University Press, 2001).

_____ *Kritik der Urteilskraft* (Hamburg: Felix Meiner Verlag, 1959).

Kerman, Joseph, *The Beethoven Quartets* (New York: Alfred A. Knopf, 1967).

Keneally, Thomas, *Schindler's Ark* (London: Hodder and Stoughton, 1982).

Kivy, Peter, "Critical Study: Deeper than Emotion," *British Journal of Aesthetics*, 46 (2006).

_____ *Music Alone: Philosophical Reflections on the Purely Musical Experience* (Ithaca, New York: Cornell University Press, 1990).

_____ *New Essays on Musical Understanding* (Oxford: Clarendon Press, 2001).

_____ "On the Banality of Literary Truth," *Philosophic Exchange*, 28 (1998).

_____ *Osmin's Rage: Philosophical Reflections on Opera, Drama, and Text*. 2nd edn. (Ithaca, New York, and London: Cornell University Press, 1999).

_____ *Philosophies of Arts: An Essay in Differences* (Cambridge: Cambridge University Press, 1997).

_____ *Sound Sentiment: An Essay on the Musical Emotions* (Philadelphia: Temple University Press, 1989).

_____ *The Corded Shell: Reflections on Musical Expression* (Princeton: Princeton University Press, 1980).

_____ *The Fine Art of Repetition: Essays in the Philosophy of Music* (Cambridge and New York: Cambridge University Press, 1993).

_____ *The Performance of Reading: An Essay in the Philosophy of Literature* (Oxford: Blackwell, 2006).

_____ *The Possessor and the Possessed: Haydn, Mozart, Beethoven, and the Idea of Musical Genius* (New Haven: Yale University Press, 2001).

Kivy, Peter (ed.), *Essays in the History of Aesthetics* (Rochester: Rochester University Press, 1992).

Kivy, Peter (ed.), *The Blackwell Guide to Aesthetics* (London: Blackwell, 2004).

Lamarque, Peter, and Stein Haugom Olsen, *Truth, Fiction, and Literature: A Philosophical Perspective* (Oxford: Clarendon Press, 1994).

Le Huray, Peter, *Authenticity in Performance: Eighteenth-Century Case Studies* (Cambridge: Cambridge University Press, 1990).

Le Huray, Peter, and James Day (eds.), *Music and Aesthetics in the Eighteenth and Early-Nineteenth Centuries* (Cambridge: Cambridge University Press, 1981).

Lessing, Gotthold Ephraim, *Laocoon: An Essay upon the Limits of Painting and Poetry*, trans. Ellin Frothingham (New York: Noonday Press, 1957).

Levinson, Jerrold, *Music, Art and Metaphysics: Essays in Philosophical Aesthetics* (Ithaca, New York: Cornell University Press, 1990).

Melden, A. I. (ed.), *Ethical Theories: A Book of Readings* (New York: Prentice-Hall, 1950).

Mill, John Stuart, *Utilitarianism*, ed. Oskar Piest (New York: Liberal Arts Press, 1957).

Mozart, Wolfgang Amadeus, *Letters of Mozart and His Family*, trans. Emily Anderson, 3 vols. (London: Macmillan, 1938).

Plato, *The Dialogues of Plato*, trans. B. Jowett, 2 vols. (New York: Random House, 1937).

—— *The Republic of Plato*, trans. Francis MacDonald Cornford (New York and Oxford: Oxford University Press, 1960).

—— *The Republic of Plato*, trans. John Llewelyn Davies and David James Vaughan (London: Macmillan, 1950).

Pope, Alexander, *Selected Works*, ed. Louis Kronenberger (New York: Random House, The Modern Library, 1951).

Randel, Don Michael (ed.), *The Harvard Dictionary of Music* (Cambridge, Mass.: Harvard University Press, 1978).

Reese, Gustave, *Music in the Renaissance* (New York: Norton, 1954).

Robinson, Jenefer, *Deeper than Reason: Emotion and its Role in Literature, Music, And Art* (Oxford: Clarendon Press, 2005).

Robinson, Jenefer (ed.), *Music and Meaning* (Ithaca, New York: Cornell University Press, 1997).

Rothenberg, David R., "The Marian Symbolism of Spring, ca. 1200–1500: Two Case Studies," *Journal of the American Musicological Society*, 59 (2006).

Russell, Bertrand, *Mysticism and Logic and Other Essays* (London: George Allen & Unwin, 1951).

Santayana, George, *The Sense of Beauty* (New York: Random House, The Modern Library, 1955).

Schenker, Heinrich, "The Spirit of Musical Technique," trans. William Pastille, *Theoria*, 3 (1988).

Schmieder, Wolfgang, *Thematisch-systematisches Verzeichnis der Musikalischen Werke von Johann Sebastian Bach* (Leipzig: Breitkoph und Härtel, 1950).

Schopenhauer, Arthur, *The World as Will and Representation*, trans. E. F. J. Payne, 2 vols. (Indian Hills, Colorado: The Falcon's Wing Press, 1958).

_____ *The World as Will and Idea*, trans. R. B. Haldane and J. Kemp, 4th edn. (London: Kegan Paul, Trench, Trübner, 1896).

Schroeder, David P., *Haydn and the Enlightenment: The Late Symphonies and their Audience* (Oxford: Clarendon Press, 1990).

Shostakovich, Dmitri, *Testimony: The Memoirs of Dmitri Shostakovich*, trans. Antonina Bouis, ed. Solomon Volkov (New York: Harper & Row, 1979).

Solomon, Robert, *Spirituality for Skeptics: The Thoughtful Love of Life* (Oxford: Oxford University Press, 2002).

Strunk, Oliver (ed.), *Source Readings in Music History* (New York: Norton, 1950).

Sullivan, J. W. N., *Beethoven: His Spiritual Development* (New York: Vintage Books, 1960).

Szpilman, Wladyslaw, *The Pianist*, trans. Anthea Bell (New York: Picador, 1999).

Thayer, Alexander Wheelock, *The Life of Ludwig van Beethoven*, 2 vols. (Carbondale, Illinois: Southern Illinois University Press, 1960).

Uehling, Theodore E, Jr., *The Notion of Form in Kant's "Critique of Aesthetic Judgment"* (The Hague: Mouton, 1971).

Index

aboutness 168–70
absolute music 17–18, 70–1
  and aboutness 168–70
  and agency 132, 133–4, 136–9, 140–2, 147–9
  as agreeable art 47–9
  appeal, explanation of 120
  and behavior 132, 135–6, 224–5
  as decorative art 244–8
  definition of 170–2
  and emotions 99
  as empty pleasure 242, 243–4
  existence of 155–6, 157–8
  expression theory of 19
  as fine art 30–6, 41–2, 47–8, 49, 183–4
  and garden-variety emotions 84, 88, 98, 224–5, 226–7
  and ideational content 35–8
  and informational learning 198–9
  interpretation of 26
  mood-arousing conditions 87–8
  and mood changes 87–90
  moral force of 218, 232
  and morality 215
  narrative theory of 4, 18–19, 23, 24–5, 174–5
  persona theory 101–5
  persona theory:refutation of 105–14
  problem of 119–21
  as pure sonic structure 20–3
  and rapt attention 202–3
  recognition of meaning 131, 133
  and recognitional learning 195–8
  repetition in 108–10, 210–11
  Schopenhauer's theory of 183, 184–8
  Schopenhauer's theory: failure of 190–1, 193–4
  as story-telling 240–1
  theories of description 4
  as wordless drama 20
advertising blurbs 217

aesthetic emotion 248–51
affective appraisal theory 226–7
Affektenlehre 37–8, 51–2
agency
  indeterminacy of 140–2, 147–9
  and narration 131–2, 133–4, 140–2
  representation of 132, 136–9
agreeable art
  absolute music as 47–9
  music as 31–5, 43–4, 47–9
akrasia (weakness of will) 151–2
Alceste (Gluck) 16
Ambros, Wilhelm August 54
  absolute music 70–1
  architecture 70
  music 70–1, 72–3, 74–5
  musical aesthetics 67
  musical boundaries 69–70, 72
  painting 70
  poetry 70, 71
  sculpture/plastic art 70
Amenda, Karl 166
'Analytic of the Beautiful' (Kant) 38, 50
Anthropology from a Pragmatic Point of View (Kant) 35
Apel, August 18
architecture 70
Aristotle 126–7
  and epistemic moral force 219, 220, 221
  informational learning 191–2
  music and emotions 224
  on pleasure 253–4, 255, 258
  recognitional learning 189–90, 191, 192–3
  on representation 188–90, 191–2
Arnheim, Rudolph 68
art
  art/craft distinction 180–1
  music as 180–3, 205–7
  and religion 248–53
Art of the Fugue (Bach) 161

artistic interpretation
  principle of charity 114–17
artworks
  ineffability of 36
  literary 220–1, 222
  and moral knowledge 220–1, 222
Avison, Charles 225

Bach, Johann Sebastian 111, 161
  music, reuse of 10–12
Bamberg Codex 180 n.
Basner, Elena 173
Beaumarchais, Pierre 218
beauty 50, 73–4
Beethoven, Ludwig van 210–11,
  242–3
  and genius 25
  and program music 166–8
  repetition in 109, 110
  see also String Quartet in F Minor
Beethoven: His Spiritual Development
  (Sullivan) 230
behaviour 132, 135–6
  moral 224–9
behavioral moral force 219, 224–9
Bell, Clive 22–3, 94, 248–50, 251
Bentham, Jeremy 238
Bernstein, Lawrence F. 54
Bonds, Mark Evan 66, 67
Bouwsma, O. K. 65
Brahms, Johannes 102–5, 107, 115,
  116, 195
Braunbehrens, Volkmar 3
Budd, Malcolm 252
  demystification strategy 206, 207–8,
    209
  on Eroica Symphony (Symphony
    No. 3, Beethoven) 211
  value of music 205, 206, 207

Caccini, Giulio 15
Camerata 14–15
Cantata 110 (Unser Mund sei voll
  Lachens, Bach) 10–12
Carroll, Noel 107
  mood arousal hypotheses 85–7
  mood arousal hypotheses: refutation
    of 91–7
  music and moods 81, 82, 84–5, 98,
    99

music and motion 86–7, 92–3,
  96–7
Carter, Tim 14 n. 11
Casti, Giambattista 3–5: see also First
  the Music, and then the Words
character: music and 230–3
character-building moral force 219,
  230–3
Charpentier, Gustave 141
cinema 68
clumsiness 143–5
Cone, Edward T. 101–2
Council of Trent 13–14, 235–6, 239
Cours complet d'harmonie et de
  composition (Momigny) 20
crafts 181
Critique of Judgment (Kant) 27, 32–5

Da Ponte, Lorenzo 5, 17, 218
Danto, Arthur 168, 169–70
Davide penitente (Mozart, K. 426) 17
Davies, Stephen 247
  garden-variety emotions 227–8
decorative arts 50–1, 244–8
description: theories of 4
disinterested perception 40–1
drama: music and 210–12

emotions 80–1
  and absolute music 99
  aesthetic 248–51
  and behavior 224–5
  garden-variety 81, 84, 88, 98,
    224–8
  representation of: in music 55–9
emotivism 60–3, 69, 98
empty pleasure 239–41
  absolute music as 242, 243–4
  story-telling as 243, 244
enhanced formalism 60, 64–5, 75,
  88–9, 98, 201
  and clumsiness of music 144
  human agency, representation
    of 138
  patterns in absolute music 136
Entführung aus dem Serai, Die (Mozart,
  K. 384) 17
Epicurus 253, 258
epistemic moral force 219, 220–4, 229

Eroica Symphony, *see* Symphony No. 3 (Beethoven)
Essay on Criticism (Pope) 236
ethical hedonism 253
Euler, Leonhard 32
expression theory 19
extreme formalism 60–4, 66–7

fantasias 50
Fay, Laurel E. 172
fine arts
    absolute music as 30–5, 41–2, 47–8, 49, 183–4
    and form 31–6
    ideational content of 36–8
    vocal music as 29, 35–6
First the Music, and then the Words (Salieri) 3, 12
    libretto 5–7
    musical joke 5–7, 9, 10, 16–17
    plot 5–6
formalism
    extreme 60–4, 66–7
    musical 42, 49–52, 53, 54–64
    see also enhanced formalism
Forster, E. M. 241–2
free beauty 50
free fantasias 50
fugues 110–12

genius 25, 247, 259
Gluck, Christoph Willibald 16
Great Mass in C-minor (Mozart, K. 429,) 17
Grenzen der Musik und Poesie: (The Boundaries of Music and Poetry, Ambros) 54, 67
Grundlegung zur Metaphysik der Sitten (Foundations of the Metaphysics of Morals, Kant) 219, 220, 221, 229

Hamlet (Shakespeare) 151–2
Handel, Georg Friedrich: music, reuse of 8–10
Hanslick, Eduard 7, 8, 9, 23, 26, 97, 246
    emotivism 60–3
    emotivism: argument against 69, 98

extreme formalism 60–4, 66–7
music: representational content of 66
musical formalism 53, 54–5
musical formalism: negative thesis 55–9, 64–5
musical formalism: negative thesis, reaction to 60–4
    on opera 112
Haydn, Joseph 223
hedonism 253, 259
Hegel, G. W. F. 17–18, 29, 183–4
Herder, Johann Gottfried xii, 23
Heydrich, Reinhard 216
historicism, doctrine of 24, 25
Homer 68–9
Hosenfeld, Captain Wilm 217
Howard's End (Forster) 241–2
Howeis, Reverend H. R. 225
Hume, David 73, 166

imagination 39
'Immer leiser wird mein Schlummer' (Brahms, Op. 105, No. 2) 102–3
indeterminacy 147–50
informational learning 191–2, 193
    and fictional narrative 198–9
Intermezzo in B–flat minor (Brahms, Op. 117, No. 2) 103–5, 107, 115, 116, 195
interpretational charity, principle of 114–17
Ion (Plato) 180–1

James, Henry 149–50
James, William 250
Jennens, Charles 8
Joseph II, Holy Roman Emperor 3

Kant, Immanuel 27, 245–6
    aesthetic ideas (ineffability of) 51–2
    Affektenlehre 37–8, 51–2
    on decorative arts 50–1
    and epistemic moral force 219, 220, 221, 229
    free beauty 50
    free fantasias 50
    ideational content of fine art 36–8

Kant, Immanuel   (*cont.*)
  ideational content of music   35–8,
    51
  music as agreeable art   31–5, 43–4,
    47–9
  music as fine art   30–41, 42, 44,
    47–8, 49, 50, 183
  musical formalism   42, 49–52
  pure judgment of taste   38–41, 42–3
  on vibrations   32–5, 42, 43, 44–7,
    48, 49
  on vocal music   35–6
Karl, Gregory
  interpretation of Shostakovich's
    Tenth Symphony   158–61
  interpretation of Shostakovich's
    Tenth Symphony: refutation
    of   161–5, 173
  and musical persona   158–61
Kerman, Joseph   121, 166
King Lear (Shakespeare)   144–5
Kristeller, Paul Oskar   29, 181–2

Lamarque, Peter   221–2, 240
Laocoon (Lessing)   67–9
le Huray, Peter   20
Leonore Overture No. 3
  (Beethoven)   109
Lessing, Gotthold Ephraim   67–9
Letter to Menoeceus (Epicurus)   253
Levinson, Jerrold   102, 104, 222
  garden-variety emotions   227–8
  and musical persona   107, 108
literary artworks: and moral
    knowledge   220–1, 222
literary personae   106, 108
Louise (Charpentier)   141, 152–3

Mahler, Gustav
  and Charpentier's *Louise*   141,
    152–3
  see also Symphony No. 9 (Mahler):
    Second Movement
Marriage of Figaro (Beaumarchais)   218
Maus, Fred Everett   121, 155–6
  on Beethoven's String Quartet in F
    Minor, Op. 95:   121, 122–5,
    127–9, 195
  and recognitional learning   196–7

meaning: recognition of   131, 133
Messiah (Handel)   8–10
Mill, John Stuart   238–9, 253, 255–6
Missa Pape Marcelli (Palestrina)   14
Momigny, Jerome-Joseph de   20, 21–2
Monteverdi, Claudio   14
moods   87–90
  appropriateness of music to   89
  characteristics of   82–3
  music and   72–3, 74–5, 82–5,
    88–9, 98, 99
moral behaviour   224–9
moral force   218–20
  behavioral   219, 224–9
  character-building   219, 230–3
  epistemic   219, 220–4, 229
moral knowledge
  literary artworks and   220–1, 222
  music and   220–4
morality   215
motion   86–7, 92–3, 96–7
Mozart, Wolfgang Amadeus   3, 17,
    143, 144, 218, 222–3
  on role of music in opera   15–16
  see also Quartet in D Minor
music
  abstractness of   207, 208–9
  aesthetical properties of   62, 97–8
  affective content   80
  and affective states   81
  as agreeable art   31–5, 43–4, 47–9
  as art   180–3, 205–7
  canonical listening   49, 88, 93–6, 99
  and character   230–3
  and drama   210–12
  and emotions   55–9, 80–1, 224
  as fine art   30–41, 42, 44, 47–8, 49,
    50, 183
  ideational content of   35–8, 51
  ineffability of   4, 26, 51–2
  and moods   72–3, 74–5, 82–5,
    88–9, 98, 99
  and moral behavior   224–9
  and moral knowledge   220–4
  and motion   86–7, 92–3, 96–7
  mystery of   205–13
  non-aesthetical properties of   62–3
  in opera   15–16
  power to move hearers   205–9
  as representation   183–8

representational content 66
and ritual 203−5
value of 205−7
see also absolute music
Music and Morals (Howeis) 225
musical aesthetics 67
musical agency uncertainty
principle 195
musical boundaries 69−70, 72
musical formalism
Hanslick and 8, 26, 53, 54−5
Hanslick's negative thesis 55−9,
64−5
Hanslick's negative thesis: reaction
to 60−4
Kant on 42, 49−52
Musical Joke (Mozart, K. 522) 143,
144
musical personae 101−7, 108, 195
fugues 110−12
and principle of interpretational
charity 114−17
and repetition 108−10, 112−13
in Shostakovich's Tenth
Symphony 158−61
musical representation theory
(Schopenhauer) 192, 193−4

narrative theory 4, 18−19, 23, 24−5,
174−5
Newcomb, Anthony 131−2, 156
agency, indeterminacy of 140−2,
147−8
agency, representation of 132,
136−7
behavior patterns 132, 135
clumsiness of music 143−4
interpretation of Mahler's Ninth
Symphony 131−2, 139−42,
195
interpretation of Mahler's Ninth
Symphony: refutation
of 132−9, 143−54
meaning 145−6
narration 131−2, 133−4, 140−2
recognition of meaning 131
and recognitional learning 196−7
Nicomachean Ethics (Aristotle) 219, 220,
221, 254, 255
Nottebohm, Gustav 166

Of Musical Beauty (*Vom
Musikalisch-Schönen,* Hanslick)
emotivism 60−3
musical formalism 8, 26, 53, 54−5
musical formalism: negative
thesis 55−9, 64−5
Olsen, Stein 221−2, 240
opera 19, 112
development of 14−15
music in, role of 15−16
Orchestral Suite No. 4 (Bach) 10−12

painting 70
Palestrina (Giovanni Pierluigi da
Palestrina) 14
Payzant, Geoffrey 60
personae
literary 106, 108
theory of 101−5
theory: refutation of 105−14
see also musical personae
Phaedo (Plato) 237
Phaedrus (Plato) 180−1
philosophical aesthetics 182
philosophical hedonism 259
Pianist, The (Szpilman) 216−17
plastic art 70
Plato vii, 107, 237
and art/craft distinction 180−1
music and emotions 224
pleasure 237−44, 252
concept of 237−9
defense of 253−6
empty 239−41, 242, 243−4
justification for 256−8
types of 241−4
Poetics (Aristotle) 126−7, 188,
191−2
poetry 70, 71, 181, 191−2
Pope, Alexander 236, 239−40
Prima la musica, e poi le parole, see *First
the Music, and then the Words*
program music 113
criteria for 165−7
Symphony No. 10 (Shostakovich,
Op.93) as 164−5
progress, doctrine of 24, 25−6

Quartet in D Minor (Mozart, K.
421) 20, 21−2

Quarteto Serioso, *see* String Quartet in F Minor (Beethoven, Op.95)

rapt attention 202–3
Rasoumowski Quartets (Beethoven) 25
recognitional learning 189–90, 191, 192–3
and fictional narrative 195–8
religion 259
art and 248–53
and epistemic moral force 220, 221, 222
and ritual 203–4
text setting 14, 235
see also Council of Trent
repetition 108–10, 112–13, 210–11
representation 55–9, 66, 183–90, 191–2
Republic (Plato) vii, 107, 180–1, 224
ricco d'un giorno, Il (Salieri) 17
rituals
religious 203–4
subscription concerts as 204–5
Robinson, Jenefer 110, 116, 156
affective appraisal theory 226–7
and musical persona 102–7, 112, 158–61, 195
and recognitional learning 196–7
on Shostakovich's Tenth Symphony: hope in 158–61
on Shostakovich's Tenth Symphony: refutation of 161–5, 173
Rosenkavalier, Der (Strauss) 143, 144
Russell, Bertrand 250

Salieri, Antonio 3, 17: see also *First the Music, and then the Words*
Santayana, George 73–4
Schauspieldirektor, Der (Mozart) 3
Schenker, Heinrich 110, 112
Schindler's List (film) 216, 229
Schmieder, Wolfgang 11 n.
Schopenhauer, Arthur
Haldane/Kemp translation 185–6
musical representation, theory of 192, 193–4
theory of absolute music 183, 184–8

theory of absolute music: failure of 190–1, 193–4
Schroeder, David P. 223
sculpture 70
Shakespeare, William 151–2
King Lear 144–5
Shostakovich, Dmitri 158–65, 167, 172–3
Shostakovich, Maxim 173
Sibley, Frank 97
Solomon, Robert 231, 260
stage plays
analogy with Beethoven's Op. 95: 124–5, 127
analogy with Beethoven's Op. 95: refutation of 125–7, 128
idealized notion of 124
Stephanie, Gottlieb 17, 18
story-telling 240–1
as empty pleasure 243, 244
Strauss, Richard: *Der Rosenkavalier* 143, 144
String Quartet in F (Beethoven, Op. 18) 166–7
String Quartet in F Minor (Beethoven, *Quarteto Serioso*, Op.95) 121–30, 195
action as explanation 129–30
action as explanation: refutation of 129, 130
analogy with stage play 124–5, 127
analogy with stage play: refutation of 125–7, 128
subscription concerts 204–5
Sullivan, J. W. N. 230, 231, 232
Sulzer, Johann Georg 19
Symphony in G–minor (Mozart, K. 550) 222–3
Symphony No. 3 (*Eroica*, Beethoven) 110, 210, 211
Symphony No. 5 (Beethoven) 109, 110, 242–3
Symphony No. 9 (Mahler): Second Movement 131–54, 195
agency, indeterminacy of 147–8
authorial intent 152–4
clumsiness of music 144–5
meaning of music 145–7
Newcomb's interpretation of 131–2, 139–42, 195

Newcomb's interpretation:
        refutation of 132–9, 143–54
weakness of will 151–2
Symphony No. 10 (Shostakovich,
        Op.93) 167
Karl and Robinson's interpretation
        of 158–61
Karl and Robinson's interpretation:
        refutation of 161–5
musical personae in 158–61
as program music 164–5
Symphony No. 83 (Haydn) 223
Szpilman, Wladyslaw 216–17

Taruskin, Richard 172
Testimony (Shostakovich) 162, 172
Turn of the Screw, The (H. James)
        149–50

understanding 39

vibrations 32–5, 42, 43, 44–7, 48, 49,
        87
vocal music: as fine art 29, 35–6
Vogt, Carl 71
Volkov, Solomon 162, 172

Wackenroder, Wilhelm Heinrich 22,
        23
weakness of will *(akrasia)* 151–2
Weitz, Morris 53
Well-tempered Clavier, Book I
        (Bach): Fugue XVI in G minor
        111
Wilde, Oscar 220
Wollheim, Richard 137
Wolterstorff, Nicholas 248, 251